HARVARD-YENCHING INSTITUTE STUDIES
XX

STUDIES IN CHINESE INSTITUTIONAL HISTORY

BY

LIEN-SHENG YANG

Professor of Chinese History

Harvard University

HARVARD UNIVERSITY PRESS
CAMBRIDGE, MASSACHUSETTS
1963

DISTRIBUTED IN GREAT BRITAIN BY
OXFORD UNIVERSITY PRESS
LONDON

Library of Congress Catalog Card Number 61-8844

PRINTED IN THE UNITED STATES OF AMERICA

FOREWORD

This volume contains nine of my articles selected from the *Harvard Journal of Asiatic Studies*, 1946–1957. Except for the one on dynastic configurations, which is of a rather general nature, all deal with problems in the history of Chinese political, social, and economic institutions. The articles are collected here to make them more readily available to students of Chinese history. At the end of the volume, corrections of misprints and mistakes are noted together with additional bibliographical and related information to bring the content up to date. The system of numbering these notes refers in each case to the relevant *HJAS* volume and original pagination, as well as to the continuous foot pagination added in the present collection.

Several of the articles are general surveys covering centuries or even millennia of Chinese history. In theory, a broad survey should base itself on detailed studies of various shorter periods, such as the courses of major and minor dynasties. But such studies are not always available. Meanwhile, a preliminary account of certain institutions through the ages may serve to stimulate further investigation. Indeed, the field of Chinese institutional history is like a vast beach after ebb tide. Whatever value these articles may have, they are hardly more than a few pebbles or shells gathered by one beachcomber in the course of a decade. It is hoped that they may encourage and aid fellow scholars to make more valuable findings.

L. S. Y.

September 1960

CONTENTS

TOWARD A STUDY OF DYNASTIC CONFIGURATIONS IN CHINESE HISTORY

Lien-sheng Yang

Harvard University

Students of Chinese history generally recognize in the rise and fall of dynasties a recurrent pattern which they call the dynastic cycle. Obviously a dynasty may experience a number of declines and revivals before the completion of its cycle. A detailed graph of a given cycle, taking account not only of the dynasty's general rise and fall but also of the minor ups and downs in between, may be termed a dynastic configuration. A study of such configurations, if they reflect fairly accurately what happened, will deepen our understanding of the dynastic cycle. The drawing of such a configuration, however, is no simple matter. I offer here some preliminary considerations of the major problems involved.

The first problem is: what are the dynasties to be included in our study? Chinese history is full of dynasties, long and short, Chinese and alien. The ruling houses which governed the whole or nearly the whole of China may be called major dynasties, and those which controlled only a portion of it, minor dynasties. When modern scholars speak of the dynastic cycle, they tend to refer to the cycles of major dynasties of considerable length; this may be justifiable, since obviously not all dynasties may be treated on the same basis. Nevertheless, it seems worthwhile to plot configurations for the minor dynasties in periods of disunity, including such independent states as the Seven Powers in the Period of Warring States and the Ten Kingdoms in south China during the Five Dynasties. It will be extremely interesting if one can correlate differences of configuration with differences in territory.

Chinese tradition distinguishes a dynasty of the legitimate line of succession, *cheng-t'ung* 正統, from a dynasty of usurpation or a puppet dynasty, *chien-wei* 僭偽. The standard adopted for this distinction, however, may vary in accordance with the time

1

of the historian. A classical example is the differing treatment of the history of the Three Kingdoms, Wei, Shu, and Wu. During the Western Chin period, Wei was considered the legitimate dynasty because it received from Han the throne which it transmitted in turn to Chin, and also because Wei occupied the heart of China at that time, the Yellow River Valley. By the time of the Eastern Chin this view was already questioned, and legitimacy based on blood relationship began to receive stress. Since the Eastern Chin achieved only a partial revival, naturally there grew up some sympathy for Shu which had been in a similar situation of *p'ien-an* 偏安 " partial security " or " security at one corner." [1] Later, the contrast between the geographical standard and that of blood relationship became still sharper, with SSU-MA Kuang (Northern Sung) crediting Wei with legitimacy, and CHU Hsi (Southern Sung) giving it to Shu, as a continuation of Han. [2] This significant difference in the history of thought perhaps can never be settled permanently. For our purpose, it is important to remember that legitimacy need not restrict the scope of historical study. For instance, the reign of WANG Mang may as well be studied as a short major dynasty like the Sui.

The second problem is: what are the beginning and end of a dynasty? Chinese tradition in general dates the beginning of a dynasty from the time when it declared a dynastic title, in most cases the declaration being in effect a claim to the Mandate of Heaven. However, a dynasty may already have existed as a state before this official beginning. Such is the case of Ch'in, the first imperial dynasty, and on this score Ch'in differs widely from Sui, although the two dynasties are similar in several other ways. [3]

[1] This point has been made in the *Ssu-k'u ch'üan-shu tsung-mu t'i-yao* 四庫全書 總目提要 (Commercial Press ed.) 1.987, on the *San-kuo chih*.

[2] A collection of literature on *cheng-t'ung* may be found in the *Ku-chin t'u-shu chi-ch'eng* 古今圖書集成 vol. 452, " Ti-t'ung pu " 帝統部. It is interesting to note that, unlike other sections, this section contains only *i-wen* 藝文 but no sub-section called *tsung-lun* 總論 which is supposed to be devoted to more or less orthodox views. In the short preface to the section, the compilers of the encyclopaedia explained this omission on the ground that there were no orthodox views on this subject, which was only too true under the Manchu dynasty.

[3] For a comparison of the two dynasties, see Derk BODDE, review of Woodbridge BINGHAM, *The Founding of the T'ang Dynasty*, in *JAOS* 61 (1941).4. 294-295.

Early beginnings are also found in the alien dynasties and, as far as we can tell, the two very ancient dynasties, Shang and Chou. This similarity between alien and ancient Chinese dynasties is worthy of note. In our study it seems advisable to include the pre-" imperial " period of a dynasty, although one may wish to distinguish this part of the configuration from the rest somehow, e. g., by charting with different colors.

The end of a dynasty involves the interesting problem of *chung-hsing* 中興, " revival or restoration." According to tradition, a revival may come after a complete break, such as the case of the Eastern Han, Eastern Chin, and Southern Sung. It may follow the pacification of a major rebellion. Thus after the rebellion of AN Lu-shan, the T'ang dynasty was restored under Su-tsung 肅宗 (756-762), who was canonized as Hsüan Huang-ti 宣皇帝, evidently to compare him with King Hsüan (827-782 B. C.) of the Chou dynasty who had achieved a revival. For the Ch'ing dynasty, people speak about the T'ung-chih restoration [4] after the T'ai-p'ing rebellion. In this case, the hope of revival may have been expressed even in the year-title T'ung-chih, i. e., to be the same as Shun-chih.[5] Generally speaking, it is difficult to achieve a complete restoration and the revived phase tends to be less glorious than the earlier phase. The Eastern Han is probably the only exception.

Incidentally, the historical expression *chung-hsing* only means

---

[4] In her doctoral thesis " The T'ung-chih Restoration " (Radcliffe College, 1950) Mary WRIGHT devotes a section to a comparison of a few earlier restorations.

[5] Cf. LI Tz'u-ming 李慈銘, *Yüeh-man-t'ung jih-chi pu* 越縵堂日記補, *Hsin-chi hsia* 辛集下 17a-b. The year-title originally adopted was Ch'i-hsiang 祺祥, which was criticized by the Grand Secretary CHOU Tsu-p'ei 周祖培 as being redundant in meaning. According to LI, the Grand Secretary first wished to propose Hsi-lung 熙隆 or Ch'ien-hsi 乾熙, obviously alluding to the years of K'ang-hsi and Ch'ien-lung. This source of information seems authoritative because at that time LI lived in Chou's house as tutor of his son.

However, in the *Ch'ing-shih t'ung-su yen-i* 清史通俗演義 by TS'AI Tung-fan 蔡東藩 (1935), p. 478, it is stated that the Dowager Empress Tz'u-hsi liked the year-title T'ung-chih because it implied " joint-governing " or co-regency of the two dowager empresses. This of course cannot be considered an official interpretation. Nevertheless it seems likely that the court adopted the year-title because of its ambiguity. Also we may recall that the early years of Shun-chih were also under a regency. I am indebted to Professor William HUNG for discussion on this point.

" *re*vival " rather than " revival in the middle of a dynasty " as one might guess. Tradition [6] prefers to pronounce the character *chung* in falling tone instead of level tone, the meaning being " second " (same as *chung* 仲) and therefore " again " or " another." This meaning of *chung* can be found also in year-titles. For instance, the last two years (56-57) of Emperor Kuang-wu of the Eastern Han are known as Chien-wu Chung-yüan 建武中元, i. e., another era of Chien-wu. Emperor Wu of the Liang Dynasty had the year-titles Ta-t'ung 大通 (527-528) and Ta-t'ung 大同 (535-545), and repeated them as Chung Ta-t'ung 中大通 (529-534) and Chung Ta-t'ung 中大同 (546), respectively.

In Chinese history there are cases when a dynasty is continued in a manner even short of a partial security, and for this precarious continuation its protagonists may still wish to claim a revival. A notable example is that of the Ming princes who established themselves in south China after the Manchu invasion, although what they actually accomplished was a brief survival rather than a revival. Revivals or survivals, it seems only fair for the historian to include them in the study of dynastic configurations, again bearing in mind the difference in territory. This applies to the alien dynasties as well as the Chinese. Thus the Khara-Khitai should be studied along with Liao, and the independent Mongolian princes in the Ming period may be considered survivals of Yüan.[7]

---

[6] HU Ming-yü 胡鳴玉, *Ting-o tsa-lu* 訂譌雜錄 (*Ts'ung-shu chi-ch'eng* 叢書集成 ed.) 2.15.

[7] In a book entitled *Chung-hsing lun-lüeh* 中興論略 published in 1910 by a certain Manchu scholar Hsing-yüan 興元 from Peking, the term *chung-hsing* is used in a broad sense, covering complete and partial revivals, of Chinese and alien dynasties and even feudal states. A miscellaneous group of unsuccessful attempts is recorded in the last two chapters as an appendix and labeled as *Chung-hsing yü-hsü* 中興餘緒 i. e., revivals which amounted to mere survivals. Since this book was written toward the end of the Ch'ing dynasty, it is natural that the author should wish to use the term *chung-hsing* in a rather loose sense, hoping that some kind of revival or survival might be achieved by the Manchus.

A loose use of the term *chung-hsing*, however, is found in an early history. In *Nan Ch'i shu*, 2.9a, we read: "The Sung dynasty had eight rulers and lasted sixty years [420-479]. Four times the normal line of succession was broken and three times they achieved a revival." (宋氏正位八君,卜年五紀,四絕長嫡,三稱中興。)

The inclusion of both major and minor dynasties in our study, and also the pre-dynastic survivals, makes it necessary to consider configurations which overlap each other in time. The overlapping may be external or internal. Internal overlapping is typical in dynastic changes by way of abdication. First, the founder of the new dynasty, or his father, served as a powerful minister under the old dynasty. Finally, his influence became so overwhelming that the last ruler of the old dynasty was obliged to abdicate. This was the normal process of passing on the throne from the Han to the Sung dynasties inclusive. In such cases, we must be careful in our interpretation of the configuration of the old dynasty. For instance, toward the end of the two Han dynasties, there were signs that the central government had become strong, and these would be reflected in the configuration. But the strength was chiefly to the credit of WANG Mang [8] and TS'AO Ts'ao, who acted in the name of their masters. The upswing in the configurations indicates the rise of the Hsin dynasty and the Wei dynasty rather than a revival of Han.

External overlapping may exist between two dynasties, or among several dynasties or states,[9] either Chinese or alien. In comparing their configurations, we may find factors which favored co-existence and factors which led to conquest. Obviously, one situation which has promoted co-existence is that in which two dynasties were both fairly strong and prosperous and had mutual respect for each other. The long peace between Northern Sung and Liao which lasted from 1004 to 1122 is an excellent illustration.

Old-fashioned Chinese scholars were inclined to study Chinese dynasties as isolated entities, and in their studies of relations with the non-Chinese states their views tended to be overly influenced by the key role played by China in East Asia. Fortunately,

[8] As observed by Hans BIELENSTEIN in "The Restoration of the Han Dynasty," *BMFEA* 26 (1954).159, "Actually, since Wang MANG held all the power under Emperor P'ing, he also deserves the credit of the improvement during this time."

[9] An interesting article that bears on the general subject of the rise of states is that by Karl W. DEUTSCH, "The Growth of Nations: Some Recurrent Patterns of Political and Social Integration," *World Politics* 5 (1953).2.168-195.

modern scholars have already been making attempts to correct this bias. In the West, works of Owen LATTIMORE and Karl A. WITTFOGEL [10] are good examples. In China, CH'EN Yin-k'o 陳寅恪 [11] in his brilliant volume on the political history of the T'ang dynasty has demonstrated the interlocking nature of the rise and fall of foreign races and the interaction between civil government and national defence. Students of Chinese history will do well in broadening their scope of study to include configurations of all non-Chinese states which had direct or even indirect contacts with China.

We come now to the third and perhaps the most important problem: what is the basis of grading or standard of measurements? Two obvious pairs of criteria are unity and expansion, and peace and prosperity, in other words, *wen-chih* 文治 and *wu-kung* 武功 or civil and military achievements. Of course, these two kinds of merit somehow contradict each other because unity and expansion often involves war, which is against peace. In general, Chinese tradition expects military merits from the founder of a dynasty, and civil achievements from his successors, thus distinguishing *ch'uang-yeh chih chün* 創業之君 and *shou-ch'eng chih chu* 守成之主. Expansionist emperors in the middle of a dynasty were often criticized for their ambition. For instance, after the death of Emperor Wu of Han, the court proposed to honor him with the temple name of *Shih-tsung* 世宗, the " Epochal Exemplar." To this proposal, strong objection was raised by the classical scholar HSIA-HOU Sheng 夏侯勝, who denounced the late emperor for the disasters which he had brought upon the people through his ambitious wars. [12] Although this objection was not favorably received, it expressed the Confucianist view against expansion by force. An adequate national defense, however, was considered necessary. And when the character *wu* 武 " martial " was used in an imperial designation, it was generally intended to be compli-

---

[10] Owen LATTIMORE, *Inner Asian Frontiers of China*, 1940; Karl A. WITTFOGEL and FENG Chia-sheng, *History of Chinese Society, Liao (907-1125)*, 1949.

[11] *T'ang-tai cheng-chih shih shu-lun kao* 唐代政治史述論稿 (1944), pp. 94-116.

[12] *Han shu*, 75.3a-4a. Also see Homer H. DUBS, " Chinese Imperial Designations," *JAOS* 65 (1945) .26-33 for proposed translations.

mentary. For the purpose of showing the configuration, the modern student may draw two different curves based on the civil and military criteria, or one curve to indicate the average of the two. The use of two curves has its advantage. For instance, they may reveal a lag of the civil peak behind the military peak in the configuration, as suggested by the tradition which expects different kinds of achievements from dynasty-founders and from their successors.

Occasionally Chinese historians describe a glorious era in terms of cultural activities in such fields as philosophy, art and literature. Whether this is justifiable leads us to an interesting problem. Some years ago, the celebrated American anthropologist Arthur L. KROEBER made a study of configurations of culture growth and became rather disappointed at finding only a partial correlation between national solidarity and cultural achievement.[18] On this highly complicated subject I wish to offer only a couple of general suggestions. First, there is the problem of defining the " culture " in culture growth. I believe, in making such a study, it may be useful to distinguish (1) a kind of cultural activity or a division of culture, such as poetry, (2) a particular form or genre in the division, such as lü-shih 律詩 or regulated verse, and (3) cultural activities in general. The configurations of culture growth in these three senses need not coincide, as the causes of their rise and fall may vary.

Second, there is the problem of quantity and quality. Students in the history of art, literature, and philosophy chiefly concern themselves with quality rather than quantity. This approach may be adequate in their separate fields. For a full understanding of cultural history, however, we should like to learn not only about the best results achieved by the outstanding masters but also about the standard reached by the average work, and the total volume of achievements by all the participants in cultural activities. Generally speaking, although there are great masters who appear to have lived out of the period of their speciality (e. g., BACH and polyphony), the history of art, literature and phi-

---

[18] *Configurations of Culture Growth*, 1944.

losophy reveals a rather close correlation between quality and quantity. For instance, in Chinese literature, tradition associates *fu* 賦 or rhymed prose with Han, *lü-shih* or regulated verse with T'ang, *tz'u* 詞 or song-words with Sung, and drama with Yüan. These are believed to be the periods that produced the most and the best. This correlation is understandable since the period that produced the most had a good chance to produce the best.

Whether a division of culture is especially favored or disfavored in a given society, and developed early or late in history, involves many factors—material as well as ideological—which can not be easily generalized. The rise and fall of a particular form in a cultural division can be interpreted to some degree by what I call a game theory. A particular form of art or literature is subject to a set of rules just like any competitive game which requires skill. Under the rules there are a limited number of possibilities to be realized by the player. Those who realize the best possibilities become the outstanding masters. Of course, those are also outstanding who invent a new game with many possibilities or modify an old game to make it more interesting. When people have exhausted the possibilities, or at least the good possibilities, the game (or the form of art or literature) will decline.

This point of exhaustion of possibilities has already been made by the seventeenth-century scholar Ku Yen-wu 顧炎武. His famous *Jih-chih lu* 日知錄 [14] contains the following remarks on "Shih-t'i tai-chiang" 詩體代降 ["Periodical Changes in the Style (or Form) of Poetry"]:

That the Three Hundred Poems (i. e., the *Shih ching*) had to be replaced by the *Ch'u tz'u* 楚辭, the *Ch'u tz'u* replaced by the poetry of Han and Wei, and in turn replaced by the poetry of the Six Dynasties and that of Sui and T'ang was natural. To follow the style (or form) of a period requires resemblance to the literature of that period—this is called conformation. That poetic and prosaic literature was different from period to period had a reason which made the change unavoidable. When the literary style of an era has been followed from a long time, it becomes intolerable for everybody to echo the same word. Now history has passed thousands of years; how can one imitate all the worn-out expressions of the past and still call the result poetry! Therefore, if one's work is [entirely] dissimilar to those of the ancients, it misses being poetry. On the other hand, if it is [entirely] similar to works of

[14] *Jih-chih lu* (SPPY ed.) 21.18a-b.

8

the ancients, it misses being one's own work. That the poetry of LI Po and TU Fu was particularly outstanding among T'ang authors was because their poetry succeeded in being both similar and dissimilar [to traditional poetry]. He who understands this principle can be called a critic of poetry.

In KROEBER's *Configuration of Culture Growth* (p. 763) we also read, " The value culmination comes at the moment when the full range of possibilities within the pattern is sensed. . . . The pattern can be said to have fulfilled itself when its opportunities or possibilities have been exhausted." It may be observed that although this principle of exhaustion of possibilities can be applied to either a whole division of art or literature or to a particular form or style within the division, it is more effective when applied to the latter.

This is illustrated by KU Yen-wu's discussion quoted above. The modern scholar WANG Kuo-wei 王國維 made a similar observation and added, " Hence I dare not believe the remark that literature of later times is inferior to that of earlier times. But in speaking about one style (or form) of literature, this theory is irrefutable." [15] In other words, the opportunities within a given poetic form or style are limited, whereas the possibilities of poetry as a whole appear to be too numerous to be exhausted.

Normally it takes a peaceful and prosperous era to permit many people to devote themselves to art and literature.[16] But whether they wish to play one game or another is a different proposition. Consequently, the correlation is likely to be only partial between the dynastic configuration and a culture configuration which represents a division of art or literature or a style or form within the division. As for cultural activities in general, in terms of quantity if not quality, at least in China there seems to be a considerable correlation between their high points and the peaks in the dynastic configuration. The period of Warring States is

[15] *Jen-chien tz'u-hua* 人間詞話, 1937 ed., p. 37.

[16] This traditional view should not be considered one-sidedly materialistic, because the Chinese tradition also recognizes the principle of challenge and response, e. g., as expressed in the saying " Wen ch'iung erh hou kung " (文窮而後工)—" One's literary writings excel only after experience of poverty (or hardships)," or as expressed in more general terms in *The Works of Mencius* (LEGGE, *The Chinese Classics*, Vol. II), pp. 447-448.

sometimes cited as a major exception to this thesis, because cultural activities were abundant in that period of disunion. But the correlation will immediately become clear if we ignore the royal house of Chou and turn our attention to the Seven Powers. When the terms of reference are clearly defined, it becomes possible to include in the civil criterion various cultural achievements, or what the Chinese call *sheng-ming wen-wu chih chih* 聲明文物之治.[17]

With our criteria defined, we may proceed to obtain a general picture of the configuration first by reading through the annals of the standard histories. The historian's comments at the end of an annal, known as *lun-tsan* 論贊, not infrequently discuss the emperor's position in the history of the dynasty. Such discussions are often stereotyped in form. Nevertheless, they are important because they represent a traditional evaluation. The following comments paraphrased from the *Hsin T'ang shu* may serve as examples:

On T'ai-tsung 太宗 (627-649): Among the twenty rulers of the T'ang dynasty, three are remarkable. Of the three, Hsüan-tsung 玄宗 (713-755) and Hsien-tsung 憲宗 (806-820) both failed in the last part of their reigns. So outstanding was T'ai-tsung's greatness!

On Tai-tsung 代宗 (763-779): In the reign of Tai-tsung, there were still remnant rebels. Able to complete the suppression and to maintain the accomplishment, he may be considered a ruler of medium caliber (中材之主).

On Hsüan-tsung 宣宗 (847-859): Hsüan-tsung excelled in his judgment of affairs. But he relied too much on his fault-finding ability and completely lacked the spirit of benevolence. Alas! The T'ang dynasty began to decline from his time.

On Chao-tsung 昭宗 (889-903): In history the last ruler of a dynasty was not necessarily stupid or tyrannical. When the causes of disaster had accumulated for a long time and the time of collapse happened to occur in his days, even a wise and brave ruler could not save the situation. What a pity! Chao-tsung was such a case.

---

[17] For instance, see *Sung shih* 3.14a.

10

In apparent imitation of these passages, the *Ming shih* observes that among the sixteen Ming rulers, outside of T'ai-tsu 太祖 (1368-1398) and Ch'eng-tsu 成祖 (1408-1424), only Jen-tsung 仁宗 (1425), Hsüan-tsung 宣宗 (1426-1435) and Hsiao-tsung 孝宗 (1488-1505) are remarkable. In the annals, Ming Shih-tsung 世宗 (1522-1566) is labeled a ruler of medium caliber and Emperor Chuang-lieh 莊烈帝 (1628-1644) is lamented exactly as was the last ruler of T'ang.[18]

The traditional historian occasionally comments on the appropriateness of the posthumous imperial designation. For instance, the *Sung shih* remarks that in Jen-tsung's 仁宗 (1023-1063) benevolence and Hsiao-tsung's 孝宗 (1163-1189) filial attributes, they certainly lived up to their temple names. The *Sung shih* also approves the temple name Li-tsung 理宗 (1125-1264) as suitable because the emperor made great efforts to promote the Neo-Confucianist thinking called *li-hsüeh* 理學.[19] Such remarks on appropriateness are relatively few, obviously because the eulogistic words used in the imperial designations were in most cases excessive and cannot be taken literally. To grasp the true meaning of a temple name, it is sometimes necessary to check the precedent usages in earlier dynasties. For instance, Sung Shen-tsung 神宗 (1068-1085) and Ming Shen-tsung (1573-1619) are comparable because each of the two emperors trusted a minister who introduced reforms. Under the Ch'ing dynasty, had the Hundred-Day Reform in 1898 been more successful, the Kuang-hsü emperor might have received the temple name Sheng-tsung rather than that of Te-tsung 德宗.

Concerning the imperial career, tradition recognizes a close relationship between successful emperors and long-lived emperors. This tradition goes back to the chapter " Wu-i " 無逸 " Against Luxurious Ease " in the *Book of Documents*, in which the Duke of Chou is reported to be addressing King Ch'eng. In the address, references are made to three Shang kings who restored the glory of the dynasty from a preceding low ebb, and who reigned for seventy-five, fifty-nine and thirty-three years respectively.[20] The

---

[18] *Ming shih* 15.12b, 18.13a-b, 24.11b-12a.   [19] *Sung shih* 12.19b, 35.25a, 45.19b.
[20] LEGGE, *The Chinese Classics*, vol. 3, *The Shoo King*, pp. 464-473. Incidentally,

Sung scholar SU Che 蘇轍 [21] expressed doubts about such a correlation for later periods, pointing to such rulers as Liang Wu-ti (502-551) and T'ang Hsüan-tsung (712-756) as examples of long reigns which ended in disaster. However, another Sung scholar, SHAO Yung 邵雍, [22] noted with pride and satisfaction that the first four Sung emperors together actually reigned as long as a century. On the whole, there seems to be a rather close correlation between a long reign and success, because in most cases at least a part of the long reign did constitute a peak in the configuration.

The importance of long reigns applies to alien dynasties as well. "Of the rulers of the Liao dynasty," says the *Liao shih*, [23] "Sheng-tsung 聖宗 (983-1030) was about the only one who enjoyed a lengthy reign and lasting fame." For the Chin dynasty, the glorious reigns were those of Shih-tsung 世宗 (1161-1189) and Chang-tsung 章宗 (1190-1208). As described by the poet YÜAN Hao-wen 元好問, [24] "During the fifty years of Ta-ting (1161-1189) and Ming-ch'ang (1190-1195) [etc., the emperors'] godlike merits and sage virtues filled three (i. e., several) thousand documents (神功聖德三千牘，大定明昌五十年)." For the Ch'ing dynasty, students are familiar with the fact that the three periods of K'ang-hsi, Yung-cheng, and Ch'ien-lung covered a record length of 134 years (1662-1795). Although it is normal for a dynasty to have an early peak in its configuration, this early plateau is extraordinary. This long period of consolidation and expansion undoubtedly helped to make the Ch'ing dynasty a stable and lasting dynasty of conquest.

Corresponding to the relationship between long reigns and success, traditional historians also associate short reigns with decline. The length of a reign and that of a dynasty is difficult to interpret, because the factors involved tend to be numerous and complicated. In traditional terms, the factors were often vaguely grouped into those belonging to *T'ien* 天 "Heaven, or

this tallies with TOYNBEE's rhythm of disintegration in three-and-a-half beats (*A Study of History*, abridgement by D. C. SOMERVELL [1947], pp. 548-549).

[21] *Luan-ch'eng chi* 欒城集, *Hou-chi* 後集 (*SPTK* ed.) 7.2b-3b.

[22] *Sung shih* 40.14a.

[23] *Liao shih* 17.9b.

[24] *I-shan hsien-sheng wen-chi* 遺山先生文集 (*SPTK* ed.) 8.17a.

Nature " and those belonging to *Jen* 人 " Man." The human factors cited in tradition are usually based on common sense and consequently are easy to understand. The *T'ien* factors, however, are rather slippery for comprehension, often in terms of such semi-mystical concepts as the Five Elments, *ch'i-yun* 氣運 " vitality and fortune " or *ch'i-shu* 氣數 " vitality and number."

Traditional interpretation of these concepts may be naturalistic or mechanical. The compounds *ch'i-yun* and *ch'i-shu* are often synonymous, but the character *shu* " number " in *ch'i-shu* in itself suggests a mechanical view expressed in figures. Perhaps the most famous example is the remark by Mencius, " It is a rule that a true royal sovereign should arise in the course of five hundred years, and during that time there should be men illustrious in their generation." [25] But the most gigantic scheme is probably that of SHAO Yung,[26] which covers not only cycles of mankind but also that of the universe, which was supposed to last 129,600 years (known as a *yüan* 元). A lesser known scheme of somewhat smaller scale is one invented by WANG Po 王勃 in the seventh century. According to WANG,[27] the dynasty that had the Earth Power (or Virtue) should last a thousand years, that which had the Metal Power should last nine hundred years, the Water Power six hundred years, the Wood Power eight hundred years, and the Fire Power seven hundred years. The Yellow Emperor had the Earth Power, and the cycle started by his reign was completed with Han, which had the Fire Power. The minor dynasties after Han should not count, and the T'ang dynasty should begin another cycle with its Earth Power and should last

[25] *The Works of Mencius*, p. 232. In his *History of China* (1885), p. 58, Robert K. DOUGLAS says, " There is a popular belief among the Chinese that two hundred years is the natural life of a dynasty." However, I am unable to identify his source of information.

[26] For a description of SHAO's scheme, cf. FUNG Yu-lan, *A History of Chinese Philosophy*, trans. by Derk BODDE, Vol. 2 (1953), pp. 469-476. For a discussion of cycle theories in Chinese philosophy, cf. Hsü Ping-ch'ang 徐炳昶，我國的循環論哲學 in *Che-hsüeh p'ing-lun* 哲學評論 8 (1943) .2.662-679.

[27] *Hsin T'ang shu* 201.14a. For a comprehensive discussion of the Five Elements and the corresponding Five Virtues or Powers of Rulers in Chinese history, cf. KANO Naoki 狩野直喜，五行の排列と五帝德に就いて *Tōhōgakuhō, Kyōto*, 3 (1933) .1-32; 5 (1934) .50-86.

a thousand years. To a modern student, such mechanical schemes undoubtedly will sound ridiculous.

The following observation by the Ch'ing scholar CHAO I 趙翼 [28] seems to derive from the concept of *ch'i-yün* ("vitality and fortune"), in a rather eloquent application. How far his views can be endorsed is of course another matter. The topic of his discussion was: "Most Emperors of the Eastern Han Failed to Live Long."

When the "vitality and fortune" of a dynasty were excellent, the rulers in general lived long, had sons early, and had many of them. The case of the Eastern Han dynasty, however, was not so. Emperor Kuang-wu lived to the age of sixty-two, Emperor Ming forty-eight, Emperor Chang thirty-three, Emperor Ho twenty-seven, Emperor Shang two, Emperor An thirty-two, Emperor Shun thirty, Emperor Ch'ung three, Emperor Chih nine, Emperor Huan thirty-six, and Emperor Ling thirty-four. Prince Pien came to the throne at seventeen, and in the same year was murdered by TUNG Cho. Only Emperor Hsien, after his abdication, survived until 234 when he died at the age of fifty-four. These were the ages of the emperors. Since the rulers did not live long, their successors certainly would be still young. When a young ruler died without heir, if there was already a dowager empress serving as his regent, she naturally would wish to put a small child on the throne in order to continue her control. . . .

In general, the peak of Han was in the period when its capital was in the west at Ch'ang-an. Coming down to the time of Emperors Yüan and Ch'eng, the "vitality and fortune" already began to decline. Therefore, when Emperor Ch'eng died without heir, Emperor Ai was called in to succeed him. When Emperor Ai died without heir, Emperor P'ing was called in to succeed him. When Emperor P'ing died without heir, WANG Mang put the young prince Ying on the throne. This is what PAN Ku in his history referred to in saying that "three times the national lineage was broken." Emperor Kuang-wu was a descendant of LIU Fa, Prince Ting of Ch'ang-sha, and originally belonged to a collateral line. The case may be compared to that of a tree-trunk several hundred years old, which suddenly issued a new bough. Though the bough might appear extremely flourishing, its vitality was already limited. When branches grew from this bough, they would be still smaller, weaker, and more easily broken. After Chin moved south, most rulers came to the throne when young. After Sung moved south, also there were many cases when outside princes were called in to succeed to the throne. These were caused by a decline in "vitality and fortune" and could not be controlled by human efforts.

CHAO's interpretation of vitality and fortune was naturalistic rather than mechanical, and while relying heavily on the *T'ien*

[28] *Nien-erh-shih cha-chi* (*Ssu-pu pei-yao* ed.) 4.15a-b.

14

factor he did not ignore the human side of the picture. For instance, his point on the selfishness of dowager empresses was based on human psychology.

In another passage [29] where he discussed the many young rulers of Chin, he repeated the same thesis of vitality and fortune, but also added, " Nevertheless, the Eastern Chin dynasty lasted eighty to ninety years. That was through reliance on the assistance of the great ministers." This is a good point; in the above discussion we may have over-emphasized the role played by the emperor, but not by intention. We start with the imperial annals because they provide us with a short survey. The emperor serves as a focusing point but need not occupy our whole attention. Obviously there were emperors in history who were mere figure heads. And of course even the most energetic emperor could not govern a vast empire like China singlehanded.

The general picture obtained from a reading of the annals may or may not be accurate. To ensure some degree of reliability, the rough configuration should be subjected to what may be called multiple checking. As far as possible, information should be found concerning the territory, the number, intensity and results of foreign and civil wars, the population, the cultivated land, works for water conservancy, the currency, the price level, the number and intensity of natural calamities and the efforts made to meet such a challenge, the number of successful and unsuccessful candidates in the civil service examinations, the number of able ministers and benevolent administrators, etc.

A few studies along such lines have been made by modern scholars, for instance, in the study on internecine wars by LI Ssu-kuang 李四光,[30] on water works by CHI Ch'ao-ting 冀朝鼎,[31]

---

[29] *Ibid.*, 8.4a-b.

[30] The Chinese version of LI's article is in *Ch'ing-chu Ts'ai Yüan-p'ei hsien-sheng liu-shih-wu sui lun-wen chi* 慶祝蔡元培先生六十五歲論文集, 1933, 1.157-166. Its English version (J. S. LEE, "The Periodic Recurrence of Internecine Wars in China," *China Journal of Science and Art*, March and April, 1931) has been discussed by LIN Yu-t'ang, *My Country and My People* (1935), pp. 28-34, and by Owen LATTIMORE, *Inner Asian Frontiers of China* (1940), p. 532.

[31] *Key Economic Areas in Chinese History, as Revealed in the Development of Public Works for Water-Controls*, 1936.

on land tax by WANG Yü-ch'üan 王毓銓,[32] on floods and droughts by YAO Shan-yu 姚善友,[33] on price levels in T'ang and Sung times by CH'ÜAN Han-sheng 全漢昇,[34] and on portents during the Western Han period by BIELENSTEIN [35] and EBERHARD.[36] The works by CH'ÜAN, BIELENSTEIN and EBERHARD are especially interesting because they represent the first serious attempts to draw configurations under single dynasties based on one criterion. It is true that many figures in Chinese historical works cannot be accepted at their face value. For instance, population figures and land acreage tended to have fiscal significance rather than reflecting the real situation. Reports on portents and calamities may have been omitted or fabricated. But in many cases such figures can be made meaningful. Handled with care, they are by no means non-touchables.

In general, the above-mentioned and other modern studies have made contributions in advancing interpretations on the basis of geographical areas and social groups—in other words, on the stage and actors of history. These factors were not unknown in the Chinese tradition, but their effective use in historical interpretation is relatively new. Traditional scholars tended to identify a dynasty with the whole country and also with all classes. Nominally this may be true, but actually a dynasty was likely to have its basis in certain areas and certain groups of people. Further,

[32] "The Rise of Land Tax and the Fall of Dynasties in Chinese History," *Pacific Affairs* 9 (1936).

[33] "The Chronological and Seasonal Distribution of Floods and Droughts in Chinese History, 206 B.C.-A.D. 1911," *HJAS* 6 (1942).273-312; "The Geographical Distribution of Floods and Droughts in Chinese History, 206 B.C.-A.D. 1911," *FEQ*, 2 (1943).4.357-378; "Flood and Drought Data in the *T'u-shu chi-ch'eng* and the *Ch'ing shih kao*," *HJAS* 8 (1944).214-226.

[34] CH'ÜAN Han-sheng article on price fluctuations during the T'ang period in *CYYY* 11 (1943).101-148, on price fluctuations under the Northern Sung in *CYYY* 11 (1943). 337-394; on the great changes in prices during the first years of the Southern Sung in *CYYY* 11 (1943).395-423; on the inflation and its effects on prices toward the end of the Sung dynasty in *CYYY* 10 (1942).193-222.

[35] Hans BIENLENSTEIN, "An Interpretation of the Portents in the Ts'ien Han shu," *BMFEA* 22 (1950).127-143, and "The Restoration of the Han Dynasty," *BMFEA* 26 (1954).158-62.

[36] Wolfram EBERHARD, "The Function of Astronomy and Astronomers in China during the Han Period," paper written for the Second Conference on Chinese Thought, 1954.

these were the first things the dynasty would attend to, although it also had an interest in holding the empire. In this sense, a dynasty may be considered a composite entity of geographical and social forces. The interests in the capital and at court may be different from local interests. For instance, a decline of central control often means more freedom for the local rich and powerful. Also such matters as whether the political center and the economic center coincide have great influences over institutions of the dynasty. As for social groups, it is useful to keep in mind a distinction between the ruling classes and the ruled, the gentry and the peasantry, the civil and the military groups, etc. The presence of geographical and social differences, however, provides chances both for conflict and for cooperation. It is the duty of the historian to find out how the cooperative and conflicting forces worked under a dynasty. The study of dynastic configurations naturally leads one to the problem.

In applying the multiple checking, we may come across interesting features of Chinese society. For example, in the matter of price, a low and steady price level (the price of grain in particular) was usually considered a sign of prosperity. Although as early as the period of Warring States people already were aware of the principle *ku-chien shang-nung* 穀賤傷農 i. e., " low grain prices hurt the farmers," [37] there was no fear of overproduction and depression as people have in the modern West.

Only after making all the necessary checkings can we compare and interpret the different configurations intelligently. Only then can we tell in what sense Chinese history from dynasty to dynasty has been a repetition of the same cycle or different cycles. If we are contented with the thesis that the rise and fall of a dynasty involve both cyclical and non-cyclical factors (not necessarily those of *T'ien* and *Jen*), it is still desirable to find out the relative importance of the two types of factors for each dynasty. Otherwise, to speak about the dynastic cycle without going into the configurations would be too abstract to be useful. Dynasties rise and fall just as man is mortal. What is important is to learn something useful from the achievements and failures, in other words the careers, of mortal dynasties.

[37] Nancy Lee SWANN, *Food and Money in Ancient China* (1950), p. 139.

17

SCHEDULES OF WORK AND REST IN IMPERIAL CHINA

LIEN-SHENG YANG

HARVARD UNIVERSITY

Introduction

This article is an attempt to survey the schedules of work and rest, or work and play, through the twenty-one centuries of imperial China. The study is divided into two parts. The first deals with office hours and official holidays—in other words, with the daily and annual schedules of the officials and of the emperor, affecting everybody who had contact with officialdom. At the end of this section there are given some general accounts concerning the schedules of students and of the Buddhist and Taoist clergy, because these were groups closely related to the official class. The second section covers the business and labor hours of the farmers, merchants, craftsmen, servants, and slaves, as well as their holidays and festivals. For the sake of simplicity, the first section is labeled " Official Holidays and Office Hours " and the second " Business Hours and Working Hours."

These matters are, I think, of fundamental social and economic importance. The ratio between an individual's work and play is an index—though not, of course, an absolute one—of what he gives to and takes from society. From another point of view, we can apply what may be called the equation of three W's: Welfare equals Wage divided by Work. Of course, in applying this rough formula we must take into consideration such factors as real and nominal wages, previous training of the worker, intensity of work, and working conditions. Sometimes it may be difficult to distinguish work from play; for instance, a ruler may enjoy thoroughly the time he devotes to making decisions, and an artist the time he devotes to his masterpiece. Nevertheless, from the point of view of the society, the person is working if he is performing the duty required by his role. Working schedules of different social classes, therefore, should reflect the pattern of contribution made by each group to society.

18

(1) Official Holidays and Office Hours

This section will be limited for the most part to the normal schedules of the official class, because obviously the working schedule need not be identical for every official—his post may be a busy one or one with leisure. Further, the schedule may change according to whether the country is at peace or in a state of emergency.[1] There may be seasonal differences in the summer schedule and winter schedule. Moreover, even the normal schedule cannot be maintained always with the same rigidity or faithfulness. A lazy ruler or official may often fail to keep his office hours or to hold court, whereas a conscientious emperor or official may work day and night. With these modifications in mind, we may proceed to describe and discuss the normal practice.

First, we may ask, was there a regular holiday comparable to Sunday in traditional China? The answer is yes. Under the Han dynasty, officials were allowed to take one day off in every five days. The holiday was known as *hsiu-mu* 休沐 " a day for rest and for washing one's hair." [2] This practice was followed as late as the Sui dynasty. A change, however, had taken place in south China sometime in the period of disunion following the fall of the Han dynasty; we know that at least the Liang dynasty in Nanking observed a regular holiday only once in every ten-day period.[3] Such was the rule from the T'ang dynasty through the Yüan dynasty, and these holidays, known as *hsün-chia* 旬假 or *hsün-hsiu* 旬休, were observed on the tenth, the twentieth and the last day (i. e., the twenty-ninth or thirtieth) of the moon.[4] A further reduction was made in Ming and Ch'ing times when the

---

[1] For instance, in the first years of the Southern Sung dynasty, which was a time of emergency, officials were required to remain in the office on holidays. Cf. *Sung hui-yao kao* 宋會要稿, " Chih-kuan " 職官 60.15a-b.

[2] Examples can be found in *Han shu* 46.11b, 50.12a, and in *Hou Han shu* 74.3b.

[3] The Ch'ing encyclopaedia *Yüan-chien lei-han* 淵鑑類函 123.37b-38a contains a poem on *hsün-chia* 旬假 "holiday in a ten-day period" by Liu Hsiao-ch'o 劉孝綽 of the Liang dynasty, and another poem by Chiang Tsung 江總 of the Sui dynasty beginning with the line 洗沐惟五日 " The day for bathing and washing one's hair occurs on the fifth day." Chiang Tsung originally served under the Ch'en dynasty, but probably wrote the poem under the Sui.

[4] *T'ang hui-yao* 唐會要 (*TSCC* ed.) 82.1518-1521; *T'ung-chih t'iao-ko* 通制條格 22.4a.

19

regulations provided for no such holidays at all. (Sunday was introduced as an official holiday only in the Republican era.)

How can we interpret this continuous reduction of regular holidays in Chinese history? Two easy answers readily come to mind. First, these changes may have reflected a long-run increase in government duties (or perhaps in red tape) to be handled officially. Second, there may have been a tendency in Chinese history for the emperor to be more and more of a slave-driver toward his officials. In general, these interpretations seem to apply to the Ming and Ch'ing periods, when the governing power became more centralized than in earlier dynasties. The case of the T'ang dynasty was rather different, because, as we shall see, it made very liberal allowances of festival holidays and other vacations.

To understand the change from the Han system of having one day off in every five days to the half rate under the T'ang, we have to consider another factor, namely, the residence of the officials. As far as can be determined, it was customary for an official in Han times to live in his office rather than in his home.[5] Thus, in theory, he could transact business any time day or night, although normally he would hold office only early in the morning and late in the afternoon.[6] Since most officials lived in their office quarters, the holiday " for rest and for washing one's hair " would amount to a short home leave for those who had their families within reach.

According to examples recorded in history, on such a holiday, a poor but incorruptible official would walk home because he could not afford to ride in a cart or a boat. A social-minded man would first visit relatives and friends on his way home.[7] It was undoubtedly rare for an official to refuse to take a holiday. The following story, being an exceptional case, is interesting and instructive.

[5] Shang Ping-ho 尚秉和, *Li-tai she-hui feng-su shih-wu k'ao* 歷代社會風俗事物考 (1938), pp. 351-353.

[6] This is reflected even in the *Shuo-wen* definition of the word *shen* 申 (3-5 P.M.) as the time for officials to work further on government affairs left over from the morning (吏以餔時聽事申旦政也). Cf. *Shuo-wen chieh-tzu ku-lin* 說文解字詁林 14B.6643b-6647a.

[7] *Hou Han shu* 106.12a.

In the Former Han period, Hsüeh Hsüan 薛宣 served as the prefect of P'ing-i 馮翊, a prefecture near the capital. On the day of the summer or winter solstice, all officials took a holiday, but CHANG Fu 張扶, chief of the police section (賊曹掾), refused to do this and sat in his office to work as usual. Thereupon, the prefect Hsüeh Hsüan issued him an instruction which read: " In general, rituals should esteem harmony and mankind should be social. It has been a long tradition for officials to rest on a day of solstice in accordance with the government regulation. Although there may be official business in your section, your family also expects you to have personal feelings of affection. You would do better to follow the majority to be with your wife and children, and prepare some food and wine to entertain your neighbors and have a good time." The chief of police became very ashamed of himself, as the other subordinate officials applauded this instruction.[8]

The requirement for officials to live in their offices probably continued for some time after the Han dynasty. This may be illustrated by a case under the Wei dynasty in the third century, when a harsh official refused to grant a day's leave to a subordinate to visit his sick father, who lived very near to the office. WANG Ssu 王思, the Minister of Finance (大司農), had become very suspicious in his old age. When the subordinate asked for leave because his father was critically ill, the Minister remarked irritably, " I have heard of cases in which a man claims his mother is ill when he really merely misses his wife. This must be it! " Next day the father of the subordinate died, but the Minister expressed no regret.[9]

Changes probably took place under the Northern and Southern dynasties when it became the regimen for officials to take turns of night duty in their offices—a practice that lasted through the rest of imperial China. From T'ang times on, it was customary for officials to be in their offices in the morning, or in the morning and afternoon, and then to return home. Of course, if it was a day for a court gathering, officials in the capital would first appear at the imperial court early in the morning before they went to their

[8] *Han shu* 83.4a-5a.
[9] *T'ai-p'ing yü-lan* 太平御覽 634.2a.

offices. Since most officials lived with their families, there was little need for a short leave every five days. Moreover, it would seem only fair to reduce the regular holidays because the officials now spent less time in their offices.

In addition to the regular Sunday-like holiday, festival holidays were also provided in government statutes. In the T'ang and Sung periods, there were major and minor festivals each allowing one, three, five, or seven holidays. High on the list were the New Year and the Winter Solstice, seven days each. For the T'ang period, all together I count fifty-three festival holidays in a year, including three days for the birthday of the emperor, and one each for the birthdays of the Buddha and Lao-tzu.[10] The Sung allowed fifty-four such holidays, but only eighteen days specified as *hsiu-wu* 休務 or " without business; " presumably the other days were at least partly for business as usual.[11] The Sung did not consider the birthdays of the Buddha or Lao-tzu as legal holidays, probably reflecting a decline in the influence of Buddhism and Taoism.

The Yüan dynasty recognized sixteen festival holidays.[12] In Ming and Ch'ing times, festival holidays were at first even fewer than the Yüan. The government statutes list only three major festivals, the New Year, the Winter Solstice, and the Emperor's birthday.[13] Actually, the fifth day of the fifth moon and the mid-autumn festival also became important. But the main change under the Ming and Ch'ing was the introduction of a long New Year or winter vacation that lasted about a month. For officials all over the empire, a day around the twentieth day of the twelfth moon would be chosen by the Imperial Astronomer for them to " seal up their government seals " (*feng-yin* 封印). About a month later, another day would be announced for the " opening of the seals " (*k'ai-yin* 開印).[14] During this period, officials would

---

[10] Niida Noboru 仁井田陞, *Tōryō shūi* 唐令拾遺 (1933), pp. 732-735.

[11] *Sung hui-yao kao, Chih-kuan* 60.15a.

[12] *T'ung-chih t'iao-ko* 22.4a.

[13] *Ming hui-tien* 明會典 (*Wan-yu wen-k'u* 萬有文庫 ed.) 43.1235-1236; *Ta-Ch'ing hui-tien shih-li* 大清會典事例 (Kuang-hsü ed.) 92.1a-6b.

[14] Derk Bodde, tr., *Annual Customs and Festivals in Peking as Recorded in the Yen-ching-sui-shih-chi by Tun Li-ch'en* (1936), p. 95.

still go to their offices occasionally, but the handling of judicial cases would be entirely suspended. The winter vacation may be considered a compensation for the loss in regular and festival holidays.

In the government statutes, home leaves and similar vacations were provided to take care of one's duties to the family and clan on such occasions as, for instance, the marriage or death of a close relative. Most liberal were the provisions under the T'ang dynasty, which included: [15]

a) Home leave of 30 days (exclusive of travel) in 3 years if parents lived 3000 *li* away; 15 days in 5 years if parents lived 500 *li* away.

b) For the capping ceremony of one's son, 3 days leave; for a relative, 1 day.

c) For the marriage of one's son or daughter, 9 days leave, exclusive of travel; for other close relatives, 5 days, 3 days, or 1 day.

d) For the death of one's parent, a forced retirement from office for 3 years; in case of military officers, 100 days.

e) For the death of other close relatives, a leave of 30, 20, 15 or 7 days; for distant relatives, 5 days, 3 days, or 1 day.

f) For the death of one's tutor (a teacher who had actually taught one), 3 days leave.

g) For a privately tabooed day (*chi-jih* 忌日, birthday or day of death of one's parent or grandparent), 1 day's leave.

h) In the 5th moon, a " farming vacation " (*t'ien chia* 田假) of 15 days, and a " vacation for making clothes " (*shou-i chia* 授衣假) of 15 days in the 9th moon.

Most of these rules appear to have been followed also in Sung times, except for the last item. In the Ming and Ch'ing periods, many such leaves were omitted entirely or were *ad hoc* and had to wait for the permission of the emperor.[16] The only rule that was observed quite rigidly was the forced retirement for three

---

[15] *Tōryō shūi*, pp. 736-749.
[16] *Ming hui-tien* 5.115-116; *Ta-Ch'ing hui-tien shih-li* 296.1a-2a.

years (actually twenty-seven months) following the death of one's parent.[17] These changes seem to indicate an increasing or continuous emphasis on one's duty to the emperor and to one's parents, with relatively less regard to other social relations, such as duty to other relatives and to one's tutor. This appears to be a feature in the ethics of Ming and Ch'ing times.

On the daily schedules, it is interesting to note that the position of the chief official of a local government resembled that of the emperor in many ways. Under the Ming and Ch'ing dynasties, this resemblance was reflected even in similarities between the building plans of their offices (of course, on quite different scales).[18] In a local yamen, as in the imperial palace, there were gates and courtyards in front, with small rooms for subordinates and police guards on the two sides. Then there was the *ta-t'ang* 大堂 or " main hall " corresponding to the Main Throne Hall (*cheng-tien* 正殿) of the emperor, chiefly used for ceremonial or other formal occasions. The *erh-t'ang* 二堂 or " second hall " corresponded to other throne halls (especially the *hou-tien* 後殿) of the emperor, used more often for fulfilling everyday duties. In a small yamen, the second hall or a part of it was often designated as the *ch'ien-ya fang* 簽押房 or " chamber for signing documents." This personal office or study could be used by the official to go over documents or to consult his confidential secretaries, either during the regular office hours in the morning or at any optional working time in the afternoon or evening. The emperor would also designate an inner hall or chamber of study for similar purposes, although it was not known as *ch'ien-ya fang*. The back part of a yamen, which served as living quarters of the family of the chief official, corresponded to the rear palaces of the imperial consorts.

The emperor's schedule normally began with court gatherings

---

[17] The emperor might require the official to return to service before the completion of the mourning period. This was known as *to-ch'ing ch'i-fu* 奪情起復 " to call back to service in violence to feelings " (also shortened to *ch'i-fu*, which means simply " call back to service "), and it was considered appropriate only when there was a military emergency. In general, the practice was resorted to more commonly in the T'ang and Sung periods than in later times.

[18] Building plans of local yamen are often included in gazetteers.

early in the morning. Meetings of ceremonious nature tended to be held on festival days or at intervals of three (3, 6, 9) or five (5, 10) days. Less formal gatherings could occur every other day or even every day. The hour was often frightfully early, about five or six o'clock in the morning. It would be considered late if a court gathering took place at seven or eight o'clock. Under the Manchu dynasty, the emperor occasionally held court in the famous Yüan-ming Yüan outside Peking, and many officials in the city had to get up about midnight in order to get there in time. In general, the Manchu rulers maintained these early office hours quite faithfully, which fact doubtless played its part in helping to make the Ch'ing a stable and lasting dynasty though alien.[19]

The example of the Manchu rulers, however, was not regularly imitated by local government officials, although they were supposed to follow a similar schedule in their respective offices. There was laxity even in the Yung-cheng reign, when the emperor maintained an extraordinarily close supervision over his provincial governors. According to an official handbook for the local governments (the *Chou-hsien shih-i* 州縣事宜)[20] issued in this reign, many prefects and district magistrates simply failed to hold court in the morning. The handbook urged them to reform, but with what results one can only wonder.

To announce the beginning (and sometimes the end) of office hours, the central government normally used drums or bells. Local governments, especially those on the district and prefectural levels, generally resorted to the less august sound of wooden clappers (*ch'uan-pang* 傳梆) or the ringing of a gong (*ta-tien* 打點).[21] Clerks and runners were obliged to be ready at the court on time, subject to the penalty of beating. Under the Yüan dynasty, the powerful minister Sang-ko 桑哥 (Sengge) applied this rule rigidly even to subordinate officials in his ministry; once

---

[19] Regulations on the days and hours for court gatherings are found in statutes of various dynasties such as the *T'ang hui-yao* 24.455-458. For a summary of the practices under the Ch'ing dynasty, see Chen-chün 震鈞, *T'ien-chih ou-wen* 天咫偶聞 (1907 ed.) 1.2b-4a.

[20] *Huan-hai chih-nan* 宦海指南 ed., 9b-10a.

[21] Ts'AI Shen-chih 蔡申之, "Ch'ing-tai chou-hsien ku-shih" 清代州縣故事, *Chung-ho yüeh-k'an* 中和月刊 2(1941).10.73-74.

the celebrated artist and scholar CHAO Meng-fu 趙孟頫 actually received a beating for arriving after the morning bell. Only after CHAO's complaint to higher authorities did Sang-ko limit the punishment to clerks and lesser employees.[22]

For the promotion of officials, service time (known as *lao* 勞, "industry") was taken into consideration together with distinguished service (known as *kung* 功, "merit"). This was true at least as early as the Han period.[23] However, it is not clear from what dynasty the government introduced books of attendance for officials and others to sign. An example is found in Yüan times when officials, clerks, and guards at government treasuries were required to record their attendance in the so-called *mao-yu wen-li* 卯酉文曆 ("journal from 6 A. M to 6 P. M.").[24] Similar registers of attendance seem to have become regularly used in many offices in Ming and Ch'ing times. For officials on periodic night duty the T'ang dynasty had the *chih-pu* 直簿 "night duty register," which probably had existed in earlier times.[25] Sometimes night duty became a mere fiction, as in the Northern Sung period when officers of the four imperial libraries were accustomed to evade their night duty by making a false report of stomach trouble. As a result, the night duty register (*su-li* 宿曆) of the imperial libraries acquired the nickname of *hai-tu li* 害肚曆 "journal of suffering from stomach trouble." [26]

Of course, a really conscientious official would not only keep his office hours but add to them many extra working hours. As an illustration, I shall cite the working schedule of TSENG Kuo-fan when he was governor-general of Liang-kiang, directing the campaign against the Tai-p'ing rebels. As shown in his diary, entry of the 19th day of the 8th moon, in the first year of T'ung-chih (1862),[27] TSENG Kuo-fan decided that the following items should constitute his daily schedule:

---

[22] *Yüan shih* 172.6a.

[23] ŌBA Osamu 大庭脩, "Kandai ni okeru kōji ni yoru shōshin ni tsuite" 漢代における功次による昇進について, *Tōyōshi kenkyū* 東洋史研究 12 (1953) 3.14-28. A. F. P. HULSEWÉ, *Remnants of Han Law*, Vol. 1 (1955), p. 47.

[24] *T'ung-chih t'iao-ko* 14.5a-b.

[25] *T'ang hui-yao* 82.1516.

[26] *Meng-ch'i pi-t'an* 夢溪筆談 (SPTK ed.) 23.5b-6a.

[27] *Tseng Wen-cheng kung shou-shu jih-chi* 曾文正公手書日記 14.₊1b.

Morning—Receive guests, paying attention to their appearance and words; draft memorials; check list of officials recommended for appointment or promotion; call rolls and supervise military drills; write letters that have to be done with his own hand; read books; practice calligraphy.

Afternoon—Read today's documents; revise draft letters; approve and comment on draft documents going to subordinate officials; check and take notes on financial accounts.

Night—Review poetry and classical-style prose; approve and comment on draft documents going to subordinate officials; check items of affairs that should be memorialized to the throne.

TSENG Kuo-fan also decided that special attention should be paid to civil government and military affairs in the morning, to financial affairs in the afternoon, and to literature and learning at night. In general, his diary indicates that these were the types of work he did every day, although with variations from time to time. I may add one thing: to balance his work, he played one or two games of *wei-ch'i* or *go* every day. But since he was not a particularly strong player, presumably he played rather casually and the game probably did not take much of his time. It is evident that he attended to his duties most diligently and conscientiously. His example influenced many others of his time.

As the conscientious head of a family, TSENG Kuo-fan drew up working schedules not only for himself but also for other members of his household. According to the autobiography of his youngest daughter,[28] when he was governor-general in Nanking in 1868 he laid down the following schedule for young females in his household:

After breakfast, "food affairs" (*shih-shih* 食事)—preparation of dishes, sweets, wine, soya sauce, etc.

Late morning (10:00-12:00), "clothing affairs" (*i-shih* 衣事)—spinning cotton or making hemp thread.

After lunch, "fine work" (*hsi-kung* 細工)—embroidery and other fine needlework.

Evening (6:00 to 9:00 and later), "coarse work" (*ts'u-kung* 粗工)—making clothes, and shoes for men and women.

The boys in the household were to do four things for their studies: *k'an* 看, i.e., read silently; *tu* 讀, i.e., read aloud; *hsieh* 寫, i.e., practice calligraphy; and *tso* 作, i.e., compose. TSENG

---

[28] *Ch'ung-te lao-jen pa-shih tzu-ting nien-p'u* 崇德老人八十自訂年譜 6a-b.

Kuo-fan himself was going to supervise: some duties were to be supervised daily, others every few days, and others monthly.

This leads us to the schedules of students and pupils in imperial China. The students who studied in the imperial college (T'ai-hsüeh 太學 or Kuo-tzu-chien 國子監) were treated almost like officials, and also received a considerable number of holidays.[29] The number of such students was not very large, more often in the hundreds than in the thousands. Most students and pupils pursued their work in both morning and afternoon hours at private tutoring schools, and enjoyed holidays only during major festivals. In Ming and Ch'ing times, private schools also had a New Year or winter vacation of about a month.

In connection with school schedules, attention may be called to a point that is generally overlooked in the history of education in China, which is that schools for farmers' children tended to operate only in non-farming seasons. In the Han work Ssu-min yüeh-ling 四民月令 [Ordinances for the Four Classes],[30] which deals primarily with schedules of the farming population, it is stated that youths between the ages of nine and fourteen should go to elementary schools in the first moon, eighth moon, and eleventh moon, and those between fifteen and twenty should go to advanced schools in the first and tenth moons. In T'ang times, the " farming vacation " of fifteen days in the fifth moon and the fifteen-day " vacation for making clothes " in the ninth moon also applied to students in the imperial college, apparently to accomodate those who came from the countryside. In the Sung period, country schools for the farmers' children were known as tung-hsüeh 冬學 " winter schools," because they were open only in winter times.[31] The term tung-hsüeh is actually in use even at present.

[29] In T'ang times students were to take tests on the day before the regular holiday at the end of a ten day period; cf. Tōryō shūi, pp. 274-276. Under the Ming dynasty, students of the two Imperial Colleges enjoyed regular holidays on the first and the fifteenth day of the moon (Nan-yung chih 南雍志 9.4a-b, Kuo-tzu-chien chih 國子監志 43.21a).

[30] Ch'üan Hou Han wen 全後漢文 47.1a-8a.

[31] Ch'ü Hsüan-ying 瞿宣穎, Chung-kuo she-hui shih-liao ts'ung-ch'ao 中國社會史料叢鈔, Chia-chi 甲集, (1937), p. 815.

Schedules of work and rest for Buddhist and Taoist priests were rather rigid because of their communality. The most striking item in the annual schedule for Buddhist monks was the practice of *hsia an-chü* 夏安居 " summer retreat " which was borrowed from India. From the fifteenth day of the fourth moon to the fifteenth day of the seventh moon, Buddhist monks were required to stay in their respective monasteries. The interpretation was that in the summer months itinerant monks might suffer from heavy rains or that they might unwittingly commit the crime of killing living creatures.[32] Certainly the former and probably the latter were more likely to happen in India than in China. Nevertheless this rule was observed for many centuries in China, especially during T'ang and Sung times. The beginning and ending of the " summer retreat " were both marked by large vegetarian feasts in different monasteries.

To announce time for daily schedules in temples and monasteries, bells and drums were used, and their punctual sounds proved helpful to laity in the neighborhood as well. Some Buddhist monks actually assumed the duty of waking people in the morning by beating an iron plate or knocking a *mu-yü* 木魚 " wooden fish." In the Sung period, they were most active in the capital, not only waking people by sounding their instruments but also shouting whether it was fine, cloudy, or raining, and what kind of court gathering there was going to be on that particular morning. They did so irrespective of the weather, braving rain and snow. Each of these dawn-announcing monks had his own particular round to make, and from time to time they made a door-to-door collection of donations from shops and households.[33]

Monastic life was supposed to be quiet, but it was hardly so during festivals or on such days as the first and the fifteenth day of the moon, when the temples and monasteries would have their gates wide open for burners of incense. On certain days of festival,

[32] MOCHITSUKI Shinkō 望月信亨, *Bukkyō daijiten* 佛教大辭典 1.79c-80c; *Meng-liang lu* 夢粱錄 (*TSCC* ed.) 3.19-20, 4.24. The Buddhist rule against killing was also responsible for the designation of days and months in which no butchery was allowed—a practice that prevailed under many dynasties.

[33] *Tung-ching meng-hua lu* 東京夢華錄 (*TSCC* ed.) 3.7; *Meng-liang lu* 13.114-115.

the place might become a busy and noisy market or fair. The clergy also had their schedules of collecting donations by paying a visit to their patrons with token presents. This was rather different from the donations collected by the dawn-announcing monks as rewards for a service. It is, moreover, incorrect to assume that the monks were otherwise entirely parasitic. This was certainly not true with those Zen monks in late T'ang and early Sung times who followed the principle of " a day without work, a day without meals " (一日不作,一日不食).[34] During many periods in Chinese history when monasteries were rich, the clergy went into money-lending and other business activities on a considerable scale. Several money-raising institutions in China seem to have originated in monasteries.[35]

(2) Business Hours and Working Hours

The annual schedule of the farmer was a major concern of the ruler as well as the farmer himself. In order to facilitate the work of this chief producer, the government from antiquity had assumed the function of devising a calendar, which amounted to a detailed working schedule. In addition, rulers in ancient times were expected to promote and harmonize the cosmic forces of the season so as to help the people. This view predominated under the Han dynasty more than in later times; still, ceremonial promotions of agriculture were resorted to even until the end of the Ch'ing dynasty. For instance, on the day before the Beginning of Spring, local government officials would ceremoniously beat an earthen ox made for the purpose of announcing the arrival of the season for agriculture. On a chosen day in the spring, the Emperor, followed by his court, would personally perform the ceremonial ploughing to set an example for the people. More practically, local officials were to supervise the farmer's work and to encourage him. Of course, there were also the deadlines set for the payment of taxes, which the farmer could not afford to ignore.

Two matters that occasionally interfered with the farmer's

---

[34] A motto devised by the T'ang monk Huai-hai 懷海 (720-814).

[35] Lien-sheng YANG, " Buddhist Monasteries and Four Money-raising Institutions in Chinese History," *HJAS* 13 (1950).174-191.

schedule were forced service and lawsuits. For the most part of the period from the Han dynasty to the middle of the T'ang, the people were required to render a considerable amount of labor and military services. It is true that from antiquity thinkers constantly warned against drafting the farmer for corvée except in non-farming seasons, but unfortunately this advice was often disregarded. In the more recent periods of imperial China, the tendency was for soldiery to become an independent occupation and for labor service to be commuted into money payments. In the long run, this reduction of interference may have favored an increase in food production, and indirectly an increase in population.

That lawsuits were costly was proverbial in imperial China. This was particularly true for the farmer, who was easily victimized by red tape and corruption. For example, in the second century when the Han dynasty was declining, the farmer found it extremely difficult to have a legal case settled in the city. He would not be announced unless he appeared during the short court hours in the early morning or late afternoon, and even then he could not see the magistrate unless he presented a gift. He was often detained in the city for days and months, and it became necessary for his relatives or neighbors to bring him provisions and support. As estimated by the second-century scholar WANG FU 王符,[36] this situation cost the working time of as many as 300,000 persons per day in the Han empire. Though this may have been an exaggeration, it is beyond question that lawsuits could seriously interfere with the farmer's schedule. Remedies were attempted in later times but were rarely successful. An interesting provision was made under the Sung dynasty when farmers were not allowed to present civil lawsuits in their working seasons. This was known as *wu-hsien* 務限 " reservation made for the working time," which lasted from the first day of the second moon to the first day of the tenth moon.[37]

[36] *Ch'ien-fu lun* 潛夫論 (*SPPY* ed.) 4.26b-29a.

[37] Lawsuits accepted up to the last day of the first moon were to be tried by the end of the third moon (*Sung hui-yao kao, Hsing-fa* 3.46a-48a; *Sung hsing-t'ung* 宋刑統 13.7a-b). Under the Yüan dynasty, the *wu-hsien* lasted from the first day of the third moon to the first day of the tenth moon (*Yüan tien-chang* 元典章 53.36a).

The daily schedule of the farmer was to work in the field from sunrise to dark. This was interrupted only by the noon meal which was brought to him by his family in accordance with an ancient custom. The farmer's wife might collaborate in the field to a greater or lesser degree, varying with local practice. But she was always the spinner and weaver, and her work might last till midnight if she could afford the oil. Sharing of light by spinning and weaving females was another custom traceable to antiquity.[38]

In places where collective farming was practiced, such as the Szechwan area in Sung and Yüan times, a "farm drum" and a "farm clepsydra" were used to mark the time. Poems were written by Sung scholars on these and other farming implements.[39] In a Yüan work devoted to agriculture,[40] we read, "The weeding drum (薅鼓) is seen when one enters Szechwan. It is used first to cause [the farmers] to assemble, then to give rhythm to their work and keep them from conversations which might hinder their work. The sound of the drum is powerful and brisk, varying in speed and pitch but having no melody. It is continuously heard from morning till evening." Apparently the weeding drum was an effective means of regulating and encouraging farming work. However, it was not well known in other parts of China where collective farming was rare or nonexistent.

Unlike the schedule of the farmer, which remained stable throughout imperial China, that of the merchant underwent substantial change. The long-range historical trend was toward an increase in commercial activities and therefore toward the lengthening of business hours. From Han to the middle of T'ang, the government designated market places in the cities where merchants were to congregate and do business. Merchants of the same trade were supposed to dwell in the same lane in the market place, and the government exercised extensive control and supervision. Market time began only at noon in accordance with an ancient

[38] *Han shu* 24A.4b; Nancy Lee SWANN, *Food and Money in Ancient China* (1950), p. 129.

[39] *Lin-ch'uan chi* 臨川集 (*SPPY* ed.) 11.3a-5a; *Wan-ling hsien-sheng wen-chi* 宛陵先生文集 (*SPPY* ed.) 51.1b-3a.

[40] WANG Chen 王禎, *Nung shu* 農書 (*Wu-ying-tien chü-chen-pan ch'üan-shu* 武英殿聚珍版全書 ed.) 10.11a-b, with an illustration.

custom. In the T'ang period, the market place opened at noon upon two hundred beats of a drum, and closed seven quarters before sunset upon three hundred beats of a gong. This rule was gradually relaxed from the ninth century. By the twelfth century it was normal for large cities to have commercial activities from early in the morning till late in the night. Merchants were no longer restricted as to either time or place. Parallel to the relaxing of government control over city markets was the development of markets in the suburbs, known as *ts'ao-shih* 草市 or " hay-markets," which were under little control from the beginning.[41] Of course, in Sung and later times there were still, as in earlier periods, periodic fairs and markets in small towns and villages, which tended to last only a part of the day because there was no need for them to be continued longer.

Merchants normally would continue their business on holidays, and especially on festival days, because these were the best days to do business. This was true for for merchants who maintained shops as well as for hawkers and peddlers. One major exception to this rule had to do with the New Year, when nearly every business would take a vacation for at least a day or two, including even the restaurants and medicine shops; the latter were expected to keep somebody in the closed shop to answer emergency calls for prescriptions. Toward the end of the Ch'ing dynasty and in the early years of the Republic there began the custom of keeping a number of shops open to carry on business during the New Year holidays. Known as *lien-shih* 連市 " continuation of business," this practice at first was somewhat frowned upon as an indication of over-eagerness for extra profit.[42]

The working schedule of the craftsman normally embraced the whole day, like that of the farmer. Of course, the day could be long or short according to the season, and this fact was acknowledged from early times. For instance, under the T'ang dynasty, government statutes recognized the third and seventh moons as periods for " long work " (*ch'ang-kung* 長功); the tenth, eleventh, twelfth, and first moons as periods for " short work " (*tuan-kung*

[41] KATŌ Shigeru 加藤繁, *Shina keizai shi kōshō* 支那經濟史考證 1.299-421.
[42] *T'ien-chih ou-wen* 10.11a.

短功); and the other four moons as periods for " medium work " (*chung-kung* 中功).[43] Presumably the government attached different weight to work done in the different months. In more recent times, roughly from the Sung period on, it became common for craftsmen in cities to work at night as well as in the daytime. This development appears to be similar to the change in the merchants' schedule, but the practice was much less extensive. Night work was required only for indoor crafts, and for about half the year (e. g., from the ninth moon to the third moon), as a compensation for the shorter daylight of that part of the year.[44] There seems reflected here a lag in industrial development behind commercial development.

The heaviest working schedule in trade or industry invariably fell on the apprentice, whose position was no better than that of a slave or servant. These three together formed the lowest groups among the ruled classes. Of course, slaves and servants belonging to rich and powerful households might in some cases live an easier life than an ordinary commoner. But to the labor that could be exacted from them there was practically no limit. The famous " Contract for a Slave " (" T'ung-yüeh " 僮約) by WANG Pao 王褒 (first century B. C.) has been translated and annotated in English, and more recently in Japanese.[45] The numerous tasks listed in the contract could hardly have been performed by a single individual; still, the document can be viewed as reflecting a collective picture. Less well known is a document by the Sung scholar HUANG T'ing-chien 黃庭堅 headed " Po-hsi i-wen " 跛奚移文 or " Memorandum for a Lame Maid-Servant." [46] The lame woman was procured to serve HUANG's sister after her marriage. She walked so clumsily that she annoyed nearly everybody. HUANG, however, succeeded in persuading her that she could do plenty of work without walking, and put down in partly rhymed prose her different tasks, which may be summarized as follows:

---

[43] *T'ang liu-tien* 唐六典 (1836 Japanese ed.) 7.9b.

[44] *Shina keizai zensho* 支那經濟全書 2.642, 649.

[45] C. Martin WILBUR, *Slavery in China During the Former Han Dynasty* (1943), pp. 382-392; UTSUNOMIYA Kiyoyoshi 宇都宮清吉, *Kandai shakai keizai shi kenkyū* 漢代社會經濟史研究 (1955), pp. 256-374.

[46] *Yü-chang Huang hsien-sheng wen-chi* 豫章黃先生文集 (*SPTK* ed.) 21.3b-6a.

In the morning she is to enter the kitchen, wash the pots and pans, and select vegetables. In cutting meat, slicing fish, making dough, cooking noodles and rice, etc., she is to follow specific instructions. If there is any misconduct on the part of fellow maidservants, such as scratching their dirty skin or hair above the dishes or stealing a taste of food, it should be reported.

After eating she is to wash the dishes several times, on both sides, dry them clean and put them back in good order. After noontime, during which she is at leisure, she should wash clothes, making sure that she uses the correct tubs for dirty and clean (i. e., upper and lower) garments. White clothes should be bleached, and colored clothes should be dyed bright. Both should be starched and ironed.

When evening approaches, she is to call in the cattle and chickens, and close and lock the gates to prevent thieves. She should feed the cats and dogs, and seal up mouse holes. She will be held responsible if a bird, cat, dog, or mouse touches any food or container.

When spring silkworms have had their third sleep and are spinning on a frame, she should see to it that they are kept warm day and night. Taking the various kinds of fibres such as those of hemp, rattan, and plantain, she should work constantly with them making thread or cloth.

In hot weather she should fan the air and prepare iced and honeyed drinks. She should burn mugwort to drive away mosquitoes, and keep flies away from the plate of fruits on ice. When fruits are raw, she should guard the trees; when they are ripe and picked, she should guard the baskets. No birds should touch them. Nor should she taste any lest she be blamed or ridiculed by the womenfolk or catch stomach trouble.

When it is cold, she should warm up the clothes and bedding with a brazier. She should also warm her hands before she uses them to soothe others' itching or pain.

When she has nothing to do, she should lean against a wall and make shoes or slipers. When other servants are called, she should transmit the call from the master or mistress and respond on behalf of the servants.

35

For the schedule of an apprentice I have translated and appended at the end of this article a *Manual for Apprentices in Trade*, found in an almanac dated 1905.[47] Unlike the Contract and the Memorandum, which are mixed with remarks intended to be humorous, the Manual is completely serious and therefore more realistic. Interestingly enough, several of the same duties appear in all three documents.

For the various ruled classes, holidays were few except for major festivals such as the New Year. For merchants and craftsmen who lived in the shops, a home leave was normally every few years. Working in the shop, at regular intervals they would also be served better food than usual, for instance on the first and the fifteenth day of the month. Such matters were conventionalized by custom and often regulated by the guild of the profession. This was true for both merchants' and craftsmen's guilds.

Most interesting was the special holiday in honor of the deity of the trade or profession. It was often celebrated with pomp and zeal. Shops belonging to the guild shared the expenses of banquet, theatrical performance, and procession. For the farmer, it was the *she-jih* 社日, the day for the god of the soil, which recurred in the spring and the fall. Expenses for its celebration constituted a regular item in the budget of the farmer from as early as the Chou period.[48] After sacrificial offering to the god of the soil, the meat and wine were shared by members of the community, and if it was a year of good harvest, every household would have the job of helping its intoxicated member home. It was a day of absolutely no work for anybody, including school children and women, because superstition had it that those who failed to take the day off would become stupid and clumsy.[49] The observation of the *she-jih* declined from the Yüan period. It has been suggested that this may have resulted from prohibition of mass worship by the

---

[47] *T'ien-pao-lou chi-ch'i hung-tzu-t'ou t'ung-shu* 天寶樓機器紅字頭通書 or *Almanac with Red Characters Machine-Printed by the T'ien-pao-lou*. It is interesting to note that in the Cantonese dialect the two characters 通書 are often pronounced like 通勝 (" to win completely ") because *t'ung-shu* suggests the homophonous 通輸 (" to lose completely "), which is a tabooed expression.

[48] *Han shu* 24A.6b; *Food and Money in Ancient China*, pp. 140-142.

[49] *Chung-kuo she-hui shih-liao ts'ung-ch'ao, Chia-chi*, pp. 478-505.

alien Mongolian dynasty.[50] Still it was not uncommon for the farmers to observe an annual festival in a village temple, though the god of the temple and the date of celebration would vary from place to place. As pointed out above, the important holidays in Ming and Ch'ing times were at the time of the New Year, the fifth day of the fifth moon, and the mid-autumn festival. These three major festivals, known as *san ta-chieh* 三大節, were universal for all classes.

Conclusion

The general picture that emerges from the above survey can perhaps be described as "change within tradition," if I may borrow the title of an illuminating article by Professor E. A. KRACKE, Jr.[51] Schedules of work and rest in imperial China underwent certain changes due to such factors as religious influences in the earlier periods, and the rise of commerce and increase in centralization of political power under the later dynasties. Nevertheless, the continuation of a lasting political, social, and economic order is unmistakable, and this is amply reflected in the schedules of both the ruling and ruled classes. A more comprehensive study, for instance, including such groups as soldiers, actors, fishermen, etc., may reveal more interesting details, but probably will not alter the general picture.

Apparently the various groups of people in imperial China found it natural to observe regular schedules of work and rest. Ancient tradition emphasized the virtue of *ch'in* 勤 or diligence; for instance, in the *Book of History*, certain ancient rulers are praised for being diligent in state affairs and frugal in their households.[52] The *Tso chuan* quotes an ancient saying, "People's weal depends on diligence; with diligence, there is no want." [53] The early philosophers expounded some basic principles related to schedules of work and rest. For instance, when Confucius com-

[50] *Li-tai she-hui feng-su shih-wu k'ao*, p. 443. Imperial decrees prohibiting such worship (*ch'i-shen sai-she* 祈神賽社) were issued in 1317 and 1319 (*Yuan tien-chang* 57.43b-45b).

[51] E. A. KRACKE, Jr., "Sung Society: Change within Tradition," *FEQ* 14 (1955) 4.479-488.

[52] LEGGE, *The Shoo King* 3.60.

[53] LEGGE, *The Ch'un ts'ew with the Tso Chuen* 5.318.

mented on a festival for driving away evil spirits, which had the whole state excited, he recognized the value of rest and pleasure as a means of relaxing strain from work.[54] Another principle, that of division of labor, was clearly recognized by Mencius as illustrated in his debate against the thought of the so-called agriculturalist school (*nung-chia* 農家).[55] At least as early as Chou times, the four major professional classes had already become standard: the scholar-official, the farmer, the craftsman, and the merchant.

Modern Westerners sometimes criticize the Chinese for their lack of a sense of time in their daily affairs. One must remember that China was an agricultural state in a pre-machine age where there was little need to be particular with time to the minute or second. The traditional emphasis on diligence and the habit of observing schedules of work and rest probably helped China to maintain a long lasting empire, and these factors will undoubtedly prove helpful in the industrialization and modernization of the country.

Appendix

A Manual for Apprentices in Trade
(" Hsi-ku hsü-chih 習賈須知 ")

[Translated from the *Almanac*[56] of 1905 published in Fo-shan, near Canton]

Whoever leaves his home to learn a trade, no matter what role he plays, should always be diligent and careful. Whenever his seniors talk, he should listen attentively and not interrupt. If they speak on respectable subjects with dignity, he should humbly accept [their words]. If they speak only jokingly for pleasure, he may disregard their words with a smile. If the apprentice's mistakes are mentioned, he should bend his head down and say, " Yes, yes." He should remember to correct such mistakes and by no means should he repudiate the criticisms or argue obstinately.

No matter whether it is a fellow worker (a journeyman or apprentice) of the same shop or a friend who does not belong to the trade, if he is older than the apprentice himself, the latter should address him according to his age as " elder uncle," " younger uncle," or " big brother," and may not call him by his personal name, which is contrary to etiquette. People's nicknames (花號) are extremely important [to avoid].

---

[54] Legge, *The Lî Kî* 2.167.
[55] Legge, *The Works of Mencius* 2.248-250.
[56] See note 47.

The apprentice should not open his mouth casually, because he who talks much is bound to err. It is best to be solid and quiet. He should by all means avoid slandering or quarreling with people; neither should he sing " wooden-fish songs " (木魚歌曲) or speak of this or that woman. Indeed he should be watchful against all these. He should not talk about fellow workers' short-comings behind their backs, or make a display of his own strong points. If Mr. A speaks about the shortcomings of Mr. B, the apprentice should only listen and not comment, nor should he later to Mr. B's face mention Mr. A's criticisms to show his own intimacy [with Mr. B], lest ill feeling may develop between the two [other] persons. This is of paramount importance.

He should set his mind upright, and not be selfish or greedy. Gambling is a thing he should not learn. Even if others gamble, he should neither be an onlooker nor tell outsiders about the gambling. As for visiting prostitutes and opium smoking, these two things most easily harm both body and character, and should not be touched at all. When he is not occupied, he should stay in the shop with his mind at peace, waiting for [his seniors'] call for service, and not take the opportunity to go out in the streets to have fun, watch theatrical performances, or peep surreptitiously at people's wives or daughters. These things he should not do even if, having some business to attend to for the shop, he happens to have such opportunities on the way; because he might thus hinder the business and be blamed for it.

All the tasks in the shop cannot be anticipated, so that he must be ready to make adjustments according to the situation, and by no means should he be lazy. Of the tasks he should not choose between the light and the heavy. Light tasks are of course easy to do; heavy tasks should also be done in accordance with one's own strength. If the work is beyond his strength, he should discuss the matter with the manager, and should not overstrain lest he hurt himself. He should think thrice (i. e., several times) before he does anything.

Concerning such matters as lamp oil and candlelight he should be most careful, because of course the commodities in the shop are valuable, and the lives of persons are even more important. In using oil he should take care not to pour any away; although this seems a small matter, it is tabooed in business circles as something extremely unlucky. So by all means be careful! In winter there should always be a candle in each lantern. If the old candle is used up he should light [a new] one, blow it out, moisten [the wick] with oil, and place the candle back in the lantern. Further, he should keep boxes of paper lighters (紙煤) and matches for the night.

Each morning, after the fifth watch he should be alert to wake up on time. As soon as the last drums finish (收擂) he should get up, light the lamp in the kitchen, and start the fire to boil water for making tea. Then he should light the lamps along the passages. Then he should pull his bed apart lightly, lest the noise disturb the sleep of others. If some fellow apprentices have not yet awakened, he should rouse them in a low voice, so that they will not be blamed for getting up late. In this way he shows his friendly concern for others.

The apprentice himself should wash his face quickly, light the lamp in front of the god, and burn sticks of incense. Then he should wash the teacups, and when the water is boiling, make tea and offer some to the deity. If there are water-pipes left on tables or on the sides of chairs, these should be removed and put back into the wooden tub for the water-pipes. Of the other miscellaneous objects, if any looks out of place it should be put back properly.

If those who sleep in the cashier's office are up, he should pull apart their beds for them and dust the counter, and the tables and chairs everywhere. He should change the water in the basins and moisten the writing brushes on the brush-stands. He should fill all the water-pipes with tobacco and change the water in them. Seeing anybody, he should say " Morning " to him.

When he has nothing to do and sits straight to the left or right of the shop front, he should not permit his shoes to leave his feet, nor stamp with his feet, nor cross his legs. When a customer comes, either an old or a new one, the appentice should respectfully serve him tobacco and tea. When the customer leaves, the apprentice should rise and stand straight. During the day, when he is upstairs, in the transverse hall, or in the rear quarters, whenever he hears a customer arrive at the front of the shop, he should go out and be ready to offer service.

When it is almost time to cook the meal and there is nothing going on in front of the shop, he should enter the kitchen to help the cook to clean the bowls and chopsticks with a towel, to make tea, and to warm the wine. When the meal is cooked, first he should see whether everything is there. If a guest has gone out in the city, it should be found out whether he will come back for the meal. Then the apprentice sets the table and places the chopsticks neatly. As soon as everybody is seated, no matter whether the apprentice himself drinks or not, he always first holds the wine pot [to pour wine for others], making sure that the mouth of the pot faces himself.

When he sits [at the table] he should not spread his elbows sidewise or lean with them on the table. If the candlelight is dim he should trim the wick. If there are seniors or guests at the table, the apprentice should keep an eye on their bowls. If any one of them is about to finish his bowl, the apprentice should leave his seat, go to the side of the senior or guest to receive his bowl, fill it with more rice, and return the rice bowl with both hands. He himself should finish eating quickly, and not be the last one at the table. If the guest raises his chopsticks and says, " Please eat slowly " (i. e., " Excuse me for finishing early "), the apprentice should offer him a cup of tea, using both hands. If the guest has finished and left the table, the apprentice should get water for him to wash his face. If every one has finished, he should put the chairs back and remove the dishes carefully. If there are grains of rice left on the table, these must be picked up with the fingers before the table can be mopped. The mopping should be done toward oneself. After the table leaves are put down and the floor swept, the apprentice, seeing everything is in order, may go to the kitchen to help the cook to clean things up; then he should go back to the front part of the shop.

When at leisure, he should collect [soiled] clothes and wash them. Whenever clothes are dried in the sun, he should carry a piece of cloth to clean the bamboo rods used as clotheslines, lest the rods be dirty and stain the clothes. When he has nothing to do, by no means should he go upstairs to take a nap during the day, but should go out to the front of the shop and wait for orders.

Every day at noon he should make tea. The cup should be filled about two thirds, not too full. A cup should be offered to every one. By no means should he make distinctions and fail to offer it to any one. In the afternoon he should put oil in the lamps in front of the deities in various places and wipe clean the outside of the lamps. He should remove the ends of incense sticks from the incense burners and polish the burners. He should put oil in the unused lamps, but not over-fill them.

If it is cloudy and is going to rain, he should go up to the sun-porch to put aside the articles that are being exposed. He should also search for umbrellas and hats, clean them, and put them in convenient places for use. If they have been used, they should be spread and dried at night and put back when dry. If it is a fine day and evening is approaching, he should go up to the sun-porch to collect the clothes and miscellaneous articles that are being dried. He should put them in order and take good care of them.

When evening falls, after supper and after everything in the kitchen is taken care of, having seen that the accounts are completed he should set up the beds in the cashier's office. If there is a guest, he should set up the guest bed. He should empty the chamberpots from various places. At about the second watch he should boil water and make tea, and offer a cup to every one. Then he should wait at the shop front to help close it up. If he still has surplus energy, he should practice the abacus and calligraphy. If there is anything [about these] he does not understand, he may ask questions freely.

At bedtime, if there is a guest, the apprentice should light a lamp to conduct him to his bed. Waiting until the seniors have all gone to bed, he can then set up his own bed. Before sleeping, he should have ready matches or ignited paper-lighters. Of the perpetual lamp and nightwatch incense he should take special care. He should also keep ready a few candles at the foot of the perpetual lamp, so that he may hold them to throw light while going the rounds to check the door and windows during the nightwatch. If the fire in the portable stove or the kitchen stove is not out, he should pull out the firewood and pour water over it to extinguish the fire; only then will it be safe. The lamps and candles should not be completely used up, else they may not be ready when needed during the night. Seeing that everything is in order, he may blow out the lamp and go to sleep.

For the first and fifteenth days of each month, he should buy incense and candles and have them ready the preceding afternoon. After supper he should remove the tables and chairs in the whole shop and sweep the floors. He should use hot water to wipe the articles, except for the scales and weights since copper and iron objects should not be exposed to water. On the first day and the fifteenth day he should get up at the fifth watch and boil water, wash his face, make tea, and wake those who are to worship the deities so they can get up and wash their faces. Then he should light the lamps in front of the deities at various places, have the candles and incense ready, and wait for the ceremony of worshipping the deities. He should prepare incense, candles, paper shoes (silver ingots), and lanterns, and follow [the seniors] going to the temple for worship.

Whoever serves as the cook (火頭) should get up even earlier than the others, strike a fire to light the kitchen lamp, start a fire and boil some water, and then make tea. Then he may pull apart his own bed, only lightly [so as not to make much noise]. Having washed his face, he should boil water in the boiler to wash the dishes. They should be washed one by one, and certainly should not all be put in the basin [at one time] lest they be broken in

41

handling. The stove, the rice-boiler cover, and the cupboard should all be mopped clean very carefully. Nothing should be handled roughly. Having boiled water and made tea, he may go to buy food [to go with the rice]. Whenever one buys such food, one should consider the scale of the business of the shop and determine the amount and quality of food accordingly. He should ask the manager and other seniors for instructions about this. When the time comes, he cooks the rice and prepares the dishes. As to whether the dishes should be sour, salty, or otherwise, he should by all means carefully consider the habits of the various fellow workers, and not insist on his own preferences or be partial to certain persons.

When the rice is cooked, the fire can then be used to make tea or warm wine. When the water is boiled, he should fill the tea pail with it. In warming wine, depending on the weather, he should be careful to adjust the temperature accordingly. When the table is set, if there are cats and dogs, they should be fed early. After the meal is over, he should personally check the bowls, plates, cups, and chopsticks, and wash them properly. He should fill the water urn; this is not restricted as to time—the urn should be refilled as soon as it is empty, so as to be prepared for emergency. Then he should use a hand sweeper to clean the stove mouth, the stove base, and the foot of the portable stove [with bellows]. The dust there should all be cleaned up. Then he should collect clothes to wash and starch, and remember to fold them [when dry] and put them away.

When there is no firewood in the kitchen, he should select [from another place] short, thin pieces and keep them for making tea, so as to avoid having a lot of smoke get into the tea jar and lead people to call it "roasting goose" (燒鵝). If he is not occupied and there is some task, whether or not it is supposed to be done by him, [the cook] should do it, the same as with the apprentices. Before sleeping, he should cover the water urn tightly and close up the cupboard to prevent soilage by bugs and cockroaches.

This essay comments only on the regular daily work. As for sharpness of wit in call and response, or question and answer, I cannot comment exhaustively, and hope my readers will exert themselves to be alert in these things.

The guest bed must be kept clean. When the guest has got up, the apprentice must first roll up the mosquito net so as not to keep the human exhalations there and cause bedbugs. He should also look at the quilt, and if he finds bedbugs and the like, these should be removed so as not to bother others. The quilt, mat, and pillow should be rolled up together, to be opened again only when a guest comes. At other times, when at leisure, he should wash the mosquito net, pillowcase, and sheet for the guest bed; then, naturally, few bedbugs will come. If, otherwise, there are many bedbugs and mosquitos, the guest who sleeps there will surely suffer.

If there is a guest who takes the morning ferry, some food should be purchased for him the night before. As soon as the fifth watch is heard, the apprentice should get up and cook the meal, warm some wine, and make tea. Having made the table ready, he should go to the guest's bed with a lamp and wake him up. Then the guest gets up, washes his face, and eats. The apprentice should wait on him to help him to more rice and offer tea. Then he pours water for the guest to wash his face. When the guest leaves, the apprentice carries his umbrella and baggage for him and sees him off at the ferry. Only then can the apprentice be said to have fully shown his respect.

HOSTAGES IN CHINESE HISTORY

INTRODUCTION

The use of hostages as security existed as an institution in China until the middle of the seventeenth century. From the famous exchange of hostages between Chou and Cheng recorded in the *Tso chuan* under 720 B. C.[1] to the sending of Korean hostages to the Manchu rulers between 1637 and 1645,[2] numerous examples of the exchange or surrender of hostages can be cited. Chinese and alien dynasties have both found the system useful.

Hostages in Chinese history may be somewhat arbitrarily classified into the following groups:

1. "Exchanged hostages"—to guarantee a friendly relationship between two states or two other groups.

2. "Unilateral hostages"—to guarantee allegiance and loyalty.
   a. "External hostages" might be taken by one of two belligerent parties from another during negotiation for an armistice or surrender. In more peaceful times, hostages might be taken by a powerful state from a weak state, by a suzerain from its vassal states or dependent tribes, or by a lord from a group of individuals at the time when they were offering their allegiance.
   b. "Internal hostages" might be taken by a ruler from his military or civil officials, especially from those who were stationed along boundaries or sent out on an expedition.

---

[1] James LEGGE, *The Chinese Classics* 5.17.

[2] *Simyang-ilgi* or *Shinyō nikki* 瀋陽日記 (*Mammō sōsho* 滿蒙叢書 9), Tōkyō, 1921, is an official diary kept by secretaries to the hostage princes in Mukden. *Simyang-sange* or *Shinyō jōkei* 瀋陽狀啓 (*Keishōkaku sōsho* 奎章閣叢書 1), Keijō 京城, 1935, contains letters from these secretaries reporting to Korea. There are many interesting details in the two books. TAGAWA Kōzō 田川孝三,瀋館考 in *Oda sensei shōju kinen Chōsen ronshū* 小田先生頌壽紀念朝鮮論集, Tōkyō, 1934, presents a valuable study based on these and other sources.

In all instances the hostage was normally a member of the sender's family, in the majority of cases, his son. Hostages from several families might be required on a single occasion. An extreme case in ancient China was the following interesting situation which developed in 502 B. C. after two officials from the State of Chin had insulted the Marquis of the State of Wei during the negotiation of a covenant:

The marquis wished to revolt from Chin, but had a difficulty with the great officers. Wang-sun Chia 王孫賈 made him halt in the suburbs; and when the great officers 大夫 asked the reason, the marquis told them the insults of Chin, and added, "I have disgraced the altars. You must consult the tortoise-shell, and appoint another in my place. I will agree to your selection." The great officers said, "It is the misfortune of Wei, and not any fault of yours." "There is something worse," said the duke. "They told me that I must send my son and the sons of my great officers as hostages [to Chin]." The officers replied, "If it will be of any benefit, let the prince go, and our sons will follow him carrying halters and ropes on their backs." It was then arranged that the hostages should go; but Wang-sun Chia said, "If the State of Wei has had any misfortunes, the mechanics and merchants have always shared in them. Let [the sons of] all classes go." The marquis reported this to the great officers, who were willing to send all, and a day was fixed for their setting out. The marquis [in the meantime] gave audience to the people 國人, and made Chia ask them, saying, "If Wei revolt from Chin, and Chin 5 (i. e., several) times attack us, how would you bear the distress?" They all replied, "Though it should 5 times attack us, we should still be able to fight." "Then," said Chia, "we had better revolt from it at once. We can give our hostages when we are brought to distress. It will not then be too late." Accordingly Wei revolted from Chin, and refused, though Chin requested it, to make another covenant.[3]

Obviously the Marquis of Wei and his minister WANG-SUN Chia were taking advantage of this large-scale demand for hostages to irritate the people of their state, and the hostages were not sent. Nevertheless, cases involving sons of a ruler and some of his officials actually occurred in both the Ch'un-ch'iu period and later times.

Although the earliest recorded instance of the taking of hostages was on a mutual basis, exchanged hostages were rare even in the

[3] The translation is that of LEGGE (op. cit. 5.769), with romanization changed to the WADE-GILES system. Words in parentheses and Chinese characters have been inserted by me.

Ch'un-ch'iu period. In addition to the case of Chou and Cheng mentioned above, we may cite the exchange of hostages between Chin and Cheng in 610 B. C. and that between the ruler of Sung and a powerful Hua clan in 522 B. C. Hostages in later times were as a rule surrendered on a unilateral basis.[4]

In the following sections of this article, I shall outline a number of significant examples of external and internal hostages under various dynasties and conclude with a discussion of the traditional views on hostages in China.

EXTERNAL HOSTAGES

Taking hostages was a standard practice of the Han dynasty for controlling small barbarian states. Princes sent for this purpose were known as *chih-tzu* 質子, "hostage sons," or *shih-tzu* 侍子, "attending princes." The latter term was used because such hostages were often made attendants at the court or guards at the imperial palaces. They were lodged in the capital and treated kindly. On the other hand, they were subject to Chinese laws and punishments. Thus, a hostage prince from Lou-lan 樓蘭 is known to have been castrated in the reign of Wu-ti.[5]

Interestingly enough, the Hsiung-nu in Han times also required hostages from their satellites as a surety for allegiance. Certain small states in the Western Regions found themselves hemmed in between the Chinese and the Hsiung-nu and were obliged to send hostages to both powers. Since a hostage prince would usually prove friendly to the court where he had lived, he was in a good position to receive its support in a bid for power after his return. Bitter wars were at times waged between princes who had returned from the Han and Hsiung-nu, and this constituted an important phase of the struggle for control over the Western Regions between the two powers.[6] When the Hsiung-nu had been

---

[4] LEGGE, *op. cit.* 5.278, 681.

[5] *Han shu* 96A.5a.

[6] *Han shu* 96A.5a, 15b-16b, 18a-19a; 96B.12b-13b, 17b-19b. *Hou-Han shu* 118 (*lieh-chuan* 78).13a-16b.

defeated and weakened, they also sent hostages to China, notably, in 53 B. C. and in 20 B. C.[7]

A detailed study of external hostages may reveal the degree and direction of outward expansion of a dynasty. For example, at the beginning of the Latter Han era in 45 A. D., eighteen states of the Western Regions sent in hostages with tribute requesting a *tu-hu* 都護 or protector general to be stationed in that area. The Emperor, however, did not feel that China was ready to control that region and ordered the hostages to be returned.[8] Five decades later, after PAN Ch'ao had greatly promoted Chinese influence and prestige in Central Asia, more than fifty states in the Western Regions surrendered to the Han and sent hostages.[9] In the first years of the second century, when Hsien-pi leaders came to offer allegiance, *chih-kuan* 質館 or "hostage hostels" were built, presumably on the northeastern frontier, to accommodate sons from 120 Hsien-pi groups.[10]

The Han use of external hostages was followed by later Chinese dynasties, notably the T'ang which marked another great era of expansion. Hostage princes were sent from territories in all directions and were again made guards at the court as in Han times. The prince from Silla even had the privilege of serving as vice-envoy to accompany every Chinese mission to his country.[11] In 714 when the T'ang dynasty was at its peak, the Emperor Hsüan-tsung even issued a decree ordering the authorities concerned to send back those hostages who had resided in the capital for many years and might now be considered unnecessary.[12] This grace, however, amounted to only a temporary home leave as hostages were evidently required again in later years.

The Sung dynasty marked a low ebb in conquest and expansion. Nevertheless, the institution was continued and hostages were

---

[7] *Han shu* 94B.3b, 12a.

[8] *Hou-Han shu* 118.14a.

[9] *Hou-Han shu* 118.2b.

[10] *Hou-Han shu* 120 (*lien-chuan* 20).7b-8a.

[11] *Ts'e-fu yüan-kuei* 册府元龜 996.

[12] *Ibid.* 11a-b; *T'ang ta chao-ling chi* 唐大詔令集 (*Shih-yüan ts'ung-shu* 適園 叢書 ed.) 128.3a-b.

taken from miscellaneous dependent tribes (particularly Ti-
betans) on the western frontier. The hostages were not sent to
the Sung capital but were kept in the custody of local authorities.
Most cases occurred in the eleventh century. For instance, *Sung
shih* 491.20a says that in the year 1003, as many as thirty-two
barbarian groups offered hostages to the local officials in Yüan-
chou 原州 and Wei-chou 渭州 in eastern Kansu. From the epitaph
of the statesman FAN Chung-yen 范仲淹 composed by OU-YANG
Hsiu 歐陽修,[13] we learn that when FAN served as military governor of Shensi in the early 1040's, he permitted the hostage sons
from various barbarian tribes to move about freely. Apparently
grateful for his kindness or overwhelmed by his prestige, none of
the hostages took advantage of an opportunity to run away. Two
other bits of information on the use of hostages in Sung times
are from the *Sung hui-yao kao* 宋會要稿:[14] in 1017 an imperial
decree ordered a *Na-chih yüan* 納質院, lit. " Court for receiving
hostages," to be established in Fu-chou 府州 in northern Shensi.
Possibly this court was later under FAN's jurisdiction. In 1069
the father-in-law of a barbarian chief was sent back after having
served as a hostage for ten-odd years in Ch'in-chou 秦州 in western Shensi. This was already seventeen years after the death of
FAN in 1052.

Another kind of external hostage used in the Sung dynasty is
more famous. In 1126 when the Sung capital K'ai-feng was
beseiged by Jurchen troops, Prince K'ang 康王 and the *Shao-tsai*
少宰 (Junior Chancellor) CHANG Pang-ch'ang 張邦昌 were sent
as hostages to the invaders during the negotiation of peace.[15] In
the next year after the fall of K'ai-feng, the Jurchen made CHANG
Pang-ch'ang the emperor of a puppet state which existed only for
a few months. In the same year Prince K'ang became the founder
of the Southern Sung dynasty.

The Ming dynasty does not appear to have used external

---

[13] *Ou-yang Weng-chung-kung wen-chi* 歐陽文忠公文集 (*SPTK* ed.) 20.12a. I
am indebted to Professor E. A. KRACKE, Jr. for this reference.

[14] *Sung hui-yao kao* (*ts'e* 195) *fang-yü* 方域 21.5b, (*ts'e* 199) *fan-i* 蕃夷 6.7a.

[15] *San-ch'ao pei-meng hui-pien* 三朝北盟彙編 63.10a-11b; *Ta-Chin kuo chih*
大金國志 (Sao-yeh shan-fang 掃葉山房 ed.) 4.1a-b.

hostages at all. Ryūkyū being a tributary state, sons of its kings and ministers were allowed to study in the Imperial College in Nanking. These special students, however, were not treated as hostages and this privilege of study did not extend to other tributary states.[16] When the Manchu chief Nurhachi offered to send his son as hostage of the Ming in 1613, a military governor tentatively accepted the hostage and hailed the practice as the restoration of a *k'uang-tien* 曠典 " unusual institution." The Ming court, however, decided to reject the hostage on the grounds that it was difficult to ascertain whether or not he was really a son of the Manchu chief.[17]

Among the non-Chinese dynasties, the Northern Wei received external hostages from its vassal states and dependent tribes. The hostage sons of northern chieftains usually arrived in the fall and left in the spring so as to avoid the heat at the capital Lo-yang. Consequently they earned from their contemporaries in China the picturesque name *yen-ch'en* 鴈臣, lit. " geese subjects." [18] In later periods, very little is known about external hostages except that during the rise of the Yüan dynasty, the Chin ruler and quite a few military commanders of Ch'i-tan and Jurchen origin sent hostages to offer allegiance to the Mongols.[19]

The Yüan dynasty used the hostage system in a most extensive manner. The institution laid down by Činggis Qan was: " All surrendering states should send hostages, assist [Mongolian] troops, contribute provisions, set up postal stations, present household registers, and establish *ta-lu-hua-ch'ih* 達魯花赤 (*daruɣači*

---

[16] Chieftains of certain dependent tribes in Yünnan could also send their children to the Imperial College. *Nan-yung chih* 南雝志 (1931 reprint of Ming ed.) 1.40b, 42a-b, 47b-48a.

[17] *Ming shih-lu* 明實錄, Wan-li, 512.1b-2a. *Ch'ou-Liao shih-hua* 籌遼碩畫 (*Kuo-li Pei-p'ing T'u-shu-kuan shan-pen ts'ung-shu* 國立北平圖書館善本叢書) 2.33a-35a contains a memorial from the Governor CHANG T'ao 張濤, requesting the acceptance of the Manchu hostage.

[18] *Lo-yang chia-lan chi* 洛陽伽藍記 (*SPTK* ed.) 3.10a.

[19] Although there are numerous references to hostages in the *Yüan shih*, the only pertinent passage in the *Yüan-ch'ao pi-shih* 元朝秘史 is section 253 in which we read about the Chin ruler sending his sons with 200 followers to serve as *turɣaɣ* (i. e., hostages, lit. " guards ") for Činggis Qan. I am indebted to the Reverend Antoine MOSTAERT for calling my attention to this passage.

' resident commissioners ') ." Hostages were to be replaced when they were too old or dead. All these requirements were clearly stated in a decree issued to Korea in 1268.[20]

The hostages required by the Mongols apparently were to be proportional to the population. A 2 per cent ratio is indicated in the case of the surrender of YEH-LÜ Liu-ko 耶律留哥, an important Ch'i-tan leader who had served as a military commander under the Chin. With the rise of the Mongols, the Chin rulers became very suspicious of the former Liao people, and ordered that each Ch'i-tan household be sandwiched between two Jurchen households. Realizing his dangerous position, YEH-LÜ Liu-ko offered his allegiance to the Mongols. When Činggis Qan learned that the population under YEH-LÜ Liu-ko's control totaled over 600,000 (presumably most of them were Ch'i-tan), he demanded 3,000 of them as hostages.[21] Such external hostages apparently were organized into armies very much like the internal hostages which will be discussed in the next section.

Possibly under Mongolian influence, the Manchus in their early years also required hostages from Korea, not only sons of the Korean ruler, but also sons of his chief ministers. These hostages together with their families and servants were lodged in special halls in Mukden. The hostage princes on several occasions were required to accompany the Manchu ruler on hunting trips and military expeditions against the Ming, but most of the time the hostages stayed at Mukden. Serving also as special representatives of their country, the hostage princes negotiated with the Manchus such affairs as the purchase of freedom for Korean slaves and the smuggling of tobacco into Manchuria. From time to time the Manchu ruler would demand various articles, such as paper, textiles, or drugs, and the hostages either met these demands in Mukden or requested the products from Korea. Occasionally there were also secret personal demands from the Manchu

---

[20] *Yüan Kao-li chi-shih* 元高麗紀事 (*Kuang-Ts'ang-hsüeh-ch'ün ts'ung-shu* 廣倉學窘叢書, *ts'e* 26) 13a-b. I am indebted to Professor F. W. CLEAVES for this reference.

[21] *Yüan shih* 149.1a-2b.

nobles and interpreters who were assigned to receive these hostages.

In the year 1640, the Manchus decided to assign some land to the Korean hostages, asking them to cultivate it and support themselves instead of drawing provisions from their hosts as before. The Koreans protested on the ground that such a powerful suzerain as the Manchu should be able to support hostages from its vassal state, but their protest was to no avail, and they had to employ redeemed Korean slaves and Chinese peasants to cultivate the land. The Korean hostages were discharged only in 1645 when the Manchus had established themselves in Peking.[22]

INTERNAL HOSTAGES

The history of internal hostages in China is comparatively obscure. A key term, pao-kung 葆宮 or 保宮 " surety house," found in the Mo-tzu and the Han shu, and its variant pao-kuan 保官, found in the San-kuo chih, have not received much attention. Another term chih-jen 質任 " hostage " found in several passages in the San-kuo chih and the Chin shu has been misunderstood by a number of modern scholars.[23]

The passages about internal hostages in the Mo-tzu are in the last chapters on the attack and defense of a city. One passage reads, " City guards from the ssu-ma 司馬 ' marshall ' above should have their parents, brothers, wives, and children held as hostages at the lord's place; only then can the city be firmly defended. . . . Only those who have their parents, brothers, wives, and children in the pao-kung 葆宮 ' surety house ' may serve as attending officers. Officers may be entrusted with duties only when they have hostages." Another passage tells in detail how the hostages should be kindly treated and specifies the various kinds of treason for which hostages might be executed.[24]

---

[22] See note 2 above.

[23] LIANG Ch'i-ch'ao misconstrued chih-jen to mean contracts or affidavits. Another scholar misinterpreted the term as tribute paid by a vassal to his lord. The correct interpretation of the term has been given by Ho Tzu-ch'üan 何茲全 in Shih-huo 食貨 1.8 (1935) .337-339 and in Wen-shih tsa-chih 文史雜誌 1.4 (1941) .39-47. Ho however did not connect pao-kuan with pao-kung.

[24] Mo-tzu (SPTK ed.) 15.15b-18b, 25b-26a.

Although Mo-tzu the philosopher is believed to have lived some time in the fifth century B. C., the date of these chapters on city defense attributed to him is nevertheless doubtful. Since they contain many official titles and institutions of Ch'in and Han times, it has been suggested that the chapters may have been written in the Han period.[25] According to *Han shu* 19A.9b it was Wu-ti who in 104 B. C. changed the names *Chü-shih* 居室 to *Pao-kung* 保宮 and *Kan-ch'üan Chü-shih* 甘泉居室 to *K'un-t'ai* 昆臺· Apparently *Chü-shih* and *Kan-ch'üan Chü-shih* were special prisons in and outside Ch'ang-an. Both were under the charge of the *shao-fu* 少府 " small treasurer." If the term *pao-kung* did not exist prior to 104 B. C., the use of the compound is another bit of evidence for dating the passages in the Han period.

The origin of internal hostages, however, need not be identical with that of the term *pao-kung*. A fourth-century tradition dates the institution as far back as the time of the Warring States,[26] which is quite possible because the principle of *lien-tso* 連坐 " joint suretyship " was introduced by Legalist reformers in the State of Ch'in in that period. At the end of the Ch'in dynasty, troops who were sent out to fight against the various groups of rebels or revolutionists feared that their parents, wives, and children might all be killed if they surrendered to their opponents. Very probably these family members were held as hostages.[27]

To come back to the term *pao-kung*, history says that the mother of General Li Ling 李陵 was imprisoned in the *Pao-kung* after the general surrendered to the Hsiung-nu in 99 B. C.[28] Thus the place was actually used by Wu-ti as living quarters for hostages. In the reign of Hsüan-ti, however, the *Pao-kung* already served a different purpose. Two masters of the Ku-liang Commentary on the *Ch'un-ch'iu* were invited by the Emperor to lodge there and be employed as instructors of that classical commentary. This happened about a dozen years before the famous

[25] Wu Yü-chiang 吳毓江, *Mo-tzu chiao-chu* 墨子校註 15.11a, *fu-lu* 附錄 2.15a-23b.

[26] *Chin shu* 38.17a.

[27] *Shih chi* 7.12b.

[28] *Han shu* 54.19b.

Conference on Classics in 51 B. C.[29] The fact that the *Pao-kung* was used to house honored scholars suggests that it was no longer used to hold hostages. Probably the system of internal hostages declined after the time of Wu-ti.

The terms *pao-kuan* " surety house " and *chih-jen* " hostages " both appear in a passage in the *San-kuo chih*. They were used in a letter of 228 from Ming-ti of Wei to General MENG Ta 孟達 of Shu who had just deserted his own state to offer allegiance to Wei. The letter reads, " Now the whole country has been pacified and unified. . . . Consequently we have slackened the rules and regulations to show that we harbor no suspicion. Our *pao-kuan* is empty, and we have no *chih-jen* at all. You, in coming to us, should understand clearly our intention. By no means should you send your family members one after another on their way [as hostages]." [30]

Actually the Wei had required both external and internal hostages. For instance, when Ming-ti ascended the throne, he issued a decree ordering the prefectures and districts to report their status as either *chü* 劇 " strategic " or *chung-p'ing* 中平 " ordinary." Officers of Cho-chün 涿郡 in modern Hopei were prepared to report the prefecture as " ordinary." The Prefect WANG Kuan 王觀, however, insisted that it be graded as " strategic " because it bordered barbarian tribes and had constantly suffered from plunders and invasions. He knew that if the prefecture was considered " strategic " he would be obliged to send his son as hostage (*jen-tzu* 任子) to the capital, but he also knew that the people in a " strategic " prefecture were subject to lighter corvée.[31]

In this connection it may be pointed out that the term *jen-tzu* was usually used in Han times to mean " to guarantee a son " referring to the privilege of officials to recommend their sons for office. In most cases the recommended sons were made *lang* 郎, " court gentlemen," very much like the barbarian hostage

[29] *Han shu* 88.25a.
[30] *San-kuo chih*, Wei, 3.3a, commentary.
[31] *San-kuo chih*, Wei, 24.17a.

princes who were made court guards.[32] The fusion of the meanings of *chih-tzu* and *jen-tzu* was completed in the third century as is also evidenced by the compound *chih-jen*. In this period *jen-tzu* became an obligation rather than a privilege. In later times the privilege of getting appointment for one's son was still occasionally called *jen-tzu* but more often known as *yin* 蔭.

Internal hostages were required not only by Wei but also by the other two of the Three Kingdoms. The requirement usually included wives and children and occasionally other members of the famliy as well. Such hostages in Wu were known as *pao-chih* 保質 " surety hostages." [33] They were kept either in the capital or in other important cities.

, The Chin dynasty which followed the Three Kingdoms continued the system. In 265, the first year of the dynasty, the Chin Emperor abolished the requirement of hostages (*chih-jen*) from certain low-ranking military officers. In 279 when the conquest of Wu was imminent, hostages were no longer required from certain high-ranking officials. Hostages from generals, however, were not abolished until 330 under the Eastern Chin.[34]

History says the Northern Wei dynasty held sons as hostages for the first time in 526, in its capital Lo-yang. These were internal hostages taken from prefects, magistrates, senior secretaries in local governments, commanders and vice-commanders of garrison troops.[35] This measure was introduced apparently because a war between North and South China was being waged and some Wei officials on the frontier had surrendered to the opponent Liang dynasty. However, it was too late for the dynasty to derive benefit from the system. In 534 the Wei broke into two states, the Eastern Wei and the Western Wei.

Internal hostages were required regularly by the Yüan dynasty. The *Yüan shih* informs us that sons and younger brothers of feudal lords and military officers were organized into *chih-tzu*

---

[32] *Hsi-Han hui-yao* 西漢會要 (Chiang-su shu-chü 江蘇書局 ed.) 45.3a-5b, *Tung-Han hui-yao* 東漢會要 (same ed.) 26.16b.

[33] *San-Kuo chih*, Wu, 2.25b, commentary.

[34] *Chin shu* 3.5a, 3.18b, 7.6b.

[35] *Wei shu* 9.25b; *Pei shih* 4.20a.

chün 質子軍 or *t'u-lu-hua chün* 禿魯花軍 " hostage armies," *t'u-lu-hua* or *turγaγ* being the Mongolian word for hostages or guards.[36] The system was introduced by Činggis Qan and restated in 1263 by Qubilai Qaγan. Each *wan-hu* 萬戶 " myriarch " was supposed to send a hostage with ten horses, two oxen 牛二具,[37] and four peasants. A *ch'ien-hu* 千戶 " chiliarch " who actually commanded five hundred soldiers or more should send a hostage with six horses, an ox, and two peasants. A *ch'ien-hu* who did not command so many soldiers but had a prosperous household and strong youngsters met the same requirement. The hostages brought their wives and children, and any number of servants with them. It was permissible to bring more horses and oxen than required. If a hostage son was under age, he was replaced by a younger brother or nephew, but took over the service when he reached the age of fifteen. Hostage armies also included sons of *ta-lu-hua-ch'ih* or " resident commissioners."

The founding emperor T'ai-tsu of the Ming dynasty made it a rule to keep the wives and children of all military commanders who were sent out to attack cities. These family members were not to move outside of the capital, Nanking. T'ai-tsu also made two groups of guards out of youngsters of his civil and military officials and named the groups *chün-tzu wei* 君子衞 " gentlemen guards " and *she-jen wei* 舍人衞 " master guards " respectively. These measures apparently were discontinued when the empire became firmly established.[38]

A special way of taking hostages in Chinese history was to marry a princess to the son of a general (usually stationed on the frontier) so that the imperial son-in-law would stay in the capital, a hostage in fact if not in name. For instance, a son of

---

[36] *Yüan shih* 98a.5a-7b, *Hsin Yüan shih* 97.21a (where the characters are 覷魯花, *tu-lu-hua*), 98.11b-12a. The identification of *chih-tzu* and *t'u-lu-hua* is also made in the Yüan work *Li-hsüeh chih-nan* 吏學指南 included in the *Chü-chia pi-yung shih-lei ch'üan-chi* 居家必用事類全集, *hsin-chi* 辛集.

[37] In the Chin period, for taxation purposes, a *chü* consisted of three oxen (*Chin shih* 47.32a). Cf. *Li chi* (*Shih-san-ching chu-su* 十三經注疏 ed.) 41.35 where I am following the subcommentary in identifying *i-chü* 一具 with *i-ko* 一个.

[38] Liu Ch'en 劉辰, *Kuo-ch'u shih-chi* 國初事蹟 (*Chin-sheng yü-chen chi* 金聲玉振集 ed.) 5a, 34b-35a.

General AN Lu-shan was executed in Ch'ang-an in 755 when AN rebelled against the T'ang emperor Hsüan-tsung [39] and a son of General WU San-kuei was killed in Peking in 1674 when WU revealed his intention to drive the Manchus out of the Great Walls.[40] Both sons of the generals had married princesses. Such hostages may be called internal, although the position of their fathers was comparable to that of the head of a feudatory.

TRADITIONAL VIEWS

Traditional views were on the whole against the hostage system, either internal or external. On the famous exchange of hostages between Chou and Cheng in ancient times, the *Tso chuan* [41] contains the following criticism:

If there be not good faith in the heart, hostages are of no use. If parties are with intelligence and with mutual consideration, their actions under the rule of propriety, although there be no exchange of hostages, they cannot be alienated.

Another example is found in the Ku-liang Commentary: [42]

Kao 誥 "announcements" and *shih* 誓 "speeches" did not reach (i. e., were not good enough for) the Five Emperors; *meng* 盟 "covenants" and *tsu* 詛 "curses" did not reach the founders of the Three Dynasties; exchange of *chih-tzu* did not reach the Two Presiding Chiefs (i. e., Duke Huan of Ch'i and Duke Wen of Chin).

The same remark is also found in the works of Hsün-tzu.[43] Obviously the two points of argument are (1) the taking of hostages was a comparatively late institution, representing a degeneration of relationship between man and man, state and state; (2) it was not reliable as a practical measure.

Strong criticism was raised at least once against external hostages in T'ang times, when a court official, HSÜEH Teng 薛

---

[39] *Chiu T'ang shu* 200A.2b, 4b, *Hsin T'ang shu* 225A.6b-7a.

[40] *Eminent Chinese of the Ch'ing Period*, edited by A. W. HUMMEL, Washington, 1944, pp. 878-879 (biography of WU San-kuei by FANG Chao-ying).

[41] LEGGE, *op. cit.* 5.13.

[42] *Ku-liang chuan* (*Shih-san-ching chu-su* ed.) 2.4a-b.

[43] *Hsün-tzu* (*SPTK* ed.) 19.26b.

登, advised the Empress Wu to abandon the system.[44] The advice was not followed. In the famous encyclopaedia on government, *Ts'e-fu yüan-kuei* (996.7a-b), the Sung compilers made very critical comments on external hostages. The general position held by the T'ang and Sung critics was that barbarians should not be permitted to reside within China, because they might learn Chinese secrets and make trouble. The best way to deal with the barbarians was to expel them.

The system of internal hostages was sometimes frowned upon because its basic principle of joint surety was considered unfair. A fourth-century scholar-official, Tsu Na 祖納,[45] expressed the following opinion concerning hostages: " Crimes should not involve others; punishments should be limited to the individual himself. This is the grand principle laid down by ancient philosophers, and the general institution to be followed by all rulers." A similar point was made by another fourth-century scholar, Hsi Ch'ao 郗超,[46] against a current theory that joint responsibility of family members should also apply to divine retribution. He said, " If the punishment was not administered to the individual himself, but the disaster should involve [only] his relatives, laws based on this kind of principle would be not only intolerable for the institution of the sage [rulers] but also would be rejected even by Legalists like Shen [Pu-hai] and Han [Fei]." He also stressed that this was not the way Buddhism understood karma. These assertions of individual responsibility, representing a remarkable trend of thought in China, were later overwhelmed by the further development of the institution of the family. People of later times on the whole accepted the principle of joint responsibility as a matter of fact.

In spite of objections, the system of taking external and internal hostages persisted, obviously because of its usefulness. It was considered particularly effective for the control of distant

---

[44] *Hsing T'ang shu* 112.11b-12b.

[45] *Chin shu* 38.17a.

[46] Hsi Ch'ao's essay, " Feng fa yao " 奉法要, is included in *Hung-ming chi* 弘明集 (*SPTK* ed.) 13.5b. I am indebted to Dr. Hu Shih for calling my attention to this reference. For biographical data on Hsi Ch'ao, cf. *Chin shu* 67.20a-22b; 75.6b.

groups, as was observed by the historian P'EI Sung-chih 裴松之 (360-439) .[47] In theory, as long as the affection human beings have for their family members or certain other persons makes them behave in a predictable manner, there is no reason why the taking of hostages could not be continued, at least from time to time. On the other hand, the fact that it has ceased to be an institution in modern times indicates that people have finally decided it is not indispensable as a means to guarantee a friendly relationship, allegiance, or loyalty.

[47] *San-kuo chih*, Wei, 24.11a-12a, commentary.

ECONOMIC JUSTIFICATION FOR SPENDING—AN UNCOMMON IDEA IN TRADITIONAL CHINA

LIEN-SHENG YANG

HARVARD UNIVERSITY

For more than twenty-three years Professor Serge ELISSÉEFF as Director of the Harvard-Yenching Institute has made many contributions to higher education in Asia, and as Chairman of the Department of Far Eastern Languages at Harvard University he has guided the development of Far Eastern studies at Harvard with far-sightedness and leadership. One of the requirements upon which Professor ELISSÉEFF has always insisted in the training of students of the Department is a reading knowledge of both Chinese and Japanese. This requirement, particularly essential for any serious student of Chinese history, may, perhaps, be illustrated in a limited manner with even such a relatively narrow subject as that of this article, which I take pleasure in dedicating to him.

On matters pertaining to consumption and standards of living, traditional Chinese thought in general has been in favor of saving and frugality and against spending and lavishness. Human wants were recognized as something that could never be fully satisfied and, therefore, more or less as a necessary evil to be controlled or regulated. Saving was encouraged to prepare for famine, sickness, and such irregular expenses as marriages and funerals, while frugality or austerity was encouraged simply as a virtue in itself. Differences in standards of living were often justified as marks necessary for political or social distinctions. Also, in theory the morally worthy and the talented people should enjoy more. But, since this was not always the case, interpretations based upon such concepts as fate (and later, *karma*) were introduced from ancient times. Psychological examples were also drawn to discourage spending and lavishness. For instance, it was easy to raise one's standard of living but very painful to reduce it—thus it might be preferable to eat a sugar cane by beginning with the less tasty sections, especially if a sugar cane was all that one was entitled to enjoy in his whole life.[1]

In general, the above represent the predominant approaches from political, social, ethical, and religious angles. In the realm of economic thought, relatively little attention has been paid to the relation between saving and investment, especially investment in terms of the total economy. Still less attention has been paid to the possible relation between spending and economic growth. This is perhaps not strange, since even in the West such concepts as "spending for prosperity" and "paradox of thrift" are relatively new.[2] On the other hand, it should be pointed out that in certain periods of Chinese history, one finds fragments of economic thought that recognize the importance of spending in the whole circulating process or flow of economy. It is the purpose of this article to trace this interesting though uncommon idea in traditional China.

Economic justification for spending is traceable to the time of Warring States, which was a period, among other things, marked

[1] The figure of eating sugar cane is taken from a story about the celebrated artist Ku K'ai-chih (ca. 345 to ca. 406) in the *Shih-shuo hsin-yü* 世說新語 (*SPPY* ed.) C2 "P'ai-tiao" 排調 11b and *Chin shu* 晉書 92.21a:

When K'ai-chih ate sugar cane, he usually chewed it from the end to the middle. When people wondered why, he would say, "One enters into the realm of delights gradually." (*Biography of Ku K'ai-chih*, translated and annotated by CH'EN Shih-hsiang, 1953, p. 14).

I hope to discuss at another time the concept of fixed fortunes in life and the possibility of modifying them. Meanwhile, attention may be drawn to the fact that several books on fortune-telling (e. g., *Yen-ch'in-tou-shu san-shih-hsiang* 演禽斗數 三世相, 1933, a Japanese reprint of a late Sung edition) describe in detail twelve types of *lu* 祿 (lit. "salary," but also "fortune") ranging from *man-lu* 滿祿 "full fortune," with "Complete good luck and fortune, nine jars of wine, twelve strings of cash, one picul and three pecks of rice, ten catties of meat, one chest of clothing, and leisure and high position throughout life," to *p'o-lu* 破祿 "broken fortune," with "wine hard to drink, one picul of rice, four strings and nine cash, three catties of meat, a handful of ginger, three pints of soya beans, and two pieces of clothing."

[2] For a comprehensive survey of relevant views in the West, cf. Carle C. ZIMMERMAN, *Consumption and Standards of Living*, 1936, pp. 479-536. For a lucid discussion of the "paradox of thrift," cf. Paul A. SAMUELSON, *Economics: An Introductory Analysis*, 1948, pp. 269-272.

by a high level of economic activity and fermentation of thought. It has been observed by several modern scholars that the low esteem in which merchants were held—predominant from Han times on —was not quite so noticeable in this period.[3] In a recent article, Kuo Mo-jo 郭沫若 draws attention to what he calls "fossilized ideas" in favor of spending in the chapter entitled "Ch'ih-mi" 侈靡 or "Lavishness" in the *Kuan-tzu*.[4]

This chapter in the *Kuan-tzu* is badly garbled and is at places practically beyond comprehension. Commentators however have taken up the challenge and proposed many emendations and alterations, not infrequently at variance with one another. On the passages containing economic thought, several Ch'ing and Republican scholars have advanced interpretations along the line of encouragement of spending in order to promote circulation of wealth and to create opportunities for work.[5] Nevertheless, Kuo Mo-jo deserves credit for being the first scholar to devote a whole article to the study of the chapter. For the sake of convenience, I shall first review Kuo's article and then proceed to discuss the relevant passages in the chapter as well as other related texts. I shall then cite and discuss a few illustrations of "work relief" (*kung-chen* 工賑) and conclude the article with reference to materials in Japanese.

Kuo points out that the greatest significance of this chapter lies in its economic thesis. In the words of Kuo:

He (the author of the chapter) affirms enjoyment of pleasure and opposes

---

[3] Views of Professor Okazaki Fumio and Dr. Hu Shih have been referred to in my "Notes on Dr. Swann's *Food and Money in Ancient China*" *HJAS* 13 (1950) .525-527. Cf. the interesting articles by Lo Ken-tse 羅根澤, *Kuan-tzu t'an-yüan* 管子探源, 1931, Appendix 2, "Ku-tai ching-chi-hsüeh-chung chih pen-nung mo-shang hsüeh-shuo" 古代經濟學中之本農末商學說, and Ku Chi-kuang 谷霽光 "Chan-kuo Ch'in-Han chien chung-nung i-shang chih li-lun yü shih-chi" 戰國秦漢間重農抑商之理論與實際 in *Chung-kuo she-hui ching-chi shih chi-k'an* 中國社會經濟史集刊, 7 (1944).1-22. Also compare Wang Yü-ch'üan, *Early Chinese Coinage*, 1951, pp. 22-53, for an excellent summary of the development of commerce in ancient China.

[4] Kuo Mo-jo, "Ch'ih-mi p'ien te yen-chiu" 侈靡篇的研究, in *Li-shih yen-chiu* 歷史研究 1954.3.27-62.

[5] Kuo Mo-jo, Wen I-tuo 聞一多, and Hsü Wei-i 許維遹, *Kuan-tzu chi-chiao* 管子集校, 1955, A.538-631.

economy and frugality; he emphasizes circulation and opposes the despising of commerce; he advocates full employment and opposes negative relief of the poor. In order to realize full employment, he advocates heavy consumption, and even rich burial. His point of emphasis is placed on the theme that heavy consumption may stimulate heavy production, therefore he remarks very little, almost nothing, on how to proceed on the productive side, how to improve technology, etc. In principle, he takes agriculture to be the fundamental occupation; although he emphasizes commerce, he does not dare to despise agriculture. . . . Nevertheless, in spite of the author's advocation of heavy consumption and extreme lavishness, he has a restriction that should not be neglected, namely, the topmost ruler should not blindly be lavish in the same manner. This is an important restriction, which one can neither overlook nor take to be the author's self-contradiction. . . . His main goal is to enrich the masses at the bottom, to cause the middle-layer gentlemen-officials (who are also landlords) to be unable to accumulate capital for annexation (or branching out to business activities), but not to restrict the merchants.[6]

On the whole, the above summary is based on a reasonable interpretation of fragments of the text with some emendation. Kuo undoubtedly over-modernized the text by introducing unnecessarily the technical term " full employment." But a more serious problem is whether one can be sure that the whole chapter labelled " Ch'ih-mi " or even the economic passages came from a single hand. It is well known that the work *Kuan-tzu* is of a highly mixed and encyclopedic nature, including ideas of such schools as the Confucianists, Taoists, Legalists, and Cosmologists, as well as of agricultural and military specialists.[7] Especially in chapters containing dialogues attributed to Duke Huan of Ch'i and Kuan Chung, of which " Ch'ih-mi " is one, ideas and theories of others are often quoted and criticized. It is important to distinguish the criticism from its target as well as to watch for mutilation and interpolation. In a greatly garbled chapter like the " Ch'ih-mi," the reconstruction of fragmentary ideas into a scheme can at best be tentative. The above summary of Kuo actually includes a divergence of points. For instance, it is one thing to justify lavishness by referring to a possible link between spending and employment. It is another to emphasize commerce

[6] *Li-shih yen-chiu* 1954.3.37-38.
[7] Lo Ken-tse, *Kuan-tzu t'an-yüan*, 1931; P. Van der Loon, " On the Transmission of *Kuan-tzu*," TP 41.4-5 (1952) .357-393.

but not to despise agriculture. It is still another to limit lavishness as desirable for the middle wealthy group but to leave out the masses and the ruler himself. It is still another thing to distinguish the gentlemen-officials and landlords on the one hand and the merchants on the other, though both groups could equally be wealthy. These points need not constitute a cogent scheme because, as matters of attitude or policy, it is quite possible to adopt one without affirming another. Thus KUO seems to be indulging in over-schematization. For the purpose of this paper, however, the interesting part is the economic argument that links consumption with employment.

Assuming that the whole chapter was by a single author, KUO continues to discuss other passages in the chapter which deal with policies on government, law, religion, and military affairs, comparing them to ideas of the Legalists and Hsün-tzu. KUO even speculates on the date and authorship of the chapter and concludes that it was written around 190 B.C., perhaps by a disciple or retainer of the Ch'in chancellor LI Ssu,[8] who was a disciple of Hsün-tzu. KUO views the chapter as a whole as reflecting unsuccessful efforts made by the merchant class to bid for political leadership and to place themselves over the landlords, presumably in the third and the early second century B. C. According to KUO, these efforts were doomed from the beginning because, China being a continental agricultural state, before science and technology reached a certain level, the country had to rely on agriculture as the basic occupation and political leadership had to rest with the landed class. In his words, " The merchants surrendered. The theory of lavishness naturally became fossilized." [9]

In my opinion, the antagonism between merchants and landlords during this period appears to be overdrawn. Another problem is: How far should one go in adopting a materialistic interpretation of the history of thought? So far as the linkage between consumption and employment is concerned, it can be discovered by any observer who has gone deeply enough into the subject,

[8] On LI Ssu, cf. Derk BODDE, *China's First Unifier, a Study of the Ch'in Dynasty as Seen in the Life of Li Ssu*, 1938.

[9] *Li-shih yen-chiu* 1954.3.62.

and it is by no means limited to thinkers representing the merchant class. On the other hand, it seems obvious that a high degree of commercial activity can provide a favorable condition for the discovery and spread of such an idea.

In his discussion of the authorship of the chapter, KUO Mo-jo cites the following passage from the seventh century encyclopedia *I-wen lei-chü* 藝文類聚 : [10]

> CHOU Jung Tzu-hsia 周容子夏went to see Duke Huan of Ch'i with the policy of lavishness. Duke Huan asked, "Can one govern the world with a policy of lavishness?" Tzu-hsia said, "Yes. To carve firewood and only then to cook with it, and to decorate eggs and only then to boil them—this is to distribute the stored wealth and to circulate the myriad articles."

In the chapter " Ch'ih-mi " one finds the practically identical phrases, " to decorate eggs and only then to boil them, and to decorate firewood and only then to cook with it," although the words are attributed to KUAN Chung in a conversation with Duke Huan of Ch'i. It has been suggested that the *I-wen lei-chü* passage may have been taken from this chapter in the *Kuan-tzu*. KUO Mo-jo, however, feels that the passage was a story about the chapter and that it was taken from another book which is now lost. He believes that the true author of the chapter " Ch'ih-mi " was CHOU Jung Tzu-hsia (CHOU as surname, Jung as personal name, and Tzu-hsia as *tzu* or derived name), who, according to KUO, could not have lived in the time of Duke Huan of Ch'i. As has been pointed out above, KUO places the writing of the chapter at about 190 B. C. This is chiefly because the chapter refers to " woman (or women) in charge of the government: the value (lit., ' weight ') of iron being unexpectedly higher than copper," and to the imminent transition from the Water Element to the Earth Element in terms of the Five Elements. These KUO interprets respectively as referring to Empress LÜ 呂后 who governed the Han empire after the death of Emperor Kao-tsu; to the replacement of the bronze age by the iron age, which was practically completed during the early Han period; and to the fall of the Ch'in dynasty which claimed to have based its rule on the virtue of the Water Element.[11] Although these suggestions appear

---

[10] *I-wen lei-chü* 80.23a. [11] *Li-shih yen-chiu* 1954.3.27-32, 58-59.

ingenious, they must be treated with caution and reservation in view of the complicated textual problem noted above.

This chapter " Ch'ih-mi " has been partly translated into English in *Economic Dialogues in Ancient China, the Kuan-tzu,* edited by Professor Lewis MAVERICK. Instead of " Lavishness," the title of the chapter is translated as " Generous Rewards." [12] This interpretation, as well as that of the text, is largely based on the commentary attributed to FANG Hsüan-ling 房玄齡 (578-648) (actually probably by YIN Chih-chang 尹知章 of the early eighth century). It makes good sense when applied to a statement like: " He (i. e., the ruler) must be skilled in the technique of generous rewards, before he can secure the complete loyalty of the soldiers " 通於侈靡而士可戚 (p. 82). On the other hand, this narrow interpretation becomes inadequate in the following passage:

Men whose hearts have been broken cannot be expected to perform meritorious deeds. (And on the other hand) those who roll in wealth, who eat the most delicious foods, who enjoy the finest music at dinner, who boil painted eggs over a fire of carved faggots—these are the merchants and traders—they cannot be disciplined until their speculative trade is stopped. The rich live in high fashion because the poor make it possible; indeed, the rich could not lead their luxurious life all by themselves. . . . (p. 83)

Interpreting the passage as an advocation of lavishness rather than its criticism, one may emend the translation as follows:

Men whose hearts have been broken cannot be expected to perform meritorious deeds. That is why people should be allowed to eat the most delicious foods, to enjoy the finest music, to boil painted eggs over a fire of carved faggots (or, more literally, to decorate eggs and only then boil them, and to decorate firewood and only then cook with it). If cinnabar mines are not closed, merchants will not stay home [but be active]. Let the rich live in high fashion [so that] the poor will have work to do. This is how the common people make their living and eat without relying on relief. (*Read pu* 不 *for pai* 百.) It is not that they do the work merely by themselves. They are to be provided with money.[13]

---

[12] *Economic Dialogues in Ancient China.* Selections from *The Kuan-tzu,* a book written probably three centuries before Christ. Translators: T'AN Po-fu and WEN Kung-wen (Adam K. W. WEN). Expert critic: HSIAO Kung-chüan [*read* ch'üan]. The enterprise directed and the book edited and published by Lewis MAVERICK, 1954, pp. 81-85. For a review of the book, cf. Lien-sheng YANG, *HJAS* 18 (1955) 284-288.

[13] I am not certain about the exact meaning of the last few sentences. For various and varied commentaries, cf. *Kuan-tzu chi-chiao,* A.560.

In my opinion, the importance of the *I-wen lei-chü* quotation lies not so much in its providing us the name of a person who advocated the policy of lavishness as in the light it throws on the interpretation of the above, highly interesting passage.

Another interesting passage in the chapter [14] is not translated in the MAVERICK volume. It justifies rich burial:

> Lengthen the mourning period so as to occupy people's time, and elaborate the funeral so as to spend their money. Relatives visit each other [during such occasions]—this is to strengthen kinship. . . . To have large caves for burial is to provide work for poor people; to have magnificent tombs is to provide work for artisans. To have large inner and outer coffins is to encourage carpenters, and to have many pieces for enshrouding is to encourage seamstresses.

It may be noted here that a similar economic justification for spending is found also in the *Hsün-tzu* in a chapter entitled " Li lun " 禮論, which is quoted in the " Li shu " 禮書 of the *Shih-chi*. In opposition to the Mohist emphasis on frugality and advocation of simple burial, the *Hsün-tzu* and the *Shih-chi* contain a series of interesting statements of which the first two may be translated as: " Who understands that willingness to die for a principle is [a way] to nourish (i. e., to maintain and develop) life; who under stands that freely spending money is [a way] to nourish wealth! " 孰知夫出死要節之所以養生也,孰知夫輕出費用之所以養財也. Undoubtedly over-influenced by old commentaries, both CHAVANNES and DUBS in their translations of the *Shih-chi* [15] and the *Hsün-tzu* [16] respectively fail to grasp the meaning of the second of the seemingly paradoxical statements.

[14] *Kuan-tzu* (*SPTK* ed.) 12.7a-b. For commentaries, cf. *Kuan-tzu chi-chiao*, A.582-585.

[15] Édouard CHAVANNES, *Les Mémoires historiques de Se-Ma Ts'ien* 3.214-215: " Qui ne sait que, si un homme, soutien de l'état, s'expose à la mort et s'obstine dans son devoir, c'est afin de conserver sa vie? Qui ne sait que, si un homme dépense peu, c'est afin de conserver ses richesses? " Here the understanding of the sentence structure is correct.

[16] Homer H. DUBS, *The Works of Hsün-tzu*, p. 215, " He has very capable braves, willing to die, who have agreed to be temperate, in order to care for his life. Very prudent men expend his money and use it in order to care for his wealth." Here the " he " is misconstrued to mean the emperor, rather than a gentleman in general.

KUO Mo-jo in his article fails to refer to the *Hsün-tzu* and *Shih-chi* passage.

To come back to the MAVERICK volume on the *Kuan-tzu*, I wish to add that it contains, in several places, translations as well as comments concerning economic justification of spending. From " Essay 5 " we read (p. 49) : " Too much thrift restricts business; extravagance wastes goods." From " Essay 7 " we have (p. 56) : " If the ruler does not amply reward deserving persons, the people (officers) will become sluggish, and he (the ruler) will find that it does not pay (to be so miserly) ." The same characters, 用財嗇則費, are translated in a broader sense and more exactly on page 267: " parsimony causes sheer waste."

On page 330 one finds comments on " Unemployment Relief " with the following passage attributed to KUANG Chung, translated from " Essay 69 ":

If in a year the state suffers from drought or flood, and the people lose that year's produce, then palaces, houses, towers, and pavilions should be built or repaired (to give employment). Those who have no dogs in the front (yard) and no hogs in the back (those who are so poor that they cannot afford to keep dogs or hogs) should first be employed. The building of palaces, houses, towers, and pavilions is not merely to gratify the sovereign, but to stabilize the economy of the state.

In the *Yen-tzu ch'un-ch'iu* 晏子春秋,[17] a similar story is attributed to Yen-tzu or YEN Ying 晏嬰, another statesman of Ch'i:

In times of Duke Ching [the country] suffered from a famine. Yen-tzu requested that government grain be distributed [for relief], but the Duke refused. It happened that a tower was to be built for a royal villa. Yen-tzu ordered the officials in charge to pay the workers good wages, to enlarge the area of building, to allow ample time, and not to hasten the work. In three years the tower was completed and the people were relieved.

It is difficult to say whether these attributions to statesmen of Ch'i in any way reflect the relatively highly developed economy of Ch'i in the late Chou period. On the other hand, it should be observed that, although both statesmen enjoyed high reputation, their personal modes of life are reported to have been quite different. YEN Ying is traditionally depicted as an extremely

[17] *Yen-tzu ch'un-ch'iu* (*SPTK* ed.) 5.8b. On the date of the work, cf. *Ssu-k'u ch'üan-shu tsung-mu t'i-yao* 四庫全書總目提要 (Commercial Press ed.) 12.1255-1256; Richard L. WALKER, " Some Notes on the Yen-tzu Ch'un-ch'iu," *JAOS* 73.3 (1953).156-163.

frugal person. He wore the same fur coat for thirty years. When he made sacrificial offerings to his ancestors, the pork shoulder he offered was not even large enough to cover the dish. In contrast, KUAN Chung is said to have led an extravagant and even sumptuous life.[18]

To round off the above discussions on ancient China, I wish to quote a passage from the *Yen-t'ieh lun* 鹽鐵論 or *Discourses on Salt and Iron*, traditionally assumed to be a kind of verbatim record of a debate over fiscal policies between certain government officials and a group of literati in 81 B. C. The translation is that by Esson M. GALE:[19]

e. The Lord Grand Secretary: In ancient times, reasonable limits were set to the style of palaces and houses, chariots and liveries. Plain rafters and straw thatch were not a part of the system of the Ancient Emperors. The true gentleman, while checking extravagance, would disapprove of parsimoniousness because over-thriftiness tends to narrowness. When Sun-shu Ao was the prime minister of Ch'u and his wife did not wear silk nor his horses feed on grain, Confucius said: *One should not be too thrifty so as to be hard on one's inferiors.* This is how the poem *The Cricket* was written. Kuan-tzu said: *If palaces and houses are not decorated, the timber supply will be over-abundant. If animals and fowls are not used in the kitchens, there will be no decrease in their numbers. Without the hankering for profit, the fundamental occupation will have no outlet. Without the embroidered ceremonial robes, the seamstresses will have no occupation.*

The quotation from the *Kuan-tzu*, not found in the present text, of course should be understood in the light of the above discussion. For " the hankering for profit," one may suggest " secondary profit," because for *wei-li* 味利 the text should read *mo-li* 末利, as pointed out by LU Wen-ch'ao 盧文弨 (1717-1796).[20]

The idea of work relief lay dormant from some time during the Han period. It became active again with the Sung dynasty, another era of great economic development.[21] The classical case is that of the statesman FAN Chung-yen 范仲淹 (989-1052):

---

[18] *Li-chi cheng-i* 禮記正義 (*Shih-san-ching chu-su* ed.) 23 " Li ch'i " 禮器 7b-8a, 43 " Tsa-chi hsia " 雜記下 2b: James LEGGE, *The Li Ki* (SBE 27) 402, (SBE 28) 165. LEGGE, *Confucian Analects* 162-163.

[19] *Discourses on Salt and Iron*, 1931, p. 22.

[20] *Loc. cit.* but the character is erroneously given as *wei* 末.

[21] Cf. KU Chi-kuang, " T'ang-mo chih Ch'ing-ch'u chien i-shang wen-t'i chih shang-ch'üeh " 唐末至清初間抑商問題之商榷 in *Wen-shih tsa-chih* 文史雜誌 1.11 (1941) 1-12.

In the second year of Huang-yu 皇祐 (1050), the Wu region suffered a great famine. Roads were covered with bodies dead of starvation. At that time, FAN Wen-cheng 文正 (i. e., FAN Chung-yen) served as Governor of Western Chekiang. He released grain in government granaries and encouraged the people to care for and feed [the sufferers]. He was resourceful in his measures of relief. The people in the Wu region were fond of boat-racing and they were interested in helping the Buddhist church. Hence FAN gave permission for boat-racing. The Governor himself would appear and have a banquet on the lake every day.[22] From spring to summer, people went out for fun, leaving only empty lanes [behind them in the city]. Moreover, FAN summoned the abbots and other leaders of the various Buddhist temples and advised them, " In a year of famine labor is extremely cheap. You may have much constructive work done." Thereupon, many building projects were initiated in the temples. He also rebuilt government granaries and living quarters for government personnel, engaging a thousand workers a day. The Inspector of the region impeached [the Governor of] Hangchow for not paying attention to [normal] relief measures, but spending in lavish amusements and entertainments, and for the public and private building projects which wasted the people's strength. Thereupon, FAN memorialized in detail the reasons why he ordered the banquets and constructive work. They were to distribute surplus wealth and to benefit the poor. Traders and peddlers of food, and artisans and hired laborers, who relied on these public and private activities for their living, numbered several tens of thousands a day. This was the greatest measure of relief. In that year in the two Chekiang areas (Eastern and Western Chekiang) only Hangchow was peaceful and the people did not wander to other places for refuge. This was entirely due to the beneficence of FAN Wen-cheng. In recent years, it has been proclaimed as government regulation in years of famine to distribute grain from government granaries and to encourage people to launch beneficial projects. Not only famine is thus relieved, but the people's welfare is achieved thereby. This is splendid goodness [in the nature of those created] by the ancient kings.

The above story is taken from the *Meng-ch'i pi-tan* 夢溪筆談 by SHEN Kua 沈括 (1031-1095).[23] The author has been described by Dr. Joseph NEEDHAM as " perhaps the most interesting character in all Chinese scientific history," and the book as a " landmark in the history of science in China." [24] It was probably not

---

[22] This is apparently what was referred to in the lines: " Once sent out, you served as Governor for several places in turn, and [wherever you were] people always looked up to your wine pot " (一出屢更郡, 人皆望酒壺) by MEI Yao-ch'en 梅堯臣 (1002-1060) to commemorate the death of FAN. Cf. *Wan-ling Hsien-sheng wen-chi* 宛陵先生文集 (SPPY ed.) 15.3b. I am indebted to Professor James T. C. LIU for calling my attention to these interesting lines.

[23] SPTK ed. 11.6b-7d. A very convenient, collated, and annotated edition is HU Tao-ching 胡道靜, *Meng-ch'i pi-t'an chiao-cheng* 校證, 1955, in two volumes. According to HU, the year of SHEN's birth should be 1031 rather than 1030.

[24] *Science and Civilization in China* 1, 1954, pp. 135-137.

accidental that SHEN paid special attention to FAN's ingenious policy because SHEN himself had unusually deep insight into economic affairs. When he served as minister of finance in 1077, he made the following observation to the Emperor:

> The utility of money derives from circulation and loan-making. A village of ten households may have 100,000 coins. If the cash is stored in the household of one individual, even after a century, the sum remains 100,000. If the coins are circulated through business transactions so that every individual of the ten households can enjoy the utility of the 100,000 coins, then the utility will amount to that of 1,000,000 cash. If circulation continues without stop, the utility of the cash will be beyond enumeration.[25]

This remarkable understanding of velocity of circulation has been noted by a modern Chinese scholar, who proudly points out that SHEN was some six hundred years earlier than John LOCKE (1632-1704).[26]

Guide books for famine relief, from Sung times on,[27] as a rule devote a section to "work relief" (known as *i-kung tai-chen* 以工代賑 lit., "substitution of work for relief," *chi-kung yü-chen* 卽工寓賑 "implication of relief in work," or simply *kung-chen*, "work relief") illustrated by such examples as those of Yen-tzu, FAN Chung-yen, and others. The government regulation referred to in the story about FAN probably was that of 1073, making it a rule that grain and funds from the ever-normal granaries should be used in years of famine to launch projects of water conservancy to relieve the poor.[28] Similar measures were adopted in later dynasties. It is interesting to note that the decree of 1073 ordered advanced planning of such projects with the needed labor and cost figured out in detail. Under the Ch'ing dynasty, a decree of 1737 required careful estimates of city walls to be repaired in the various provinces with priority assigned to the different projects so that work relief could be introduced whenever necessary without delay.[29]

[25] *Hsü Tzu-chih t'ung-chien ch'ang-pien* 續資治通鑑長編 283.7b.
[26] P'ENG Hsin-wei 彭信威, *Chung-kuo huo-pi shih* 中國貨幣史 1953, 2.342-343.
[27] Several such works can be found in *Huang-cheng ts'ung-shu* 荒政叢書 compiled by Yü Sen 俞森 in 1690.
[28] *Wen-hsien t'ung-k'ao* 文獻通考 (*Shih-t'ung* 十通 ed.) 26.254c.
[29] YANG Ching-jen 楊景仁, *Ch'ou-chi pien* 籌濟編 (author's preface dated 1824) (1883 ed.) 13.6a-b.

This Chinese tradition may remind the reader of similar practices in the modern West. The early development of such an idea in China is certainly remarkable. On the other hand, there are basic differences between the " work relief " in early China and the policy of " spending for prosperity " in a modern country. The Chinese measure resulted chiefly from ingenuity in dealing with cases of emergency and thus remained *ad hoc* in nature, whereas the modern policy is based on much more thorough economic analysis and aimed at optimum consumption.[30] In other words, the latter represents economic justification pushed to its logical conclusion. The closest thing to an economic analysis which I can find in relatively recent Chinese literature is a remarkable but not well known essay in favor of spending written in the sixteenth century. A translation of it appears in the appendix to this article.

On the philological side, it should be noted, in conclusion, that among the commentators who understood the chapter " Ch'ih-mi " in its right vein was IGAI Hikohiro 猪飼彦博 (Keisho 敬所, 1761-1845) whose *Kanshi ho-sei* 管子補正, published in 1798, is praised highly by KUO Mo-jo.[31] The difficult passage in the " Li shu " of the *Shih-chi* was correctly understood by the Japanese scholar NAKAI Sekitoku 中井積徳 (Riken 履軒, 1732-1817 or 1816), quoted in the famous *Shiki kaishu kōshō* 史記會注考證 by TAKIKAWA Kametarō 瀧川龜太郎.[32] For comparative institu-

---

[30] Cf. Oscar LANGE, " The Rate of Interest and the Optimum Propensity to Consume," *Economica* (New Series) 5.7 (1938) 12-32. For this reference I am indebted to Dr. Fred C. HUNG, who has also made the following observation:

In western experience, under-consumption theory which advocates increased consumption to improve economic conditions usually gains popularity during times of depression or economic hardship. The more frequent occurrence of famine and other natural disasters in Chinese history may therefore explain why Chinese scholars early discovered the benevolent aspect of consumption.

This supplements rather than contradicts the thesis that economic justification of spending tends to be made when the society is experiencing, or has experienced, a relatively high level of economic development.

Whether saving or consumption is good, of course, depends on a host of factors including the social and economic structure, the stage of development, and the relation between saving and investment, as well as other circumstances. I am also indebted to Dr. Alexander ECKSTEIN for a discussion on these points.

[31] *Kuan-tzu chi-chiao* A.7, 18-19.

[32] *Shiki kaishu kōshō* 4.10-11. LIANG Ch'i-hsiung 梁啓雄, *Hsün-tzu chien-shih* 荀子柬釋, 1936, pp. 258-259, also interprets the passage correctly.

tional history, one may point to the famous case of work relief by MATSUDAIRA Sadanobu 松平定信 (1758-1829) in 1783 when he ordered dikes to be built along the Ōkuma 大隈 River to provide employment for the poor.[33] On the other hand, it must not be assumed that MATSUDAIRA was in favor of heavy spending as a general policy. Actually, the opposite was the case. In his *Bukka ron* 物價論 or *Discourses on Price* with his colleagues, 1789-1790,[34] it was his colleague HONDA Tadakazu 本多忠籌 who argued that the prohibition of lavishness would inhibit the development of commerce, while MATSUDAIRA himself stood strongly for frugality. This again illustrates the possible or even frequent discrepancy between government policy and economic thinking.

---

[33] *Dainihon nōsei shi* 大日本農政史 (also known as *Dainihon nōsei ruihen* 大日本農政類編) 1932, pp. 811-812.

[34] TOKUTOMI Iichirō 德富猪一郎, *Kinsei Nihon kokumin shi, Matsudaira Sadanobu jidai* 近世日本國民史,松平定信時代 1936, pp. 222-226, 255-256.

A SIXTEENTH CENTURY ESSAY IN FAVOR OF SPENDING

PRELIMINARY REMARKS

The following essay by Lu Chi 陸楫 of Shanghai (fl. c. 1540) is rather freely translated from his *Chien-chia-t'ang tsa-chu tse-ch'ao* 兼葭堂雜著摘抄 (*Chi-lu hui-pien* 紀錄彙編 204.2b-4a). The essay is remarkable in that it makes a distinction between the economic interests of an individual or a family and those of the world as a whole. Apparently, the author realized something in the nature of what is known in logic as " fallacy of composition," i. e., what is true for each is not necessarily true for all, and, conversely, what is true for all is not necessarily true for each.

Another interesting point is the author's reference to a passage in the *Works of Mencius* (LEGGE, pp. 269-270) where the Master was justifying his own grand style of living, " If you do not have an intercommunication of the productions of labour, and an interchange of *men's* services, so that *one from his* overplus may supply the deficiency of *another,* then husbandmen will have a superfluity of grain, and women will have a superfluity of cloth. If you have such an interchange, carpenters and carriage-wrights may all get their food from you." Of course, Mencius was quick to add that such a style of living was only too appropriate for worthies like himself.

This passage in the *Works of Mencius* includes the words *hsien* 羨 " surplus " and *pu-tsu* 不足 " deficiency " which also appear in other ancient texts, notably the *Kuan-tzu*.[1] In the *Yen-t'ieh lun*,[2] one finds the puzzling expressions *ch'ien pu-tsu* 前不足, *san pu-tsu* 散不足, and *chü pu-tsu* 聚不足. The modern Japanese scholar MIYAZAKI Ichisada 宮崎市定, in his article " En fusoku ron " 羨不足論 (" Zum chinesischen Luxus—Ein Beitrag zur Abwechselung des Luxus in China ") *SZ* 51.1 (1940).27-56, has suggested that these were all corruptions of *hsien pu-tsu* referring to unequal distribution of wealth and I am inclined to agree.

TRANSLATION OF THE ESSAY

Those who discourse on government as a rule wish to prohibit extravagance, assuming that restricted spending will enrich the people. However, as an early

---

[1] *Kuan-tzu*, Essays 52, 73, 81, *SPTK* ed. 17.2b, 22.4b, and 24.1b. The text *i pu-tsu* 義不足 in Essay 52 (17.2b) should read *hsien pu-tsu*, following the emendation by IGAI Hikohiro. Also cf. Lewis MAVERICK, *Economic Dialogues in Ancient China*: *Selections from the Kuan-tzu*, pp. 97-98, 117, 181.

[2] Chapters 28, 29, 30, *SPTK* ed. 5.15a, 6.1a-1b, 6.10a-10b. Chapter 28 is the last chapter of the *Yen-t'ieh lun* translated by P. A. BOODBERG and T. C. LIN in *JNCBRAS* 65 (1934).73-110, where *ch'ien pu-tsu* is rendered as " insufficiency [described] before " on page 110.

worthy has observed,[3] as to the wealth produced by Heaven and Earth there is a fixed amount 天地生財，止有此數. One person's loss becomes the gain of another. I do not see how extravagance is capable of impoverishing the whole world. Spoken from the point of view of an individual, his frugality can, perhaps, save him from becoming poor. Spoken from the point of view of a family, its frugality can, perhaps, save it from becoming poor. In an over-all consideration of the trend of the world, this, however, is not true. Should the ruler of the world plan only to enrich an individual or a family, or rather to enrich the whole world in an equalized manner?

I often observe broadly the trend of the world, noting that, in general, if a place is accustomed to extravagance, then the people there will find it easy to make a living, and if a place is accustomed to frugality, then the people there will find it difficult to make a living. Why? Because this is caused by the trend.

Now the wealth of the country is concentrated in Wu and Yüeh (i. e., the modern Kiangsu and Chekiang). As for extravagant custom, there is no place where it surpasses that of the people in Soochow and Hangchow, where numerous people consume fine food without tilling one inch of soil and wear embroidered textiles without touching the shuttle. This is because the custom there is extravagant and there are many people pursuing secondary occupations. Let us merely illustrate with the lakes and hills in Soochow and Hangchow. The people residing there go out to amuse themselves at these places according to a seasonal schedule. Whenever they go out, they always have painted boats, sedan chairs, delicacies, and superior wine, together with singing and dancing. This is, indeed, extravagant. On the other hand, there are numerous people, including boatmen, sedan-chair carriers, singsong boys and dancing girls, who depend on the lakes and hills for a minimum living. Therefore we say, one person's loss becomes the gain of another.

Suppose one dumps his wealth entirely into a ditch or drain, then it is advisable to prohibit this extravagance of his. But what is generally referred to as extravagance is merely the fact that rich merchants and powerful families spend much for their own houses, carts, horses, food, drink, and clothing. When they are extravagant in meat and rice, farmers and cooks will share the profit; when they are extravagant in silk textiles, weavers and dealers will share the profit. This is exactly what Mencius meant by saying " have an intercommunication of the production of labour, and an interchange of *men's* services, so that *one from his* overplus may supply the deficiency of *another.*" Why should the government prohibit this?

At present, the custom in Ningpo, Shao-hsing, Chin-hua, and Ch'ü-chow is known as most frugal. Then [according to conventional reasoning] the people there should be rich. But the people in these prefectures can not even support themselves and half of them have travelled to other places for a living. This is because the custom is so frugal that the people are unable to help each other.

In short, richness precedes extravagance and poverty precedes frugality.

---

[3] This remark seems to have been first made by Ssu-ma Kuang (*Wen-hsien t'ung-k'ao* 23.226b), although a similar conception, in different wording, can also be found in earlier texts.

The custom of extravagance or frugality comes from the people's being rich or poor. Even if [an ancient] sage ruler is to appear again, he will find it difficult to prohibit extravagance in Wu and Yüeh.

Someone may say, "This is not true. The Soochow and Hangchow area is a hub for northern and southern traffic in the whole empire to which commodities of all kinds come from every direction. Therefore, the people there can make a living on trade. It is not because their custom is extravagant." However, this is merely observing the benefit from trade without realizing that the reason why there is trade is exactly because people are extravagant. If everyone leads another in being frugal, then those who pursue secondary occupations will return to agriculture. How can people still distinguish themselves by means of trade?

Moreover, let us consider our town Shanghai. It is located out of place on the seacoast. [And yet] boats and carts pass through the place not infrequently. Thus it has earned the nickname "Small Soochow." Travelling merchants who depend on this town for a living amount to hundreds of thousands. It is exactly because the custom of the place is quite extravagant that the people there find it rather easy to earn a living.

Therefore, the main reason for the easy living in Wu and Yüeh is because of its extravagant custom. The benefit from trade merely helps it, and it does not constitute the sole thing on which people depend. If those who govern the people do so in conformity with the custom, then the ruler will not be laborious and the people will not be disturbed. How can a mere prohibition of extravagance do? Unfortunately, one can only tell this to wise men.

NUMBERS AND UNITS IN CHINESE ECONOMIC HISTORY

LIEN-SHENG YANG
HARVARD UNIVERSITY

The British scholar J. H. CLAPHAM [1] has remarked that the methodological distinctiveness of economic history "hinges primarily upon its quantitative interests." In dealing with quantities it is of course necessary to have a thorough understanding of the numbers and units in use. As a student of economic history, I have found that there are certain precautions which should be observed in the use of numbers and units in Chinese texts. The principles involved may seem to be commonplace and may not be limited to texts in the Chinese language. Constant recurrence of the same old examples and constant discovery of new ones indicate that these general precautions are nevertheless worth attention.

The first precaution is to watch out for misprints and copyists' errors. The Chinese characters for one, two, and three are easily confused because they are written with one, two, and three horizontal strokes respectively. The number four in its archaic form has four horizontal strokes and thus adds to the confusion. Archaic forms of the characters for seven and ten resemble each other even more than their modern forms. Both are represented by a cross, the only difference being that the vertical stroke in the character for ten is much longer.[2] Modern characters for ten and thousand differ by only one stroke on the top.

Numerous examples of misprints of numbers may be found in Chinese texts. To avoid such mistakes, careful Chinese have introduced what may be called alteration-proof forms of numbers. There are special forms for numbers from one to ten, and also for hundred and thousand.[3] Some of these forms can be traced back

---

[1] "Economic history as a discipline," in *Encyclopaedia of Social Sciences* 5.327.

[2] For example, see the article by LIU Fu 劉復 on a Han sundial in *KHCK* 3.4 (1932) .589.

[3] 壹貳參肆伍陸柒捌玖拾佰仟.

75

to a few centuries B. C., although the whole set of ten or more alteration-proof forms is datable only from the end of the seventh century.[4]

Among misprints in units the most important is the use of shêng 升 for tou 斗 and tou for shêng (two measures of capacity: ten shêng equal to one tou). From medieval manuscripts discovered in Tun-huang, we learn that these two characters in their semi-cursive forms are so similar to each other that the reader can easily mistake one for the other.[5] The similarity was probably noted by medieval contemporaries and precautions accordingly taken. In documents of T'ang and Sung date one finds not only alteration-proof forms (勝 and 斜) for shêng and tou but also one (碩) for shih 石, which contains ten tou.

Copyists' errors may be committed by the historian himself when he carelessly transcribes figures from documents. For example, the T'ung tien 通典 6.34b gives the total revenue in the year 780 in round numbers as follows: cash collected 30,000,000 strings, of which 9,500,000 strings were for expenses in the capital and 20,500,000 for the other parts of the Empire; grain collected 16,000,000 shih, of which 2,000,000 shih were for the capital and 14,000,000 were for the rest of the Empire. The Hsin T'ang shu 新唐書 52.1b records the same amounts of cash collection but gives different figures for the grain collection: 16,000,000 shih for expenses in the capital and 14,000,000 shih for expenses in other parts of the Empire. This is apparently an error, probably resulting from a careless transcription of the figures in the T'ung tien. Three other sources [6] put the cash collection in the same year at 10,898,000 strings and grain collection at 2,157,000 shih. Al-

---

[4] In T'ang texts the alteration-proof form 漆 is used instead of 柒. The forms 壹貳參伍陸漆 already appear individually in texts of Han or earlier date. Cf. TING Fu-pao 丁福保, Ku-ch'ien ta-tz'ŭ-tien 古錢大辭典, Tsung-lun 總論 5a and 9b.

[5] For references, see Lien-sheng YANG, "Notes on the Economic History of the Chin Dynasty," HJAS 9 (1946).130, note 116.

[6] Tzŭ-chih t'ung-chien 資治通鑑 226.18a; Ts'ê-fu yüan-kuei 册府元龜 488.1a-2b; Chiu T'ang shu 舊唐書 12.10a. These figures have been discussed by CH'ÜAN Han-shêng 全漢昇 in his article on public revenue in the T'ang and Sung periods in CYYY 20.1 (1948).193-195.

though these figures are somewhat larger than the amounts for expenses in the capital as given in the *T'ung tien,* they do support the theory that the *Hsin T'ang shu* is erroneous.

The second precaution is to distinguish pseudo numbers from real numbers. Numbers used symbolically rather than scientifically are pseudo numbers and are not to be understood in their literal sense. For example, the expression *ch'ien chin* 千金 often indicates merely a large amount of wealth and not necessarily one thousand units of gold.[7] In a famous essay on three and nine [8] the Ch'ing scholar WANG Chung 汪中 (1745-1794) has proved conclusively that in many old texts the numbers three and nine are used only to mean " several " and " many " irrespective of their literal sense.[9] LIU Shih-p'ei 劉師培 (1884-1919) has developed this thesis and has suggested that numbers like 300, 3000, 36, and 72 in ancient texts may also be pseudo numbers.[10]

On the other hand, some numbers may appear to be pseudo numbers which are actually real. First we may give *pan* 半 " half " as an example. According to the " Treatise on Officials " attached to the *Hou-Han shu,* the salary of officials in Later Han times was paid half in cash and half in grain 半錢半穀. The text gives the

---

[7] KATŌ Shigeru 加藤繁 is perhaps not justified in taking the expression *ch'ien-chin* in some T'ang texts as a real number meaning one thousand *liang* 兩 of gold in his *Tōsō jidai kingin no kenkyū* 唐宋時代金銀の研究, pp. 29, 36-37.

[8] *Shih san chiu* 釋三九 in WANG's *Shu hsüeh* 述學 (*Ssŭ-pu ts'ung-k'an* ed.) 2a-3b. In this essay in three parts, WANG distinguishes *chih-tu chih shih-shu* 制度之實數, " real numbers in institutions," from *yen-yü chih hsü-shu* 言語之虛數, " pseudo numbers in language." His interpretation of the use of *san* and *chiu* as pseudo numbers may be paraphrased as follows: " Three " is the sum of the odd number " one " and the even number " two " and therefore represents the accumulation of numbers. When a number becomes as large as " ten," it will be represented by the numeral " one " again. Therefore " nine " represents the end of counting. For similar reasoning in the West, see V. F. HOPPER, *Medieval Number Symbolism* (New York, 1938), pp. 1-11 (" Elementary number symbolism ").

[9] Professor E. O. REISCHAUER has called my attention to a similar use of the number " eight " to mean " many " in a number of compounds in Japanese.

[10] There are six short essays called " Ku-chi to hsü-shu shuo " 古籍多虛數說 in his *Tso-an chi* 左盦集 (*Liu Shên-shu hsien-shêng i-shu* 劉申叔先生遺書 *ts'ê* 40) 8.6a-9a. I thank Professor J. R. HIGHTOWER for this reference. Also see Lü shu-hsiang 呂叔湘, *Chung-kuo wên-fa yao-lüeh* 中國文法要略 (Chungking, 1942) 2.15-16 for his discussion on thirty per cent and seventy per cent, meaning roughly one third and two thirds.

amounts in cash and grain for officials of nine different ranks. Two Japanese scholars [11] have done some mathematical work with these figures and have concluded that the ratio of cash to grain was about 7 to 3. This is incorrect because they ignored the difference between husked (*mi* 米) and unhusked grain (*ku* 穀). A modern Chinese scholar [12] has shown that by taking into consideration this difference and by assuming the price of a *shih* of unhusked grain to be one hundred coins, four out of the nine cases are exactly half and half. We are not certain whether the other five contain misprints, but the " half " in this text is at least partly valid.

Another example is the use of the expressions *t'ai-pan* 太半 (or *ta-pan* 大半, lit., " big half ") and *shao-pan* 少半 (or *hsiao-pan* 小半, lit., " small half "), which are used to mean more than half and less than half in ordinary modern texts. In Han or earlier times, however, they were used to mean two thirds and one third. This may be proved by calculations of figures given in some ancient texts,[13] by definitions given in early commentaries,[14] and by references to a mathematical work probably of Han date.[15] In recently published Han documents on wood, which contain records about provisions for garrison troops on the northwestern

[11] Utsunomiya Kiyoyoshi 宇都宮清吉 and Yabuuchi Kiyoshi 藪內清：續漢志百官受奉例考 in *Tōyōshi kenkyū* 東洋史研究 5.4 (1940) .271-282.

[12] Wang Shih 王栻：漢代的官俸 in *Ssŭ-hsiang yü shih-tai* 思想與時代 32.8 (1943).

[13] For example, in *Mo-tzŭ* 墨子 15 (*Tsa-shou* 雜守) on the amounts of the daily provision for people in a beseiged city (for collations of this passage, see Wu Yü-chiang 吳毓江, *Mo-tzŭ chiao-chu* 墨子校註 15.28a-b); in *Kuan-tzŭ* 管子 (*Ssŭ-pu ts'ung-k'an* ed.) 22.2a (*Hai-wang* 海王) on the amounts of salt consumed per month by male and female adults and children.

[14] For example, the commentary by Wei Chao 韋昭 to *Shih chi* 7.28b, and the commentary by Yen Shih-ku 顏師古 to *Han shu* 24A.7b.

[15] The *Chiu-chang suan-shu* 九章算術. For discussion on this work, see Ch'ien Pao-tsung 錢寶琮, *Chung-kuo suan-hsüeh shih* 中國算學史 Pt. 1 (Peiping, 1932) .31-39.

The compounds *t'ai-pan* (or *ta-pan*) and *shao-pan* also may be found on Han bronze inscriptions; for examples, see J. C. Ferguson, *Li-tai chu-lu chi-chin mu* 歷代著錄吉金目 (Shanghai, 1939), pp. 447, 612, 819, 835, 836, 838, 843, 844, 858, 1066, 1145-1146. The example on p. 612 is even earlier than Han and, according to one authority, dates from the sixth century B.C.

frontier of China, we find *t'ai-pan* and *shao-pan* shortened to *t'ai* (written *ta*) and *shao,* meaning exactly two thirds and one third.[16]

The third precaution is to keep in mind that figures which were meant to be real numbers in Chinese history may have different degrees of reliability, which can be determined only after a careful examination of the background. Population figures and amounts of cultivated land are probably the most notorious examples. In the majority of cases there was under-reporting mainly because of the inability on the part of the government to register the land owned by and the people subordinate to powerful individuals.

In some rare cases the smaller figures were reported by local officials out of good will—that is, their desire to help the people in general. For example, in the middle of the Ming period, through a survey of land it was discovered that many people owned more than the amounts they had registered. The local officials, fearing that the central government might want to increase the already heavy taxes, converted the standard *mu* into various sizes of larger *mu* and thus deceived their superiors in their reports. According to the *Kuang-p'ing fu-chih* 廣平府志 [17] land in that

[16] Many examples may be found in LAO Kan 勞榦, *Chü-yen Han-chien k'ao-shih,* *Shih-wên* 居延漢簡考釋、釋文 (Li-chuang, 1943). LAO Kan however offers no interpretation of these shortened forms. In *Les documents chinois découverts par Aurel Stein dans les sables de Turkestan oriental* (Oxford, 1913), CHAVANNES mistranslated the *ta* in documents no. 223 and no. 226 by "grand mesure" (pp. 57-58). He also misunderstood the expression *ch'ang ssŭ-ts'un-ta-pan-ts'un* 長四寸大半寸 in documents no. 320 as "long de 4 pouces, épais d'un demi-pouce" (p. 75), which may be rendered as "4⅔ inches long." The *Liu-sha chui-chien* 流沙墜簡 (1914) 2.29a-30a contains a few examples of these abbreviations, on which WANG Kuo-wei 王國維 made no comment. Cf. Lien-sheng YANG, *op. cit.,* p. 141, note 40.

It is interesting to add that the characters *dai* 大, *han* 半, and *shō* 小 appear in old Japanese documents on acreage datable from the twelfth century. *Dai* was used to mean two thirds, *han* one half, and *shō* one third, indicating portions of a *tan* 段, which was 360 *bu* 步. Again, in 16th century documents after the survey of land under TOYOTOMI Hideyoshi, we find the expressions *daibu* 大步 (200 *bu*), *hambu* 半步 (150 *bu*) and *shōbu* 小步 (100 *bu*) referring to portions of *tan* 反 (300 *bu*). Cf. *Koji ruien* 古事類苑, *Seijibu* 政治部 72. Also *Nihon keizaishi jiten* 日本經濟史辭典 (Tōkyō, 1940), under *Daihanshō* 大半小 and *Chōtanbu* 町段步.

[17] 1745 ed. 6.2a. A text with slight differences is quoted in the *Jih-chih lu* 日知錄 (*Ssŭ-pu ts'ung-k'an* ed.) 10.2a-4a. Also see *Ming shih* 明史 27.6b.

prefecture in modern southern Hopei was converted according to its fertility at different rates, which in some cases were as large as seven or eight *mu* to one *mu*.

Examples of over-reporting can also be found in Chinese history. The increase of cultivated land from 19,404,267 *ch'ing* 頃 (100 *mu* equal to 1 *ch'ing*) in 589 to 55,854,040 in *ca.* 610 has been questioned in the *T'ung tien* 2.15c. The large population figures in the later part of the eighteenth century may have been fabricated in part to please the ambitious Emperor Ch'ien-lung.[18] It is, of course, an open secret that generals over-report the numbers of their soldiers and exaggerate their military achievements.[19]

The fourth precaution is that the same unit may indicate different amounts in different places and at different times. It is well known that official standards of weights and measures have been increased throughout Chinese history.[20] Sometimes the old units and the new ones may even be used concurrently. For example, in Sui and T'ang times, there were *ta-ch'ih* 大尺 and *hsiao-ch'ih* 小尺, *ta-tou* 大斗 and *hsiao-tou* 小斗, and *ta-liang* 大兩 and *hsiao-liang* 小兩. The ratios between the three pairs were 1 to 1.2, 1 to 3, and 1 to 3, respectively. According to T'ang regulations,[21] the small units, which were more ancient, were used for musical instruments, measurements of shadow on the sundial,

---

[18] OTAKE Fumio 小竹文夫, *Kinsei Shina keizaishi kenkyū* 近世支那經濟史研究 (Tōkyō, 1942), pp. 271-282.

[19] For a discussion on the tradition of making the numbers of heads and captives ten times larger in reports by generals in the third century, see MIYAZAKI Ichisada 宮崎市定：讀史劄記 *Shirin* 21.1 (1936).134-135.

The fabulous total (over six hundred million) of people reported (*Ming shih* 309.32b; Erich HAUER, *Asia Major*, vol. 3) to have been killed by troops of the rebel leader CHANG Hsien-chung 張獻忠 (1605-1647) has been discussed by LIU I-chêng 柳詒徵 in an article on methodology in the studies of economic history in *Shih-hsüeh tsa-chih* 史學雜志 1.4 (1929).1-5.

[20] For a summary, see WU Ch'êng-lo 吳承洛, *Chung-kuo tu-liang-hêng shih* 中國度量衡史 (Shanghai, 1937), pp. 54-76. Also see J. C. FERGUSON: "Chinese Foot Measure," *MS* 6 (1941).357-382.

[21] Reference passages from the *T'ang hui-yao* 唐會要 ch. 66, *T'ang liu-tien* 唐六典, ch. 3, *T'ang-lü su-i* 唐律疏議, ch. 26, *Po K'ung liu-t'ieh* 白孔六帖, ch. 13 and *Chiu T'ang shu*, ch. 48 are conveniently put together in *Tōryō shūi* 唐令拾遺, pp. 842-846 by NIIDA Noboru 仁井田陞.

medicine, and ceremonial caps. For all other purposes, private and official, the large units were used. However, it is possible that the small weights and measures were not limited to the uses specified in the regulations. In the diary kept by the Japanese monk Ennin 圓仁,[22] who made a pilgrimage to China in the middle of the ninth century, we find mention of sha-chin 砂金, " sand gold," in both ta-liang and hsiao-liang, or large and small taels.

In this connection, it is interesting to note that the expressions ta-shih 大石 and hsiao-shih 小石 in Han wooden documents were entirely different from these large and small units of the T'ang. Under the Han, they were the same unit, but were called large or small according to what was measured. Hsiao-shih indicated unhusked grain and ta-shih husked grain.[23] The ratio between them was 5 to 3.

Besides the official standards, different local weights and measures have been used at different places and even at the same place. A modern investigation into twenty-two villages in the district Wu-hsi 無錫 in Kiangsu finds at least 173 sizes of mu in use, ranging from 2.683 to 8.957 are.[24] (The standard mu is 6 2/3 are.) This may be an extreme case, but it is by no means

[22] Nittō guhō junrei gyōki 入唐求法巡禮行記 (Dainihon bukkyō zensho 大日本佛教全書 (ts'ê 113), pp. 176, 178 and 188. The first chapter of this important work has been translated with an introduction by Professor E. O. REISCHAUER in his " Nittō guhō junrei gyōki, Ennin's Diary of His Travels in T'ang China (838-847)" (Harvard Doctoral Thesis, 1939). In this diary there are two puzzling passages concerning the weight of sand gold. On one occasion (p. 176) four small taels of sand gold were weighed as one large tael and êrh-fên-pan 二分半. On another (p. 178), two large taels of sand gold were weighed in the market as one large tael and seven ch'ien 錢, and the seven ch'ien were allowed to be counted as 准當 ta-êrh-fên-pan 大二分半. The unit ch'ien must have been one tenth of a tael, as it still is today. The fên however could not have been the normal one tenth of a ch'ien. I suppose êrh-fên-pan stood for one quarter and ta-êrh-fên-pan for three quarters. These two fractions were also known as jo-pan 弱半 (one fourth) and ch'iang-pan 強半 (three fourths) in some old mathematical works. The Japanese monk was given the advantage of counting his 1.70 tael as 1.75 tael.

[23] Cf. Lien-sheng YANG, op. cit., p. 142, note 47. Also see Jih-chih lu 11.4b-5b and Shih-chia-chai yang-hsin-lu 十駕齋養新錄 (Ch'ien-yen-t'ang ch'üan-shu 潛研堂全書 ed.) 19.10a-b.

[24] Mu-tê ch'a-i 畝的差異 (Nanking, 1929) by CH'ÊN Han-shêng 陳翰笙 and others.

uncommon to have several weights and measures used concurrently at one place.[25] The Chinese government nominally has always tried to standardize weights and measures, but has never had much success. Apparently people of vested interests have enjoyed these discrepancies in units.

These variations may be partly accounted for by the fact that a larger unit may not contain the same number of smaller units. For example, under the Ch'ing dynasty for the survey of land a standard *kung* 弓 (or *pu* 步) contained 5 *ch'ih*. According to a memorial which was approved by the Emperor in 1750, there were in use several kinds of *kung* which ranged from 3.2 to 7.5 *ch'ih*.[26] Nor was the official standard of 240 *kung* or *pu* (i. e., sq. *pu*) in a *mu* always observed.

As for measurements of time, according to the Chinese lunar calendar, a year may have twelve or thirteen months and a month twenty-nine or thirty days. These differences were also taken care of in some institutions. Under the T'ang dynasty an able-bodied adult male was required to render labor service to the government for twenty days. In an intercalary year he had to work for two more days, i. e., ten per cent extra.[27] The Ch'ing dynasty levied various additional taxes in an intercalary year; their amounts, however, were usually smaller than a 1/12th proportion.[28] These additional charges were abolished by the Republic in 1917.[29] Under the Ch'ing dynasty, in a shorter month (*hsiao-chien* 小建) the regular monthly pay to a soldier was reduced by the amount for one day, which was supposed to make

[25] See Wu Ch'êng-lo, *Chung-kuo tu-liang-hêng shih*, pp. 298-314.

[26] *Ta-Ch'ing hui-tien shih-li* 大清會典事例 (1818 ed.), *ch.* 165. Also see *Jih-chih lu* 10.1b-2a.

[27] *Tōryō shūi*, p. 668. This sounds unfair. However, according to what was probably T'ang tradition, " Throughout a year, with the exception of the intercalary month, there are two months, namely the fifth and the tenth (one version gives the ninth), which are agricultural months and in which labor services are exempted " (trans. from *Hsia-hou Yang suan-ching* 夏侯陽算經 [Wu-ying-tien chü-chên-pan 武英殿聚珍版 ed.] A7b.) Thus the average service for the other ten months was also two days per month.

[28] Amounts are given in most local gazeteers.

[29] Chia Shih-i 賈士毅, *Min-kuo hsü ts'ai-chêng shih* 民國續財政史 (Shanghai, 1934) 7.21.

up a part of the additional payment in an intercalary month.[30] This practice may have come from an ancient tradition according to which a soldier's provisions were computed on a daily basis as was done in the Han times.[31]

The Chinese Republic has tried to standardize weights and measures since 1930 by linking them to the French or International System. One *shêng* is equivalent to one litre, two *chin* 斤 to one kilogram, and three *ch'ih* to one metre. This is called the one-two-three system. But official standards in history were not always so neat. This was particularly true under the Sung dynasty, when " short catty " 省秤, " short bushel " 省斛,[32] and " short hundred " (of cash) 省陌 were officially recognized. A short catty was four fifths of a full catty; a short bushel eighty-three per cent of a full bushel, and the short hundred was actually only seventy-seven coins. These probably represented comprom-

[30] *Hu-pu tsê-li* 戶部則例 (1851 ed.) 80.4a-b; *Ta-Ch'ing hui-tien shih-li* 203.5b, 204.16b, and other places. These deductions together with those made when a soldier was absent were known by the technical term *chien-k'uang* 建曠. This term has also been defined as the surplus amount of taxes which was collected on the extra day in a longer month but was not forwarded (*Shina hōsei daijiten* 支那法制大辭典 quoted from the *Liu-pu ch'êng-yü chu-chieh* 六部成語注解. The latter work was available only in manuscript form before its publication in 1947 in Kyōto). I have not been able to find other documentation for this interpretation.

[31] *Liu-sha chui-chien* 2.28a-29a. (For *liu-jih* 六日 in line 4 on 28b read *i-jih* 一日.) WANG Kuo-wei has concluded that the daily provision for a soldier under the Han dynasty was 6 *shêng* of grain. However, I have discovered from Han wooden documents that provisions were paid at two different rates. One was 6 *shêng* of husked grain per day (i. e., 1.8 *shih* of husked grain or 3 *shih* of unhusked grain in a full month of 30 days), and the other was 6⅔ *shêng* of husked grain per day (i. e., 2 *shih* of husked grain or 333⅓ *shêng* of unhusked grain in a full month of 30 days). The higher rate seems to have been used for officers and soldiers regularly guarding the watchtowers, whereas the lower one seems to have applied to convicts, soldiers working on agricultural colonies, and officers and soldiers who served on the frontier for short periods.

[32] In the *Shu-shu chiu-chang* 數書九章 by CH'IN Chiu-shao 秦九詔 (author's preface 1247, *I-chia-t'ang ts'ung-shu* 宜稼堂叢書 ed.) 2.1b and 11.17a, the *shêng-hu* or " short bushel " is called *kuan-hu* 官斛 and *wên-ssŭ-yüan hu* 文思院斛. *Wên-ssŭ yüan* was the bureau of manufactures under the Sung dynasty. Its title alluded to 時文思索, the first line of the inscription on a standard measure of capacity mentioned in the *Chou li* (*Ssŭ-pu ts'ung-k'an* ed.) 11.26a, which BIOT has rendered as " Ceci est le résultat des méditations et des recherches d'un prince de haute vertu." (*Le Tcheou-li* 2.505.)

ises of various kinds of units in use. The amazing thing is that
these odd units were made official and were maintained for almost
the whole period. This must have been a considerable headache to
accountants, because we find in mathematical works [33] of Sung
date sections on how to convert the short units to the full units
and vice versa.

---

[33] Mathematical works (*I-chia-t'ang ts'ung-shu, ts'ê* 41, 42) by YANG Hui 楊輝
(13th cent.) also contain several questions on such conversions. For CH'IN and YANG,
see CH'IEN Pao-tsung, *Chung-kuo suan-hsüeh shih*, 125-142; for YANG, also see LI
Yen 李儼, *Chung-suan shih lun-ts'ung* 中算史論叢 (Shanghai, 1935) 2.93-119.

NOTES ON DR. SWANN'S *FOOD AND MONEY IN ANCIENT CHINA*

LIEN-SHENG YANG

HARVARD UNIVERSITY

The economic history of ancient China to the end of the Han dynasty is a fascinating subject. Although books written in this period are limited in number, studies on them by later scholars are surprisingly voluminous. The early records often permit divergent and even fanciful interpretations, but newly discovered archæological materials, particularly ancient inscriptions on tortoise shells and bronzes and Han documents on wood, occasionally lend support to one theory or disprove another. It is desirable, therefore, to examine from time to time the current status of certain problems in this field. I am taking the occasion of introducing Dr. Nancy Lee SWANN's new book, *Food and Money in Ancient China*,[1] to attempt to review recent studies on a few problems of interest, without limiting myself altogether to the scope of the work by Dr. SWANN.

Food and Money in Ancient China is a major contribution to the understanding of Chinese economic history. In an impressive volume, Dr. SWANN, the veteran scholar of Han history, offers a translation and study of *Han shu* 24, "Treatise on Food and Money," and two related texts, *Shih chi* 129 and *Han shu* 91. The book is carefully organized to introduce these early accounts of the economic history of ancient China not only to students of Chinese civilization but also to economists and historians of the Western world. The translation is literal and faithful; the footnotes are abundant and scholarly. Among the various items of "Introductory Material" (pp. 3-90), the "Commentary on Selected Topics" (pp. 19-70) is particularly valuable because it

[1] *Food and Money in Ancient China*, the earliest economic history of China to A. D. 25, *Han shu* 24, with related texts, *Han shu* 91 and *Shih-chi* 129. Translated and annotated by Nancy Lee SWANN, Princeton: Princeton University Press, 1950. Pp. xiii + 482.

provides a historical and institutional background. Following the translation of *Han shu* 24 are careful studies of several interesting problems, technical and otherwise (pp. 360-398). Two maps showing the coin-type distribution in ancient China (by WANG Yü-ch'üan 王毓銓 [2] for the American Numismatic Society), a chronological table of contents of *Han shu* 24 (pp. 91-105), some dozen well-selected illustrations, a carefully prepared index (pp. 465-480), and a facsimile of the three Chinese texts are all helpful. The printer as well as the author deserves credit for an excellent job. The large type in which the translation of *Han shu* 24 is printed is especially pleasant to the eye.

Han shu 24AB, i. e., *Shih-huo chih* 食貨志 or "Treatise on Food and Money," is characterized as "the earliest extant economic history of China from its traditional records, about the twelfth century B. C. to A. D. 25" (p. 5). Although *Shih chi* 30, i. e., *P'ing-chun shu* 平準書 or "Balance du commerce," [3] is an earlier work, it is limited to the first part of the Former Han. As a matter of fact, the material in *Shih chi* 30 is included almost *in toto* in *Han shu* 24, and forms about one third of the latter. Here is an interesting point in Chinese historiography: the *Shih chi*, a general history of ancient China, contains a chapter of economic history dealing only with a part of one dynasty, whereas the *Han shu*, a history of the Han dynasty, as if to make up what might be expected from the *Shih chi*, goes beyond its dynastic limit to include ancient times. Students of history, of course, are too happy to have the information to find fault with such historiographical inconsistency.

The two related texts, *Shih chi* 129 and *Han shu* 91, both entitled *Huo-chih lieh-chuan* 貨殖列傳, "Sketches of the Rich," or as Dr. Rhea E. BLUE puts it, "Narrative on the Increment of Goods," [4] are identical in greater part. This justifies Dr. SWANN's weaving them together into one translation under the title "Cer-

---

[2] Also see his article "The Distribtuion of Coin Types in Ancient China," *American Numismatic Society, Museum Notes* 3 (1948).131-151.

[3] Translated by CHAVANNES in *Les mémoires historiques de Se-ma Ts'ien* 3.

[4] Rhea E. BLUE, "The Argumentation of the *Shih-huo chih* Chapters of the Han, Wei, and Sui Dynastic Histories," *HJAS* 11 (1948).1-118, esp. p. 26.

tain Rich Merchants and Wealthy Industrialists " (pp. 413-464).
However, attention should be called to the notable difference in
attitude of the two historians, Ssŭ-MA Ch'ien and PAN Ku, with
regard to what may be termed the business class. Ssŭ-MA Ch'ien
considers the pursuit of wealth as " a natural effect " (p. 421) and
something " which tallies with Tao (the natural Way) " (p. 421).
He wishes to tell us " how worthies of present generations . . .
became rich " (p. 452). With apparent enthusiasm he describes
their successful accumulation of property and their high standards
of living. Possibly in a satirical mood, he declares it shameful for
one who has failed to become a good man to fail in addition to
distinguish himself as a rich man (p. 451). PAN Ku on the contrary, is very critical of the business class. He links the development of commerce and industry with the decline of the royal house
of Chou. He assails the rich people's sinking " into evils of law-
lessness, excesses, and usurpation " (p. 461). He regrets that
" law and rulings had no restraint " (p. 419). He writes about
the merchants and industrialists " in order to transmit changes of
[different] generations " 以觀世變,[5] in other words, to illustrate
degeneration. This difference is understandable when we remember that, like his father, Ssŭ-MA Ch'ien was a believer in the
Taoist philosophy, whereas PAN Ku and his father PAN Piao were
both Confucianists. Further reasons for their differing attitudes
may be found in their historical background. In Latter Han times
when the *Han shu* was written, the Confucianist school of thought,
which stressed agriculture at the expense of other pursuits, had
been firmly established as the sole orthodoxy, whereas under the
Former Han dynasty there was still room for other points of
view as demonstrated in the debate on government monopoly of
salt and iron in 81 B. C. between scholars, mostly Confucianists,
on the one side, and officials, including some ex-businessmen, on
the other. Among other things, the officials argued that profitable
enterprises like salt and iron should be under government control.
In reply, the scholars maintained that the government should not
take the lead in such secondary and disreputable activities as

---

[5] Compare Dr. BLUE's discussion of the word *pien* 變, *ibid.* pp. 16-17.

commerce and industry.[6] Against the same background, OKAZAKI Fumio 岡崎文夫 has proposed to explain why PAN Ku devoted a long chapter on agriculture in *Han shu* 24A, a section which has no counterpart in the *Shih chi*.[7]

The importance of the *Han shu* and *Shih chi* texts translated in this volume can hardly be overstressed. Familiarity with certain passages from these chapters may be considered a requirement for every advanced student of Chinese history. Let us take, for instance, a passage on public finance at the beginning of the Han dynasty (*Han shu* 24A.8a-b):

> The Throne therefore relaxed the laws; abated restrictions; and lightened the tax *tsu* on fields to one fifteenth of the produce. Emoluments of government authorities *li* were considered, and expenses of the government offices *kuan* were calculated, in order to levy the poll tax *fu* [accordingly] upon the people (203 B. C.). On the other hand taxes-in-money and/or in-kind (*tsu-shui*) that were received on [products of] mountains and streams, orchards and ponds, and on booths [and shops] in markets all were considered [revenues] for personal maintenance from the Son of Heaven down to the enfeoffed lords and ladies (*feng-chün*) who had been granted such territory, and [these funds] were not entered in the budget of the empire. [Pp. 149-151.]

The first point I wish to stress is that, although the motto *liang-ju i-wei-ch'u* 量入以爲出 or "measuring expenditures against revenues" from the *Li chi*[8] has been repeated numerous times in Chinese documents and considered a fundamental principle to be observed by officials in charge of public finance, it must be remembered that this is true only when a budget (in a loose sense) has been determined. At the beginning of a dynasty, tax rates are as a rule fixed by measuring revenues against expenditures. Consequently on such an occasion, the rule has to be reversed. It is interesting that the character *liang* "to measure" is used in this passage in connection with the consideration of emoluments of government authorities and the calculation of expenses of the

---

[6] Esson GALE, *Discourses on Salt and Iron* (Leiden, 1931), also *JNChRAS* 65 (1934). 73-110.

[7] *SG* 3 (1922).20-31. Dr. HU Shih has also discussed this problem of economic thought. See *Hu Shih lun-hsüeh chin-chu* 胡適論學近著 (Shanghai, 1935), 1.570-576.

[8] *Shih-san-ching chu-su* ed. 12.4a; LEGGE, *The Li Ki, Sacred Books of the East* 27.221, where the phrase is rendered as "regulating the outgoing by the income."

government offices 量吏祿度官用 . The same is true when tax rates need revision in the course of a dynasty. For instance, the famous change to the *liang-shui fa* 兩稅法 or two-tax system in 780 in the middle of the T'ang dynasty is explicitly called a process of measuring revenues against expenditures 量出以制入 .[9] In other words, the modern procedure of setting an annual budget was not followed in traditional China. Instead, the nation had a static budget which was intended to be observed throughout the dynasty or at least for a great part of it. The duty of officials as tax-collectors was merely to fulfill their quotas. In this sense Max WEBER is correct in comparing Chinese officials with tax farmers.[10]

Another point worthy of attention is that as early as Han times there was already a distinction between the emperor's purse and the empire's purse. This is clearly indicated in this passage and also supported by other Han texts. The Japanese scholar KATŌ Shigeru 加藤繁 has an excellent article on this distinction under the Han.[11] Actually the same distinction was maintained at least nominally under most of the major dynasties including T'ang, Sung, Ming, and Ch'ing. Treasuries of the emperor and those of the empire were kept separate and put under the direction of different officials. Although borrowing for one purse from another sometimes occurred, an account of such transfer of funds was expected. Government officials would praise the emperor for grants-in-aid from his own purse and object to attempts to enrich it by inclusion of revenues ordinarily belonging to the state. For instance, in a memorial from the Board of Revenue in 1873, it is stated that a distinction between the state finances and the finances of the imperial household was made in the early part of the Ch'ing dynasty. From 1821 to 1857, the Board of Revenue, with the permission of the Emperor, borrowed about eight million taels from the treasuries under the Office of the Imperial Household. Between 1857 and 1873, however, the Office of the Imperial Household had requested the Board of Revenue to appropriate more and more funds for imperial use, until the total amounted to

[9] *Chiu T'ang shu* 118.14a; *Hsin T'ang shu* 145.14a.
[10] *General Economic History*, trans. by F. H. KNIGHT (New York, 1927), p. 59.
[11] *TG* 8 (1918) .159-206, 9 (1919) .62-99, 195-245.

over eight million taels. Having found it impossible to continue this kind of transfer, the Board of Revenue petitioned the Emperor to return to the old rules of maintaining the distinction between the two purses. This was granted only when the Board of Revenue promised to appropriate 800,000 taels each year for the Office of the Imperial Household.[12]

Another example illustrating the importance of the texts is the following passage from *Shih chi* 129.3b:

> Now there are those who without receiving either the presentation of precedence in dignity, or that of government emoluments, and without having remuneration due to honorary rank or to [non-political control in] enfeoffed territory *i*, yet they enjoy being classed with those who have, and who are officially designated "untitled nobility." Those who are enfeoffed [receive income for] substance from taxes (*tsu-shui*, laid on use of land converted to money from tax-in-kind or labor-in-fields). The annual rate is two hundred coins for each household; hence a lord with a thousand households receives two hundred thousand [cash, but expenses for] presenting tribute to the throne in spring and in autumn as well as those for visiting [the court of the emperor and/or the capitals of lords and ladies], all are defrayed from it. Among those without government post or grade of honorary rank (*shu-min*)—farmers, craftsmen, traveling traders, and resident merchants—on the average also each property of ten thousand [cash] brings an annual interest of two thousand. [Such a] family (*chia*, like those with enfeoffed lands) with a million households *hu* thus [derives] two hundred thousand [cash, but cost for commutation of] military and labor services, taxes (*tsu*, on fields, places of business, et cetera), and poll taxes *fu* have to come out of it. In their desire for food and clothing they indulge themselves in that which is good and fine. [P. 450.]

Before discussing the significance of this paragraph, I would like to point out two errors in the translation. First, the line " and who are officially designated ' untitled nobility ' " should read " and these may be designated as ' untitled nobility ' " or, as rendered by Dr. BLUE, " they are designated *su-fêng*." [13] My feeling is that the term *su-fêng* 素封 was probably invented by SSŬ-MA Ch'ien. The other is the first part of the sentence " [Such a] family " et cetera, which should read " [Such a] family with a million [cash] in the household thus [derives] two hundred thousand [cash]." The second correction becomes obvious when compared with *Han shu* 91.6a:

[12] *Huang-ch'ao chêng-tien lei-tsuan* 皇朝政典類纂 160.1a-2a.
[13] *HJAS* 11 (1948).36-37.

Among the common people, farmers, craftsmen, traveling traders, and resident merchants, [property of] ten thousand [cash] as a rule likewise brought an annual interest of two thousand. A family *chia* with wealth amounting to one million thus [derived] two hundred thousand [cash]. [P. 432.]

In an article in *CYYY* 10.1 (1942) .41, LAO Kan 勞榦 , the Chinese expert on Han history, has offered an interesting account of the enfeoffed lord who derived about two hundred coins from each household. The poll tax *suan-fu* 算賦 per capita was 120 cash, from which the enfeoffed lord paid 63 to the emperor as *hsien-fu* 獻賦 and retained 57. If the members of a household averaged the equivalent of four adults, then four times 57 would have made 228, a little over 200. It would be very close to 200 if the average was three adults and a half.

In note 103 on page 432, the author has made the observation, " The 20 per cent interest, HS 9 : 6a/9, seems to establish an accepted rate for the period," and added a reference to the same effect in *Han shu* 72.5b, ca. 44 B. C. From *Han shu* 91.8a and *Shih chi* 129.16a we learn that greedy money-lenders expected an interest of 33.3 per cent; and the non-avaricious ones, 20 per cent. These normal rates of interest are valuable especially because the 20 per cent rate is found in different places. This forms an important point of departure for a study of rates of returns in traditional China.

To come back to the term *su-fêng*, " untitled nobility," the character *su* is certainly the same as in *su-wang* 素王, " untitled king " and *su-ch'ên* 素臣 " untitled official," referring respectively to Confucius and Tso Ch'iu-ming 左邱明 by a school of Han commentators on the *Ch'un-ch'iu*.[14] The term *su-fêng* referring to rich people without rank appears so frequently in later texts that a modern writer even proposes to label Chinese society from Ch'in-Han times down as *su-fêng shê-hui* 素封社會 or " society of untitled nobilities." [15] Of course whether Chinese society needs a label is another question.

[14] See TU Yü 杜預, preface to the *Tso-chuan* (*Shih-san-ching chu-su* ed.) 9b-10a. The *Lun hêng* 論衡 (*Ssŭ-pu ts'ung-k'an* ed.) 13.17a, 27.14b mentions *su-wang* and *su-hsiang* 素相 , the latter term, " untitled ministers," referring to certain Confucian scholars.

[15] SUN Tao-shêng 孫道昇, articles in *Tung-fang tsa-chih* 42.5 (1946) 24-29, 42.6. 26-36.

Dr. SWANN's book is primarily a translation and study of certain historical texts and consequently cannot treat all problems in the economic history of ancient China. Nevertheless, in the commentary on selected topics, footnotes, and appended studies, the author has summarized adequately most of the major problems, making this volume really indispensable to students of Chinese history. In a few instances, however, since certain recent studies by Chinese scholars have become available, it is possible to supplement or modify the author's discussion of some topics. These include the problem of the much-debated *ching-t'ien* or well-field system (cf. pp. 116-120),[16] that of tax terms in ancient China (pp. 366-376), and that of military and labor services under the Han dynasty (pp. 49-54).

In the last few years three notable Chinese scholars have discussed at length the problem of land systems in ancient China. The first is Hsü Chung-shu 徐中舒 in his article on the origin of the well-field system 井田制度探原 in *Chung-kuo wên-hua yen-chiu hui-k'an* 中國文化研究彙刊 or *Bulletin of Chinese Studies* 4 (1944).121-156. The second is Kuo Mo-jo 郭沫若 in his *Shih p'i-p'an shu* 十批判書 (Chungking, 1945), which is a collection of ten articles on ancient China, and especially on the various philosophers. The first article (pp. 1-62), perhaps the most important one, is a self-criticism of Kuo's own studies of ancient China 古代研究的自我批判, which contains a fresh treatment of the well-field system. The third is Li Chien-nung 李劍農, who has an article on *Ch'ê chu kung* 徹助貢, three key terms in the land and tax systems of ancient times, in *Shê-hui k'o-hsüeh chi-k'an* 社會科學季刊 or *Quarterly Journal of Social Science* (the National Wu-Han University) 9 (1948).25-44. Li's *Chung-kuo ching-chi shih kao* 中國經濟史稿 or *Draft Economic History of China*, presumably also a recent work,[17] devotes a chapter (pp. 122-138) to the well-field plan of Mencius. Hsü and Kuo are

---

[16] For a summary of earlier studies, see H. D. FONG, "Bibliography on the Land Problems of China," *Nankai Social and Economic Quarterly*, 8 (1935).325-384. Also see CH'I Ssü-ho 齊思和, 孟子井田說辨 *YCHP* 35 (1948).101-127.

[17] Vol. 1 to the end of Han times, date of publication unknown, received by the Chinese-Japanese Library of the Harvard-Yenching Institute Feb. 9, 1949.

both leading scholars writing on ancient China, and Lɪ is a senior historian. These books and articles were written by the three authors apparently independently of one another. Although different on many points, their views and conclusions are not incompatible. The general belief is reconfirmed that in ancient times there were land allotment and collective farming. Fresh attempts have been made to evaluate old texts and to reconcile different traditions; new working hypotheses have been advanced to interpret changing processes rather than fixed institutions. Synthetic and dynamic approaches have thrown new light on an old problem.

Let us begin with a summary of Lɪ's work. In his *Draft Economic History of China*, he states that it cannot be denied that in ancient China there was a distinction between *kung-t'ien* 公田 and *ssǔ-t'ien* 私田, i. e. the " public field " or rather lord's domain and " private fields." The farmers, in addition to cultivating the latter which were their allotments,[18] had to collaborate on the lord's domain. As for the division of a square *li* into nine squares in order to have the lord's domain in the central square and the private allotments of eight families in the other eight, it may be considered an idealized policy or rather plan on the part of Mencius, which never existed in ancient China. Lɪ compares in sequence and in detail the various early references to the well-field system, including the *Works of Mencius*, the *Kung-yang chuan* 公羊傳, the *Han-shih wai-chuan* 韓詩外傳, the *Chou li, Han shu* 24, the *Kung-yang chieh-ku* 公羊解詁 by Ho Hsiu 何休 (129-182) and the *Ch'un-ch'iu ching-t'ien chi* 春秋井田記 by an unknown author of the Latter Han.[19] The doubtful points in the *Works of Mencius* and discrepancies between the various later accounts are pointed out. Finally, Lɪ Chien-nung suggests a background of the Mencius plan in the term *ching-ti* 井地 used frequently in Ch'un-ch'iu and Chan-kuo times referring to rectangu-

---

[18] Generally speaking, prior to the Chan-kuo era, farmers had only the usufruct, because the right of land ownership was reserved for the nobles. In theory, only the king had unqualified right to all land under heaven. The lesser the nobles were, the less complete were their rights to own land. In reality, it was of course a matter of power.

[19] *Yü-han shan-fang chi-i-shu* 玉函山房輯佚書, *ts'ê* 39.

lar divisions of land and crossing irrigation channels. He also points out that Mencius advocated the well-field system with two main goals, namely, hereditary salaries for the ruling class and a certain livelihood for the ruled. Both would be necessary for the realization of the ideal society of Mencius.

According to LEGGE's version,[20] the *Works of Mencius* reads:

> The sovereign of the Hsia dynasty enacted the fifty *mou* allotment, and the payment of a tax [*kung* 貢]. The founder of the Yin enacted the seventy *mou* allotment, and the system of mutual aid [*chu* 助]. The founder of the Chou enacted the hundred *mou* allotment, and the share system [*ch'ê* 徹]. In reality, what was paid in all these was a tithe.

At least two of the three terms, *kung* and *ch'ê*, are subject to definition. In his article in the *Quarterly Journal of Social Science* mentioned above, LI Chien-nung reviews the various interpretations of *ch'ê* and endorses that of CHU Hsi 朱熹:[21] namely, *ch'ê* means collaboration in cultivation and sharing the returns according to the number of acreage which each farmer had worked 通力合作計畝均 ㄨ. Departing from this point, LI advances the theory that *ch'ê*, *chu*, and *kung* correspond to three stages of economic development. According to him, the *ch'ê* system existed in primitive tribal communal societies when the farmers had to work on large farms and to share the harvests with one another and with their chieftains. The *chu* system was used in the second stage when land was parcelled out by the king to the feudal lords. Farmers worked collectively on the feudal lord's land, and, under the direction of their lord, contributed labor service to the royal domain. The *kung* system represented a third stage when the relation between the various layers of the feudal pyramid underwent remarkable changes. With the decline of the royal power, the king found that his royal domain was diminishing; the income therefrom became insufficient, and he had to rely primarily upon the tribute or *kung* paid by feudal lords instead of the labor service from their people. Gradually the feudal lords suffered the

[20] *The Chinese Classics* 2.240-241. In the quotations from LEGGE, I have changed his transliterations to the WADE-GILES system.

[21] *Lun-yü chi-chu* 論語集註 (*Ssŭ-pu pei-yao* ed.) 6.12a; *Mêng-tzŭ chi-chu* (the same ed.) 3.4a-b.

same fate, because their vassal ministers were expanding their own holdings at the expense of the lords. In order to make up this loss, they collected taxes per acreage within the state, which, on the part of the vassal ministers, represented a tribute to the feudal lords. Presumably, the vassal ministers collected from their farmers land tax at a fixed rate, which was also called *kung*.

Li suggests that the Chou people went through all three stages. The *ch'ê* system was used largely prior to the Chou conquest of Yin, the *chu* system was introduced gradually from the early part of the Western Chou period, and the changes to the *kung* system took place step by step in Eastern Chou times. Thus the three systems may have come in the reverse order to those of Mencius. To reconcile this interpretation with the Mencius text, he proposes that the terms Hsia, Yin, Chou, which Legge renders as founders of the three dynasties, actually point to racial or geographical distinctions rather than to chronological order. Possibly descendents of Hsia had advanced to the *kung* stage, and those of Yin to the *chu* stage while the Chou people were still in the primitive *ch'ê* stage at the beginning of the Chou dynasty. He however does not want to push this theory too far, because very little is known about the economic history of the two dynasties or two peoples, Hsia and Yin.

The whole theory is advanced as a reasonable hypothesis. Li Chien-nung realizes that he has not enough documentation. There are nevertheless certain strong points in the theory. First, it calls our attention to the fact that collective farming in a communal society would have a different significance from that in a feudal order. Second, the last stage summarizes rather well the scramble for control over fiefs and revenues between the various strata of feudal lords and their vassals in the late Chou era. We shall come to this point later when we discuss some major changes in taxation and military service in the Ch'un-ch'iu period (see below).

It appears that Li's hypothesis of three stages and his interpretation of the terms may be independent of one another. The stages may stand as a working hypothesis, although the interpretation of the terms may prove unsatisfactory. In the article he has pointed out that meanings of *ch'ê* in ancient texts generally fall into three groups: "To take, to tax (a tithe)," "to repair, to regulate," and "to prevail; general." In my opinion, these meanings, taken either individually or jointly, do not lend enough support to CHU HSI's interpretation. Even if we accept CHU's view, it still does not prove that *ch'ê* corresponds to a primitive tribal communal stage. In the case of *kung*, LI tries to reconcile two traditional interpretations: first, *kung* means tribute paid by nobles to their overlords, a meaning often attested in ancient texts, and second, *kung* means land tax at a fixed rate, a meaning which is found only in the *Works of Mencius* (LEGGE, 2.240), and is rather doubtful.

Next we can take some points made by HSÜ Chung-shu in his article on the origin of the well-field system. The first is his philological note that the original meaning of the character *t'ien* 田 is "hunting or hunting ground" rather than "farming or farm" as in the *Shuo wên* dictionary. According to him the square form of *t'ien* shows barriers of the hunting ground, and the cross the line-up of hunters. This new interpretation is plausible but not wholly convincing. It is usually difficult to determine the real "original meaning" of a word. In the case of *t'ien* it is perhaps unnecessary because both definitions are attested in very ancient texts. The real problem is to decide what *t'ien* means in a particular text. It is however wise to remember both meanings. For instance, divination concerning *fên* 焚 "burning" is found frequently in tortoise-shell inscriptions. Based on a *Shuo wên* definition of this word as *shao-t'ien* 燒田 and also a *Tso chuan* gloss on it as *huo-t'ien* 火田,[22] several Chinese scholars have jumped to the conclusion that its frequent appearance indicates the prevalence of "fire farming," i. e., the method of burning down the brush and grass before planting.[23] As clearly shown by HU Hou-hsüan 胡厚宣 in his collected articles on Shang history based on tortoise-shell inscriptions [24] the "burning" was a preparation for hunting rather than farming. The *t'ien* in *shao-t'ien* and *huo-t'ien* should be interpreted accordingly. This correction of course

[22] *Shih-san-ching chu-su* ed. 7.1a.
[23] These include LI Chien-nung in his *Draft Economic History of China*, p. 7.
[24] *Chia-ku-hsüeh Shang-shih lun-ts'ung* 甲骨學商史論叢 First Series, 1.1a-3b.

does not rule out the possibility that "fire farming" was practised in ancient China.

An interesting thesis is Hsü's contrast of what he considers Yin and Chou systems with reference to their counting method. In ancient texts like the *Chou li* and the *Tso chuan*, we may distinguish two series of units in weights and measures as well as in civil and military organizations. One has basic units in groups of four or eight; and its larger units are multiples of four. The other begins with basic units of five or ten, and increases to larger units which are multiples of five.[25] Hsü suggests that the former was primarily a Yin method and the latter a Chou practice. With this hypothetical distinction in units of counting and organization, he attempts to confirm the old tradition according to Mencius and later commentators that the *chu* system of having eight families working on nine squares was used by the Yin people and the *ch'ê* system of collecting one tithe was practised by the Chou people, because eight and ten were basic numbers in the two series respectively.

In answer to a consultation by the ruler of the state of T'êng about land reforms, Mencius said (LEGGE, 2.244):

'I would ask you, in the remoter districts [*yeh* 野], observing the nine-square division, to reserve one division to be cultivated on the system of mutual aid [*chu* 助], and in the more central parts of the kingdom [*kuo* 國], to make the people pay for themselves a tenth part of their produce [使自賦].'

Hsü Chung-shu understands the second part of the sentence as something like "and in the city and suburb areas to make the people pay a tenth part of their produce, and themselves render military service (or to contribute military taxes)." He suggests that the proposal by Mencius may have come from a plan which may have originated at the beginning of the Chou dynasty to consolidate the conquest of Shang. According to this hypothetical plan, in the newly conquered areas the victorious Chou people

---

[25] The two systems, however, were not entirely unmixed. For instance, the multipliers in a series of measures of capacity were 4, 4, 4, 4, 10 (*Tso chuan* 43.4b). The multipliers in two series of organization of individuals and households were both 5, 5, 4, 5, 5, 5 (*Chou li* 10.9b-10a, 11.1b). KAO Ming-k'ai 高名凱, in his *Han-yü yü-fa lun* 漢語語法論 (Shanghai, 1948), pp. 329-336, has also pointed out that in ancient China there were counting series in multiples of 8 or 16 and 6 or 12.

would dwell in the city and suburban areas (*kuo*) whereas the Shang people would be restricted to the countryside (*yeh*).[26] The Chou "citizens" would introduce their *ch'ê* system into their areas, paying the tithe and rendering military service (*fu*). The Shang people would be permitted to maintain their *chu* system, to collaborate on the lord's domain and in addition to pay certain taxes but not to render military service. Such reservation of military power in the hands of the ruling tribe is of course fairly common in history. As an example, Hsü points to the Hsien-pi soldiers and Chinese (Han) farmers under the Northern Dynasties.

The situation, according to Hsü, however, did not remain unchanged. Coming to the later part of the Ch'un-ch'iu period, the fusion of the Shang and Chou peoples had progressed a long way. Owing to the need of more revenue and larger military forces, the states of Lu and Chêng began to introduce new measures, which are recorded in the *Ch'un-ch'iu* and the *Tso-chuan*. In 594 B. C. Lu initiated a tax on the acre 初稅畝 (LEGGE, 5.327). In 590 B. C. it collected military levies from each *ch'iu* 作丘甲 (1 *ch'iu* = 64 *ching* 井, i. e. 64 square *li*) (LEGGE 5.336). Finally in 483 B. C. it levied additional military taxes and perhaps also other taxes by acreage 用田賦. This was intended to bring in more revenue than the previous levy on a *ch'iu* basis (LEGGE, 5.828). According to Hsü's interpretation, the land tax of 594 B. C. was collected from city and suburb areas, and the military levies in 590 B. C. were introduced in the country areas. The last change in 483 B. C. was to abolish the lord's domain and to subject the Chou and the former Yin people equally to military levies and land taxes. By this time differences between the *kuo* and *yeh* areas probably had become negligible.

In his *Draft Economic History of China*, pp. 114-120, LI Chien-nung has also discussed the three changes in 594, 590, and 483 B. C. He considers the reform in 594 B. C. the first regulation by the state of Lu requiring landlords to pay land tax on the acre.

---

[26] FU Ssŭ-nien 傅斯年 has made a similar observation and interprets the *chün-tzŭ* 君子 and *yeh-jên* 野人 in a puzzling passage in the *Confucian Analects* (LEGGE, 1.237) as the Chou people and the Shang people respectively. See *CYYY* 4 (1934). 288-289. Also see Arthur WALEY, *The Analects of Confucius* (London, 1938), p. 153.

Previously, feudal vassals made contribution to their lord only in accordance with their status irrespective of their land-holding. The reform in 590 B. C. was to collect military levies on the basis of *ch'iu,* which was a unit of land. It thus represents a similar shift from a status basis to a land basis. The new measure introduced in 483 B. C. was probably to levy on a unit of land smaller than a *ch'iu,* and consequently amounted to an increase in tax rate. LI does not speculate on the possible difference in effect in the suburban and country areas, but safely limits himself to the point that the new measures indicate changes in the object of taxation.

In the state of Chêng, according to the *Tso chuan,* Tzǔ-ch'an 子產 carried out certain land reforms in 543 B. C., which included regulations to count or group houses and fields by fives. The reforms caused loud complaints at first but eulogy afterwards (LEGGE, 5.558). In 538 B. C. the same statesman introduced military taxes by the *ch'iu* (64 *ching*) 作丘賦, which must have been an increased burden, because he was criticized as making laws under the influence of greedy desires 作法於貪 (LEGGE 5.598). These changes may be similar in nature to those in the state of Lu.

It is well-known to students of the well-field problem that the *Chou li* [27] indicates two different land systems: one uses as its basic unit the land tilled by ten farmers whereas the other uses *ching* or nine squares of one hundred *mu* each. According to commentators, they apply to different parts of the royal domain (excluding the feudal states). The former applies to land directly under royal control (*hsiang-sui* 鄉遂, presumably inner areas) and the latter, to fiefs granted to princes, ministers, and grandees (*tu-pi* 都鄙, presumably outer areas). Scholars traditionally identify the two systems with the *kung* and *chu* of Hsia and Shang respectively, and interpret the Chou system *ch'ê* as a combination of *kung* and *chu* to obtain an average of a tithe. [28] Proposing to change the identification of the two systems in the *Chou li* to the

[27] *Shih-san-ching chu-su* ed. 10.7a, 11.3a, 15.7a-b, 42.1a.

[28] WANG Ming-shêng 王鳴盛, *Chou-li chün-fu shuo* 周禮軍賦說 in *Huang-Ch'ing ching-chieh* 皇清經解 436.10a-19b.

chê and *chu* of Chou and Shang, Hsü Chung-shu has assigned new significance to old texts. Although proofs for his various points are not conclusive, his general theory may still be considered a working hypothesis from the interesting angle of conquest and acculturation.

Hsü Chung-shu also discusses the interesting term *yüan-t'ien* 爰田 (also written 轅田), "changing field." Tradition says it refers to an additional allotment in the case of inferior land, so that a part could be allowed to lie fallow. According to *Han shu* 28B.20b Lord Shang [29] in the middle of the 4th century B.C. established "changing field" in the state of Ch'in. This was evidently to encourage the opening up of new fields, which was the aim of his land policy. An earlier reference to *yüan-t'ien*, however, indicates that "changing field" was also a device by which nobles of a state obtained more land from their ruler. From the *Tso chuan* (LEGGE 5.168) and the *Kuo yü*,[30] we learn that the ruler of Chin, when he was held in captivity by Ch'in after a defeat in 645 B.C. introduced "changing field" in his own state to please those in the city and suburban areas, in other words "citizens" or nobles. In return, the nobles agreed to provide *chou-ping* 州兵, "prefectural troops,"[31] which must have meant additional military service. This discussion is interesting not only because it illustrates the close relationship between political and economic matters, but also because it points to the right way of reaching sound conclusions on such complicated problems as that of land tenure in ancient China. We cannot limit ourselves to the few references obviously bearing on land systems, but have to examine all background information which may be only indirectly related to the problem. The best solution is the one that satisfies every bit of evidence.

In 1930, KUO Mo-jo in his provocative volume, *Chung-kuo ku-tai shê-hui yen-chiu* 中國古代社會研究, denied the existence of

[29] Cf. *Food and Money in Ancient China* pp. 118-119. On Lord Shang, see J. J. L. DUYVENDAK, *The Book of Lord Shang*, London, 1928; and CH'I Ssŭ-ho 商鞅變法考 in *YCHP* 33 (1947). 163-194.

[30] *Ssŭ-pu ts'ung-k'an* ed., 9.7b-8a.

[31] A *chou* or "prefect" contained 2500 families.

a well-field system in anicent China. Fifteen years afterwards, he reversed his position. In the *Shih p'i-p'an shu,* mentioned on page 531, he gives his reasons for the revision. In the first place, he points to the character *t'ien* 田 itself as a good proof. The form of this character in tortoise-shell and bronze inscriptions, with some variations, is roughly the same as in later scripts, and is valuable as a pictograph based on a regular division of land into squares. Secondly, in bronze inscriptions of the Western Chou period, there are many records about the bestowal of land or its transfer as indemnity or for exchange, in which land is specified as so many *t'ien*—one, two, seven, ten, or fifty, for instance. The use of *t'ien* as a counting unit indicates the existence of a standard size for land. According to Kuo's interpretation, a *t'ien* was one hundred *mu.* Thirdly, the terms *tung-mu* 東畝 " eastern acre " and *nan-mu* 南畝 " southern acre " which appear in the *Shih ching* and the *Tso chuan*[32] also support a rectangular division of land, because these terms indicate whether the main roads in the country went east-west or south-north respectively. Lastly, records of certain reforms in the late Chou era either mention or imply a well-field system. In 548 B. C. in order to regulate military levies, WEI Yen 蔿掩,[33] who was *ssŭ-ma* 司馬 or marshal of Ch'u, among other things, divided the rich plains into *ching* 井 (LEGGE 4.517). LI K'uei 李悝, in the land policy he worked out for the Marquis Wên (403-387 B. C.) of Wei, " reckoned that a territory of one hundred square *li* held a total of ninety thousand *ch'ing.* "[34] Lord Shang is said to have " abolished the *ching-t'ien* ancient well-field system of land division, and opened up (i. e. broken) (350 B. C.) the crossroads running south-north and east-west. "[35] These are the main reasons for believing in the existence

[32] LEGGE 4,374. Also see Arthur WALEY, *The Book of Songs* (Boston and New York, 1937), pp. 158-159.

[33] By mistake, KUO connects the event with Tzŭ-ch'an.

[34] *Food and Money in Ancient China,* pp. 136-137. Instead of " Marquis Wên," Dr. SWANN writes duke Wen, which is perhaps a slip.

[35] *Ibid.,* pp. 144-145. Following another tradition, the author translates *k'ai ch'ien-mai* 開阡陌 by " initiated (350 B. C.) that of dividing the arable lands by the crossroads running south-north and east-west."

Ch'ien and *mai* originally may have referred to roads and paths along one thousand

of a well-field system, i. e., division of land into squares, as a standard practice in ancient China.

Kuo Mo-jo, however, considers as a Utopian ideal the plan of Mencius to have the lord's domain in the central one of nine squares. Here he has made an interesting point in arguing convincingly against the traditional interpretation of two lines from the *Shih ching*. Developing the plan of Mencius, the *Han-shih wai-chuan* [36] states that huts of the eight families were located in the central square. These homesteads occupied a total area of twenty *mu*. Thus the eight families worked only eighty instead of one hundred *mu* of the lord's land, which amounted to exactly one tenth of their eight hundred *mu*. To prove this ingenius arrangement, the *Han-shih wai-chuan* cites the *Shih ching* (LEGGE 4.375):

> In the midst of the fields are the huts,
> And along the bounding divisions are gourds.

Kuo Mo-jo says, if we study the whole stanza, the traditional interpretation does not make good sense. Instead of *lu* 廬 " huts " he proposes the reading *lu* 蘆 i. e., *lu-fu* 蘆菔 or radishes.[37] Here we may take KARLGREN's version,[38] replacing " huts " by " radishes ":

In the middle of the fields there are radishes, by the boundaries and divisions there are gourds; them we cut up, them we pickle, and present them to the august ancestors; the descendant will have long life and receive Heaven's blessing.

Similar contrasts of plants are found in other poems in the *Shih ching*, notably " Nan-shan yu-t'ai," [39] which contains no less than five examples like this one:

---

and one hundred *mu* (or conceivably *fu* 夫) respectively, and thus may have served as limits to both ownership and cultivation. That *ch'ien* and *mai* may either run south-north or east-west has been pointed out by CH'ÊNG Yao-t'ien 程瑤田, *Kou-hsü chiang-li hsiao-chi* 溝洫疆理小記 in *Huang-Ch'ing ching-chieh* 541.43a-44a. Cf. CH'I Ssŭ-ho, *YCHP* 33 (1947) .183-185.

[36] *Ssŭ-pu ts'ung-k'an* ed., 4.7b-8a.

[37] On *lu-fu*, see LAUFER " The Si-Hia language," *TP* 17 (1916) .83-86.

[38] *The Book of Odes* (Stockholm, 1950), p. 164.

[39] *Ibid*. p. 116.

On the southern mountain there are t'ai plants; on the northern mountain there are lai plants.

Without the *Shih ching* support, the whole tradition, followed in *Han shu* 24 [40] and other places, becomes more doubtful.

KUO proceeds to suggest that the nine-square plan, however, may have some historical basis. Of course, it agrees with the *K'ao-kung chi* 考工記 section of the *Chou li*. The *K'ao-kung chi* was originally an independent book separate from the *Chou li* and its date has not been well established. Based on its mention of products or crafts of practically all major states in the Ch'un-ch'iu period except Ch'i, and on the identification of some of its weights and measures with those used in Ch'i, KUO concludes that the *K'ao-kung chi* was an official compilation of the state of Ch'i in the Ch'un-ch'iu period. A nine-square land system could have existed in Ch'i, and Mencius may have heard about it. KUO's date for the *K'ao-kung chi*—in the Ch'un-ch'iu period—seems too early; his linkage of the work with the Ch'i state is nevertheless interesting. This theory may also be utilized to support the thesis of HSÜ Chung-shu that there was a Yin system in the east and a Chou system in the west.[41]

According to KUO Mo-jo, the well-field system was primarily a system of land assignment to put the farmers to work. In addition, he asserts that farmers of Shang and Western Chou times were slaves, although he admits that these slave farmers had a certain amount of freedom and were comparable with serfs in medieval Europe.[42] On the early use of certain agricultural imple-

---

[40] *Food and Money in Ancient China*, p. 124.

[41] Following commentaries of Han scholars I find in the *K'ao-kung chi* three places where dialectical expressions of Ch'i are used (*Chou li* 39.5a, two; 41.9b). However, not all dialectical expressions are identified as of Ch'i. In one place, a Shu 蜀 word is used (39.8a) and in another a Ch'u 楚 word instead of Ch'i (40.12a). If the *K'ao-kung chi* was a work representing very ancient traditions in Ch'i, one may speculate whether its detailed description of *kou-hsü* 溝洫 or irrigating channels may not indicate early use of irrigation in eastern China, in support of the thesis of WÊNG Wên-hao 翁文灝 in *Ch'ing-chu Ts'ai Yüan-p'ei hsien-shêng liu-shih-wu sui lun-wên-chi* 慶祝蔡元培先生六十五歲論文集 (1935), 2.709-712.

[42] For a different view, see HU Hou-hsüan, "The Yin dynasty was not a society of slavery" 殷非奴隸社會論 in his *Chia-ku-hsüeh Shang-shih lun-ts'ung*, First Series 1.1a-14b.

103

ments, Kuo and Hu Hou-hsüan are in agreement that foot ploughs and perhaps even ox-drawn ones, were used in Shang China. The traditional view that ox-drawn ploughs began to be used in the Ch'un-ch'iu or even Chan-kuo period seems too conservative.[43] In an article in the *Ch'ing-t'ung shih-tai* 青銅時代,[44] a sister volume to the *Shih p'i-p'an shu,* Kuo offers his translation of ten agricultural poems in the *Shih ching* into colloquial Chinese. It would be interesting to compare his translation with those in English by LEGGE, WALEY, and KARLGREN. Generally speaking, the two books by Kuo are full of new and provocative ideas of unequal value.

In Dr. SWANN's book there is a section "On Tax Terms in the Treatise" (pp. 366-376), which begins with the following paragraph:

> In translating sections of the history of the earlier Han dynasty, there continually arises [sic] perplexing problems in rendering terms and phrases which have not only general meanings but also specific ones. In the case of Han tax terms in the economic section (*Han shu* 24AB), it seems, however, that the historian has in each instance of their occurrence kept to their specific meanings. Whether or not the meanings of these tax terms in other sections of the Han history would, with or without exceptions, be found to follow the same pattern is a study for some leisure year! There seem to be no exceptions in *Han shu* 24.

The sentence next to the last shows that the author is very cautious and too modest. It might give the reader the impression that the author did not use much of the other sections of the Han history. Actually, as clearly stated in the "Introduction," "Frequent reference to other chapters of the two histories [i. e. *Shih-chi* and *Han shu*] has been made in a study and translation of the two technical discussions on economics." (page 6) On the whole, the discussion of the specific meanings of tax terms is remarkably thorough and sound.

I cannot agree, however, with the author's observation that "the historian has in each instance of their occurrence kept to

---

[43] *Shih p'i-p'an shu,* pp. 13-15; *Chia-ku-hsüeh Shang-shih lun-ts'ung,* Second Series, 1.1a-124b, esp. 77a-81b. Also see Hsü Chung-shu, *CYYY* 2 (1930).11-59.

[44] Containing twelve articles on ancient China (Chungking, 1945). The translation appears on pp. 86-102.

the specific meanings." As correctly pointed out by Professor Robert B. WARREN in his foreword, *Han shu* 24 " was essentially assembled by the scissors and paste method from contemporary or semi-contemporary reports " (page vii) . In this chapter, PAN Ku not only adopted almost the whole of *Shih chi* 30, but also quoted at length from writings by LI K'uei, CHIA I 賈誼, CH'AO Ts'o 鼂錯, and TUNG Chung-shu 董仲舒. Unless these writers and the two historians, SSǓ-MA Ch'ien and PAN Ku, all observed the same rigid rule (which is unlikely) of using tax terms only in their technical sense, the author's assumption can hardly be justified.

It is noted that the term *fu* 賦 has been translated throughout *Han shu* 24 as " military taxes " for Chou times and " poll taxes " for Ch'in and Han times. Undoubtedly *fu* had those specific meanings in the respective periods. It is, however, almost certain that it was also used in the general sense of " a tax, a levy; to tax, to levy." For instance *fu* in the compound *fu-lien* 賦斂 is apparently in the general sense. Recognizing that it may be a general term, the author still asserts, " it seems rather to be a term, or expression, to include two specific taxes, both of which went to the imperial treasury for military purposes " (page 373) . Consequently, *fu-lien* is rendered as either " military taxes *fu* and other government levies " or " poll taxes *fu* and other government levies."

Let us take a part of a sentence from TUNG Chung-shu's memorial, ca. 100 B. C.: " Reduce poll taxes *fu* and other government levies [in kind or their fiscal equivalents], and lessen labor services " (page 183) . The Chinese text 薄賦斂,省徭役 reminds the reader of similar advice given by Mencius to the ruler of Liang 省刑罰,薄稅斂 . Although LEGGE 2.135 translates the six characters as " being sparing in the use of punishments and fines, and making the taxes and levies light," in a footnote he says, " 刑罰 can hardly be separated " and " 稅斂 together represent all taxes." It is possible that TUNG may have had the sentence of Mencius in mind when he wrote his. In each case, there are two balanced verb-object constructions and the verbs are the same. If three of the objects are general terms—" taxes," " punishments," and " labor services "—should the fourth one be so

105

specific as "poll taxes *fu* and other government levies [in kind or their fiscal equivalents]"?

The character *fu* also appears alone in ancient texts in the general sense of "a tax, a levy; to tax, to levy." To illustrate this point, we will not use examples from the famous chapter "Yü-kung" 禹貢 in the *Shu ching*, nor those from the *Chou li*, because the texts themselves are open to question.[45] For Chou times, we may cite the following cases from the *Tso chuan*:

[513 B.C.] In winter, Chao Yang and Hsün Yin of Chin led a force, and walled Ju-pin, after which they laid upon the [districts of the] State a contribution of a *ku* (= 480 catties) of iron in order to cast penal tripods 逐賦晉國一鼓鐵以鑄刑鼎], on which they inscribed the penal laws prepared by Fan Hsüan-tzŭ.
LEGGE 5.732.

[484 B.C.] In summer Yüan P'o of Ch'ên fled from that State to Chêng. Before this, Yüan P'o, being minister of Instruction, levied a tax on the lands of the State, to supply the [expenses of] marrying one of the duke's daughters [賦封田以嫁公女]; and there being more than was necessary, he used the residue to make some large articles for himself; in consequence of which the people drove him out of the State.
LEGGE 5.824-825.

In his *Draft Economic History of China*, pages 117-121, LI Chien-nung has cited the same passages to prove that *fu* was not necessarily used for military purpose in the Ch'un-ch'iu period.

Coming down to the Chan-kuo period, there was already a tendency to use *fu* (originally military taxes) and *shui* (originally land taxes) interchangeably. To prove this point, LI Chien-nung mentions the expression *fu-su* 賦粟, "to exact grain" in the *Works of Mencius* (LEGGE 2.304-305), referring to JAN Ch'iu 冉求, a disciple of Confucius in the Ch'un-ch'iu period. He also calls attention to the story of an able and strict tax-collector CHAO Shê 趙奢 in *Shih chi* 81.6a, in which the terms *tsu-shui* 租稅 and *fu* appear to be synonymous.

For Han times, we may point to the interesting expression *tsu-shui-chih-fu* 租稅之賦 in a decree of 167 B.C. by Emperor Wên (*Han shu* 4.14a). The character *fu* in this phrase is translated by DUBS as "impositions."[46] Dr. SWANN's argument that

---

[45] Cf. Dr. BLUE's discussion in *HJAS* 11 (1948) .106-107.
[46] Homer H. DUBS, *The History of the Former Han Dynasty* (Baltimore, 1938), 1.255.

chih here means " and " is not convincing (p. 372). According to *Han shu* 24, in 178 B. C., when CH'AO TS'O urged the Throne to bestow honorary ranks or to pardon crimes in exchange for grain, he said this measure could result in the reduction of the poor people's *fu*. Ten years later, when his policy had been adopted and the government had stored a large supply of grain, what CH'AO TS'O requested was the exemption of farmers' field taxes *tsu*. Since there is no record on a reduction of poll taxes between 178 and 168 B. C., and since there is no good ground to assume that CH'AO TS'O first proposed the reduction of poll taxes without success and later changed to the exemption of land taxes, the most likely interpretation seems to be that the *fu* in his first memorial was a general term and that CH'AO TS'O had the reduction of land taxes in mind from the very beginning.

That the word *fu* was used as a general term in Han times can further be proved by two documents. In 12 B. C. when the Confucian scholar KU Yung 谷永 objected to proposals to increase taxation, he said, " When the people are suffering from poverty like this, regular taxes 常稅 should be reduced to give them a little relief. And yet official authorities memorialize requesting an increase in taxation 加賦. This is most contrary to classical teachings and against the people's will. It is a way of spreading hate and attracting disaster " (*Han shu* 85.19b). Obviously *shui* and *fu* here are synonymous. In an imperial decree of 7 B. C., the Emperor blamed his prime minister CHAI Fang-chin 翟方進 for " having memorialized requesting a temporary (*i-ch'ieh*, possibly general) increase in taxation: levies on the surplus land and garden fields in cities and suburbs, commutation charges for labor services, and taxes on horses, cattle, and sheep " 奏 一切增 賦,稅城郭塽及園田,過更,算馬牛羊 (*Han shu* 84.10b). Evidently CHAI Fang-chin was at least one of the " official authorities " criticized by KU Yung. Held responsible for heavy taxation and other mistakes, the prime minister committed suicide. The general or vague meaning of *fu* perhaps also applies to *Han shu* 24A.8a/10; 24B.11b/6, 14a/6, 17b/8, 17b/9, and 18a/6.[47]

[47] HSÜN Yüeh 荀悅 (148-209), in his [*Ch'ien*] *Han chi* 前漢紀 (*Ssŭ-pu ts'ung-k'an* ed.) 8.3a-b, uses the word *fu* to refer to rent paid to landlords, saying " [Under

The problem of military and labor services under the Han dynasty is very complicated. In *Han shu* 24A.15a there is a statement by TUNG Chung-shu about such services in Ch'in and Han times. This important text is unfortunately obscure. Before discussing Dr. SWANN's translation of this passage, it may be helpful to review the general position held by a few modern scholars on this problem.

In his article, "An Outline of the Central Government of the Former Han Dynasty," *HJAS* 12 (1949) .141-142, WANG Yü-ch'üan writes,

> From the people who had reached adulthood, the Emperor demanded one year's service for military training, one year for garrison duties, and annually one month of service at their home locality.

This one-sentence summary covers the main points on which WANG agrees with HAMAGUCHI Shigekuni 濱口重國 and LAO Kan. HAMAGUCHI, a Japanese authority, has published several articles on military and labor services in Ch'in-Han times.[48] LAO Kan has an important article on the Han military system in the light of Han documents on wood.[49] WANG himself has devoted many years to the study of ancient China.

Such a brief summary naturally needs elaboration. In the first place, as discussed by HAMAGUCHI,[50] the age of adulthood seems to have undergone a few changes during the Han dynasty. At the

---

the Han sometimes] the government collects land tax at the rate of one hundredth, but the people (i. e. the landlords) collect rent which amounts to two-thirds [of the harvest]." 官收百一之稅,民收大半之賦 Cf. Etienne BALÁZS, "La crise sociale et la philosophie politique à la fin des Han," *TP* 39 (1949) .83-131.

In addition to the meanings concerning tax and rent collection, *fu* in ancient texts also means "to distribute, to give." Probably as a warning, TUAN Yü-ts'ai 段玉裁 in his commentary to the *Shuo wên* 6B has called attention to this meaning. One example is *Han shu* 7.8a, 罷中牟苑賦貧民, which DUBS has correctly translated as "Chung-mou Park was abolished and [its land] was distributed among the poor people." (*Ibid.*, 2.168). I have also found numerous examples of *fu* in this meaning in Han documents on wood.

[48] *TG* 19 (1931) .84-107; 20 (1932) .140-146. *Ichimura hakushi koki kinen tōyōshi ronsō* 市村博士古稀紀念東洋史論叢 1933, pp. 1025-1045. *SZ* 46 (1935) .851-871.

[49] *CYYY* 10 (1942) .23-54.

[50] *SZ* 46 (1935) .851-871.

beginning of the Han, the draft age probably began at twenty-three.[51] After 155 B. C.,[52] it was lowered to twenty. Under Emperor Chao (86-74 B. C.), according to *Yen-t'ieh lun* 4.8b [53] the age was changed back to twenty-three. Suggesting that the last change was maintained throughout the rest of the two Han periods, HAMAGUCHI quotes from *Lun hêng* 12.16a by WANG Ch'ung 王充 of the first century A. D.:

One may ask them [i. e. government clerks, who will be unable to answer]: in ancient times feudal lords were enfeoffed to rule the various states, but now prefects and magistrates are appointed. What is the significance [of this change]? The ancients had the well-field system and the people tilled the land for their lords; but now land taxes in grain and stalks are collected. What does this mean? In each year (read *sui* 歲 for the *yeh* 業 in the text) the people are required to render labor service for one month at their home locality 居更 . What is the basis? One registers for military service (read *fu* 傅 for the *ju* 儒 in the text) at twenty-three, is subject to adult poll tax 賦 from the age of fifteen, and pays twenty-three coins as [children's] head tax (*t'ou-ch'ien* 頭錢, i. e., *k'ou-ch'ien* 口錢) from the age of seven. What is the reason?

Fu-ch'ien 賦錢 or adult poll tax amounted to one hundred and twenty cash levied on males and females from the ages of fifteen to fifty-six. *K'ou-ch'ien* was levied on male and female children from seven to fourteen.[54] Obviously there were age-groups under the Han for the collection of taxes and levies. The names of the groups however are not listed in any Han text. From Han documents on wood, especially those concerning provisions for garrison troops and their families,[55] I have worked out the following categories:

---

[51] This is based on the commentary by YEN Shih-ku 顏師古 to *Han shu* 5.3b. LI Yüan-ch'êng 李源澄, in his article 漢代賦役考 in *Kuo-li Chê-chiang ta-hsüeh wên-hsüeh-yüan chi-k'an* 國立浙江大學文學院集刊 1 (1941) .26b, questions whether this was an anachronism.

[52] *Han shu* 5.3b; Dubs 1.312.

[53] GALE, *Discourses on Salt and Iron*, p. 97, " Now Your Majesty shows his commiseration for the people by liberal regulations in the matter of corvées. One becomes subject to taxation at the age of twenty-three; at fifty-six one is exempted, the purpose is to aid the elders and to give rest to the aged." The word " taxation " should read " military (and labor) services " (*fu* 賦).

[54] For details on poll taxes, see *Food and Money in Ancient China*, pp. 366-376.

[55] LAO Kan, *Chü-yen Han-chien k'ao-shi* 居延漢簡考釋 (hereafter referred to as *Han-chien*), *shih-wên* 釋文, 2.43b-59b.

A. *Wei-shih-nan* 未使男 [56] and *wei-shih-nü* 女, "pre-service male and female"—6 years or under.

B. *Shih-nan* 使男 and *shih-nü*, "serviceable male and female" —7 to 14 years.

C. *Hsiao-nan* 小 and *hsiao-nü*, "under-aged male and female" —14 or under (i. e., A or B).

D. *Ta-nan* 大 and *ta-nü*,[57] "adult male and female"—15 or above.

Besides age-groups, Han documents on wood give us detailed information on troops stationed along the northwestern frontier of China. Their main duties were to guard the signal beacons and to cultivate land. As LAO KAN has pointed out,[58] there were primarily two kinds of regular soldiers on the frontier: *ch'i-shih* 騎士 "cavalrymen" and *shu-tsu* 戍卒 "garrison soldiers." The former came from only the boundary provinces, whereas most of the latter came from other provinces, especially those in the eastern part of the empire. *T'ien-tsu* 田卒 "farming soldiers" and *ho-ch'ü-tsu* 河渠卒 "irrigation soldiers" were probably "garrison soldiers" assigned to agricultural duties, since they came from the same area as the latter. In addition, there were convicts, as well as soldiers hired either privately or by the government. The chiefs of watchtowers (*sui-chang* 燧長) and larger watch stations (*hou-chang* 候長) were from boundary provinces.

Officers and soldiers received food, clothing, and weapons from the government. Officers and their assistants in addition received salaries of a few hundred cash a month. As I have pointed out in my article "Numbers and Units in Chinese Economic His-

[56] For *shih* 使, compare Dr. SWANN's discussion of *shih* 事 on page 54.

[57] The terms *ta-nan*, *ta-nü*, and *wu-tzŭ* (or rather *yü-tzŭ*) 吾子 appear already in *Kuan-tzŭ* 管子 (*Ssŭ-pu ts'ung-k'an* ed.) 22.5b. *Wu-tzŭ* is to be identified with *yü-tzŭ* 餘子 rendered by Dr. SWANN (p. 130) as "boys."

Those who were 57 or above and had ceased to pay poll taxes may have been called *lao-nan* and *lao-nü*, "aged males and females." In a decree in *Han shu* 69.5b, we find a reference to *ta-nan*, *nu-tzŭ*, and *lao hsiao* 老小. I have included tentatively the group of *lao-nan*, *lao-nü* in my *Topics in Chinese History*, Cambridge, 1950, p. 7, although in Han wooden documents the aged people are only classified as adults. Cf. CH'ÊN P'an 陳槃, 漢晉遺簡偶述, in *CYYY* 16(1947). 319-321.

[58] *CYYY* 10(1942). 23-37.

tory," provisions were paid at two slightly different rates. " One was 6 *shêng* of husked grain per day (i. e., 1.8 *shih* of husked grain or 3 *shih* of unhusked grain in a full month of 30 days), and the other was 6 2/3 *shêng* of husked grain per day (i. e., 2 *shih* of husked grain or 333 1/3 *shêng* of unhusked grain in a full month of 30 days). The higher rate seems to have been used for officers and soldiers regularly guarding the watchtowers, whereas the lower one seems to have applied to convicts, soldiers working on agricultural colonies, and officers and soldiers who served on the frontier for short periods." [59] Soldiers doing particularly hard work (*chü-tso* 劇作) received additional provisions (*chia-shih* 加食) of about 10 per cent.[60]

Family members of officers and soldiers whose duty it was to guard the watchtowers also received government provisions. There were also two series of rates. According to the higher series, adult males in the family received 333 1/3 *shêng* of unhusked grain per month—in other words, the same amount as the troops. Younger members and particularly females received proportionaly less. Thus an " adult female " or a " serviceable male " received the same amount of 216 2/3 *shêng* of unhusked grain per month, a " serviceable female " or " pre-service male " received 166 2/3 *shêng*, and a " pre-service female," 116 2/3 *shêng*. The lower series applied to *chien-shu yung-ku* 見署用穀 and *shêng-chiao yung-ku* 省茭用穀, presumably meaning " grain consumed (when the soldiers were stationed) in an office " and " grain consumed while (the soldiers were) making hay," respectively. In this series, an adult male received 3 *shih* of unhusked grain per month, identical with the lower rate for the troops. An " adult female " or a " serviceable male " received 209 1/3 *shêng* of unhusked grain, a " serviceable female " or " pre-service male " 166 *shêng* and a " pre-service female " 106 *shêng*.[61] From the difference in

[59] *HJAS* 12 (1949) .224, note 31.

[60] *Han-chien, shih-wên* 2.32a, 2.50b.

[61] The rates are obtained by checking mathematically the records in *Han-chien, shih-wên* 2.43b-59b. Some mistakes are found, which may have been originally copyists' errors. For instance, on page 43b, line 13, the 166 2/3 *shêng* should be 116 2/3 *shêng*, on page 45b, line 16, the total 333 2/3 *shêng* should be 333 1/3 *shêng*. Similar errors are found on pages 50b, 53b, and 59a.

rates, we can see that age-groups, in addition to determining the amount of tax levies and service drafts, also were significant in the amount of provisions issued per capita. In a similar way, age-groups have been used throughout Chinese history as a basis for issuing relief in famine years.

According to Han documents on wood, garrison, farming, and irrigation soldiers were mostly in their third or fourth decade, and consequently within the range between twenty-three and fifty-five inclusive, traditionally taken to be the draft age during most of Han times.[62] No indication is found of the ages of cavalrymen. Following a suggestion by WANG Kuo-wei 王國維, LAO Kan believes that they were probably on the whole younger than the other regular troops.[63] LAO Kan has discovered a case in which a garrison soldier was only twenty; according to LAO's explanation, he may have been called to service prior to the reign of Emperor Chao, when the draft age was twenty.[64] I have noted, however, three more cases in which garrison soldiers were twenty-two, and one case in which a watchtower chief was appointed at the age of twenty-one, ca. 14 A. D.[65] The last case indicates that HAMAGUCHI's conclusion on the Han draft age, although accepted by LAO Kan, may need qualification. Either the age was lowered again for some time after the reign of Emperor Chao, or the regulation making military service begin at twenty-three was not strictly observed.

The term ch'i-shih, "cavalryman," is best explained in the Han chiu-i 漢舊儀: [66]

When a person reaches the age of twenty-three, he becomes a regular [serviceman] 正. For one year he will be made wei-shih 衛士, [palace] guard. For another year, he will serve as either a foot soldier (ts'ai-kuan 材官) or

---

[62] It seems that although a man was discharged at fifty-six, he was still subject to poll taxes in that year.

[63] Han-chien, k'ao-chêng 考證 2.63b.

[64] CYYY 10 (1949) .37.

[65] Han-chien, shih-wên 3.42b, 3.54a, 54b. The sui-chang was appointed in Shih-chien-kuo T'ien-fêng yüan-nien jun-yüeh 始建國天鳳元年閏月. The first year of T'ien-fêng was 14 A. D., but an intercalary month is found in 13 A. D., the fifth year of Shih-chien-kuo.

[66] P'ing-chin-kuan ts'ung-shu ed. B.5b-6a. Also quoted in Han shu 1A.33b. Compare translation of the passage in DUBS 1.80-81.

cavalryman (*ch'i-shih*), to be trained in archery, chariot-driving,[67] horse-riding and field combat . . . in water regions, he will be a mariner (*lou-ch'uan* 樓船), likewise to· be trained in fighting, archery, and sailing. The foot soldier [cavalryman] or mariner will be discharged to be a civilian only when he becomes fifty-six years of age and has become old and decrepit.

Thus the term referred to one of the three kinds of soldiers under training or after training. Presumably the soldier would be subject to emergency call any time before his discharging age. In the *Han shu* we find many cases in which foot soldiers, cavalrymen, or mariners were called to service on expeditions or for other duties.

The passage from the *Han chiu-i* indicates clearly that an adult male was subject to two years' military service, one for military training, and another as *wei-shih* or palace guard. According to LAO Kan, serving as a palace guard and serving as a frontier guard were both called *wai-yao* 外徭, " outside services," and presumably one was required to serve in only one of the two capacities.[68] Accepting this interpretation, WANG Yü-ch'üan has used the flexible phrase, " one year for garrison duties."

As for the one month's labor service rendered annually at the adult's home locality, earlier and modern scholars generally agree on this point. There are, however, two unsolved problems in connection with this service. First, a series of terms, *tsu-kêng* 卒更 " the required service as a soldier," *chien-kêng* 踐更 " hired service," and *kuo-kêng* 過更 " transferred frontier service," were defined by the Latter Han commentator, JU Shun 如淳. His note at the end of *Han shu* 7.8b has been translated in DUBS 2.176-177. HAMAGUCHI Shigekuni and other modern scholars however have suggested strongly that the definitions given by JU Shun are erroneous.[69] Guided by the usage of these terms in Han texts and on the definitions by another Latter Han commentator, FU Ch'ien 服虔,[70] we may define *tsu-kêng* as a general term referring

[67] Chariots, which were so important in warfare in Chou times, gradually came to be discarded in Han times. See *CYYY* 10 (1942) .26-28.

[68] *Ibid.*, p. 36.

[69] *TG* 19 (1931) .84-107; 20 (1932) .140-146. *Kuo-li Chê-chiang ta-hsüeh wên-hsüeh-yüan chi-k'an* 1 (1941) .26b-29a. *CYYY* 10 (1942) .42-45.

[70] *Shih-chi* 106.3a-b; *Han shu* 35.5b.

to the one month's labor service, *chien-kêng* as its actual performance, and *kuo-kêng* as hiring a substitute for it, or, at least in the Latter Han period, as the substitute fee which one owed the government. The term *chü-kêng* in *Lun hêng* 12.16a, quoted above, is synonymous with *chien-kêng*.

Secondly, according to Ju Shun, the fee for hiring a substitute to render the one month's service was two thousand cash, and that for commuting a three-day frontier service was three hundred. HAMAGUCHI, LAO Kan, and WANG Yü-ch'üan agree that the frontier service under the Han was one year instead of three days. HAMAGUCHI suggests that three hundred cash was to commute the one month's *tsu-kêng* service, following again FU Ch'ien.[71] LAO Kan however has pointed out that, since the currency of the Han was not stable, possibly three hundred coins were collected at one time and two thousand at another.[72]

With this background, we may proceed to examine Dr. SWANN's translation of the following quotation from a memorial of TUNG Chung-shu in *Han shu* 24A.15a:

> Moreover, there was added to the service of one moon [a year in their counties and/or provinces during three years], and then to the following regular [conscript *tsu* service for one moon a year during two years, the one at the capital and the other in training for frontier duty, the draft] for one year in camps on frontier, and/or a year (or years) in labor services. [These requirements were] thirty fold those of ancient times, . . . [Pp. 181-182.]

This was primarily a discussion of the Ch'in system, but TUNG Chung-shu also added, " When the Han arose, [the government] followed [the institutions of Ch'in] without changing them " (pp. 182-183) . Consequently, modern scholars have tried to interpret this passage in the light of what they have found out elsewhere about the Han system. Obviously Dr. SWANN has made a similar attempt, because the translation, with the inserted words, agrees with what she describes as the Han system:

> After 155 B. C. it seems that in theory the young man registered at twenty (Chinese reckoning) , served one moon a year in his native county or province or fief for three years; at twenty-three he was called for one moon that year to guard duty at the capital, and the next year he had to spend one moon back in

---

[71] *TG* 19 (1931) .87-89.   [72] *CYYY* 10 (1942) .45.

his native parts in training for frontier duties. Thereafter in the years from twenty-five to fifty-six, besides being subject to call for service in time of war, he was responsible for as many as three days a year of frontier duty. [Page 51.]

Evidently the accounts in *Yen-t'ieh lun* 4.8b and *Lun hêng* 12.16a concerning the draft age have not been utilized here. Dr. SWANN limits the *kêng-tsu* or *tsu-kêng* service to one month in each of the first three years after registration, and interprets the one year of guard duty and one year of training as only one month in each of the two following years. These interpretations unfortunately lack documentation. The three-day frontier service is based on JU Shun's commentary, which does not seem to be reliable. Actually JU Shun also quoted the statement of TUNG Chung-shu in *Han shu* 24A.15a, which DUBS has translated as follows:

" [The Ch'in dynasty . . . moreover added to the requirements of the government] that for a month [each person] should become a soldier serving in his term 更卒; when [this period] was completed, he in turn became a regular [soldier, who served] one year as a garrison guard at the frontier and one year at service on the public works 力役 —[which service] is thirty times [more] than in ancient [times]." [2.176-177.]

The rendering of the clause " when [this period] was completed " is questionable. Otherwise, this translation represents one traditional interpretation,[73] which differs considerably from both that of Dr. SWANN and that of HAMAGUCHI, LAO, and WANG. According to the latter, the passage should be rendered as follows:

Moreover, for a month [every year] he should render his labor service 更卒, and then in addition he should serve as a regular soldier 正 (卒) for one year, and as a garrison guard for another year. These services were thirtyfold those of ancient times.

Of the three versions I am inclined to endorse the last one, but still have doubts about whether TUNG Chung-shu's statement was so specific as scholars have supposed. For instance, the interpretation by YEN Shih-ku would also make sense.[74] Follow-

[73] CH'IEN Wên-tzŭ 錢文子, *Pu Han ping-chih* 補漢兵志 (*Chih-pu-tsu-chai ts'ung-shu* 知不足齋叢書 ed.) 1b-2a.

[74] The last part of Dr. SWANN's translation of this obscure passage is also based on the interpretation of YEN Shih-ku.

ing his commentary in *Han Shu* 24.15a, the passage may also be interpreted to agree with the findings of HAMAGUCHI, LAO, and WANG:

> Moreover, for a month [every year] he should render his labor service, and then in addition he should serve as a regular soldier [for two years in his life]. The garrison duties in one year and the labor services in one year were thirtyfold those of ancient times.

This version tallies even better with the translation of the *Han chiu-i* given above. Actually, the *Han chiu-i* text also permits another rendering, which is found in DUBS 1.80-81:

> The *Han-chiu-yi* (written by Wei Hung, fl. 25-27), pt. II, 5b, says that people in their 23rd year serve first as regular soldiers 正卒, after a year they serve as guards 衞士 , and after another year as skilled soldiers 材官 or cavalrymen. They were trained in archery, driving, riding, galloping, fighting, and tactics. In his 56th year a soldier was superannuated on account of age, excused from service, relegated to the ranks of the ordinary people, and went back to his farm and village.

This interpretation gives no explanation of what the soldier was supposed to do in his first year of service. Moreover it seems too rigid, if the guard service was rendered only in the second year after reaching draft age. My version, which is based on studies by HAMAGUCHI, LAO, and WANG, avoids these difficulties.

The lengthy discussion above perhaps gives sufficient indication that there are many tangled problems in the economic history of ancient China. We can obtain a clearer picture only when more scholars have made critical studies to provide a basis for further discussion. A scholarly work like this one by Dr. SWANN will naturally prove stimulative and consequently is most welcome. In conclusion, I would like to discuss briefly a few minor points as follows:

(1) *Ch'ing-chung* 輕重 . On page 222 we read, " When Kuan Chung (d. 645 B. C.) became first minister to the duke Huan (685-643 B. C., of the feudatory of Ch'i) , he put into circulation standard weights and measures [for money]." The last part of the sentence seems erroneous. I would suggest, " he mastered the balance of demand and supply." Earlier, on page 25, Dr. SWANN has understood *ch'ing-chung* as supply and demand, and on page

226 she has translated the phrase *ch'üan ch'ing-chung* 權 as " balance the light and heavy [coins]." [75]

(2) The *wu-fên* 五分 and *san-fên* 三分 coins. Following a traditional interpretation, DUBS (1.199) and SWANN (page 378) both consider the name of the *wu-fên* coins of 182 B. C. as indicating a half-inch diameter. Ts'AI Yün 蔡雲,[76] a Ch'ing numismatic authority, however, has suggested that *wu-fên* probably indicated its weight, which may have been one fifth of its face value, *pan-liang* 半兩 or twelve *shu* 銖. He has pointed out that the 4-*shu* coins issued in 136 B. C. were also called *san-fên* (*Shih-chi* 22.14b), i. e. one third of its face value, *pan-liang*. This seems preferable to the traditional interpretation.

(3) The *ts'o-tao* 錯刀 coins of WANG Mang. On pages 324-325, there is a description of the *ts'o-tao*, " On the second denomination i. e. the *ts'o-tao* actual gold [was used] to inlay its inscription reading ' one knife value five thousand [units].' " The text of *Han shu* 24B.19b has *i-tao chih wu-ch'ien* 一刀直五千 but the inscription reads *i-tao p'ing wu-ch'ien* 平, of which only the first two characters, *i-tao*, are inlaid with gold. (See illustration facing page 379) Taking into consideration these facts, we may change the translation to read, " On the second denomination actual gold [was used] to inlay [the first two characters of] its inscription reading ' one knife ' and it was valued five thousand [units]."

(4) The round coins of WANG Mang. The discrepancy between money as described in *Han shu* 24B and actual specimens of WANG Mang currency was not limited to the gold-inlaid knife coin. A round coin valued fifty cash was issued in A. D. 7 when WANG Mang was the regent. Two years later, when he became the emperor, five additional round coins valued one, ten, twenty,

---

[75] On *ch'ing-chung*, see also BLUE, *HJAS* 11 (1948).102-104.

[76] *P'i-t'an* 癖談 (*Chiao-ching shan-fang ts'ung-shu* 校經山房 ed.) 4.10a, 5.1b-2a, also quoted in *Ku-ch'ien ta-tz'ŭ-tien* 古錢大辭典, *hsia-pien* 下編 208a-b, 209a.

Ts'AI Yün in his *P'i-t'an* 5.3a-5b raises a question about the *san-shu* 三銖 coins of 140 B. C. The problem is also discussed by KATŌ Shigeru in *SZ* 43.6 (1932).59-73. Both writers hold that coins bearing the inscription 3 *shu*, which was their weight, were issued under Wu-ti for one short period instead of two short periods. Dr. SWANN thinks that the latter was the case (pp. 377-382), and LAO Kan in *Han-chien, k'ao-chêng* 1.63b-65b expresses the same opinion. The question, however, seems still open.

thirty, and forty were put into circulation. According to *Han shu* 24B.19b-20b, the first bore the legend *ta-ch'ien wu-shih* 大錢 五十, and the other five had similar inscriptions in the pattern "descriptive word plus *ch'ien* plus value." Known specimens, however, all have the character *ch'üan* 泉 instead of *ch'ien*. *Ch'üan* and *ch'ien* are two synonymous words meaning coins in general or round coins in particular. Since *ch'üan* appears in the *Chou li* and presumably was more archaic, there was good reason for its adoption by the antiquarian WANG Mang. These six denominations and the *huo-ch'üan* 貨泉 of A.D. 14 were all the round coins issued by him, and they all bore in their legend the character *ch'üan*. In Dr. SWANN's book, an illustration of *ta-ch'üan wu-shih* may be found in Fig. 9, WANG Mang coin tree. Its size however may have been reduced.

(5) The *huo-pu* 貨布 of WANG Mang. In A.D. 9 WANG Mang issued *huo-pu*, "cloth-money" (or rather spade money), in ten denominations. Based on examination of specimens and earlier numismatic studies, the author has changed the name of the seventh large denomination *hou-pu* 厚布 into *hsü-pu* 序 (page 329). This is an excellent correction of the text in *Han shu* 24B. 21a. On the plate facing page 379, however, the inscription on a WANG Mang spade-coin is unfortunately incorrectly deciphered. The author says the coin is "inscribed *pu-huo*." Actually the inscription contains four characters *ta-pu hêng-ch'ien* 大布黃千, "big spade money valued one thousand cash." The character *huang* 黃 apparently stands for *hêng* 衡, thus the reading *hêng*. This agrees with the description of *ta-pu*, the largest denomination of *pu-huo* (pp. 329-330).

(6) *Fei-yeh* 非也 or *fei-ya* 邪. On page 464, Dr. SWANN translates the last sentence or sentences in the epilogue of *Shih-chi* 129, "Are they [merely] the so-called 'untitled nobility?' They are not." Dr. BLUE [77] however understands the *fei-yeh* in the text as *fei-ya* and renders "Is this, or is this not, what is called 'pseudo-enfeoffment.'" The latter version is preferable.

---

[77] *HJAS* 11 (1948) .25, 27, note.

NOTES ON THE ECONOMIC HISTORY OF THE CHIN DYNASTY *

Lien-sheng Yang

Harvard University

CONTENTS

INTRODUCTION

1. The official history of the Chin period

The present *Chin shu* is by no means the first history of the Chin dynasty ever compiled. No less than eighteen Chin histories, complete or in part, were preserved at the beginning of the T'ang dynasty.[1] Some covered the whole period, and others only a part of it. The most voluminous was the 110-chapter work by Tsang Jung-hsü 臧榮緒 of the Southern Ch'i (479-502).[2] This, however, like the others did not please the Emperor T'ai-tsung,[3] who issued a decree in 646[4] in which he criticized all the eighteen Chin histories[5] and ordered a recompilation.

---

* I am deeply indebted to Prof. James R. Ware for his untiring guidance which has improved this thesis in many ways.

[1] According to P'u Ch'i-lung's 浦起龍 commentary to *Shih t'ung* 史通 (*Ssŭ-pu pei-yao* 四部備要 ed.) 12.16a-b they were probably the nineteen works mentioned in *Sui shu* (All dynastic histories used in this thesis are T'ung-wên Shu chü reproduction of the 1739 ed.) 33.2a-b, 4b-5a, excluding that by Hsi Tso-ch'ih 習鑿齒. This does not seem to agree entirely with the names mentioned in T'ai-tsung's decree below. Actually there were about a dozen other pre-T'ang works on the Chin history named in *Nien-êrh shih ta-chi* 廿二史劄記 (*Ssŭ-pu pei-yao* ed.) 7.16a-17b and *Shih-ch'i shih shang-ch'üeh* 十七史商榷 (*Kuang-ya* 廣雅 *ts'ung-shu* ed.) 43.1a-2b.

[2] Biog. *Nan Ch'i shu* 54.11a-12b.

[3] The famous Li Shih-min. Biog. Giles 1196; C. P. Fitzgerald: *Son of Heaven*.

[4] *T'ang ta chao-ling chi* 唐大詔令集 (*Shih-yüan* 適園 *ts'ung-shu* ed.) 81.6a-b. The intercalary second month should read intercalary third month according to *Chiu T'ang shu* 2.17b. The decree also appears in *Yü hai* 玉海 (*Chekiang shu-chü* ed.) 46.28b and *Ch'üan T'ang wên* 全唐文 (Kuang-ya shu-chü ed.) 8.1b-2b with some changes.

[5] Fourteen of the eighteen authors are mentioned in the decree by surname, name,

119

According to *Chiu T'ang shu* [6] the order for the compilation of a new Chin history was issued in 644 and the work was completed in 646. It is not impossible that the decree in 646 was merely a confirmation of previous appointments of editors and compilers, perhaps with a desire to display the Emperor's broad knowledge in Chinese historiography. The new compilation is said to have been based largely upon the work of TSANG Jung-hsü, but references were made extensively to other works and even fictitious stories.[7] The Emperor personally wrote the four critical essays attached to the annals of Emperor Hsüan and Emperor Wu, and to the biographies of the famous writer LU Chi 陸機, and the famous calligrapher WANG Hsi-chih 王羲之. In the last essay the Emperor, himself a calligrapher, criticized authoritatively the penmanship of several earlier calligraphers.[8] The whole work thus acquired the honorific title of " imperial compilation " 御撰. The Emperor was so proud of the book that a copy of it was bestowed upon two princes of Silla to take back to their country in 648.[9] The book, at first known as *Hsin Chin shu*, soon dropped the word *Hsin* in its title and replaced the other Chin histories, which are now preserved only in fragments.[10]

or *tzŭ*. Twelve of them can easily be identified as TSANG Jung-hsü (mentioned as Hsü), YÜ Yü 虞預 (mentioned by his *tzŭ*, Shu-nıng 叔寧), HSIAO Tzŭ-yün 蕭子雲 (as Tzŭ-yün), WANG Yin 王隱 (by his *tzŭ*, Ch'u-shu 處叔), Ho Fa-shêng 何法盛 (as Fa-shêng), KAN Pao 干寶 (as KAN), LU Chi (as LU), TS'AO Chia-chih 曹嘉之 (as TS'AO), TÊNG Ts'an 鄧粲 (as TÊNG), T'AN Tao-luan 檀道鸞 (as Luan), SUN Shêng 孫盛 (as Shêng), and Hsü Kuang 徐廣 (as Kuang) all mentioned in *Sui shu* 33.2a-b, 4b-5a. The other two were probably HSIEH Ch'ên 謝沈 (*tzŭ* Hsing-ssŭ 行思, mentioned as Ssŭ) and P'EI Sung-chih 裴松之 (mentioned as Sung, misread 訟 in *T'ang ta chao-ling chi*). Neither of the two appears in *Sui shu* 33 as author of a Chin history, but HSIEH's biography in *Chin shu* 82.16a mentions his work on Chin history of over thirty chapters and P'EI's biography in *Sung shu* 64.11b mentions his Chin Annals 晉紀.

[6] 66.4b-5b; 73.12a.   [7] *Chiu T'ang shu* 66.5a-b; *Shih t'ung* 5.2a-b, 17.3a-4b.

[8] To display his deep knowledge in fine arts may have been one of the Emperor's motives in preparing these essays. According to *Liang shu* 35.9b HSIAO Tzŭ-yün, one of the eighteen authors and a calligrapher, failed to carry out his own plan to write a critical essay at the end of the biographies of WANG Hsi-chih and his son. The Emperor seems to be criticizing him for this in the decree of 646: see note 4.

[9] *Chiu T'ang shu* 199A, 18a-19a; *Hsin T'ang shu* 220.20b-21a.

[10] T'ANG Ch'iu 湯球: *Chin yang-ch'iu chi-pên* 晉陽秋輯本, *Chin chi chi-pên* 晉紀, *Chiu chia chiu Chin shu chi-pên* 九家舊晉書 (*Ts'ung shu chi-ch'êng* 集成 *ts'ê* 3805-10); HUANG Shê 黃奭: *Huang shih i-shu k'ao* 黃氏逸書攷 *ts'ê* 67-79, in which works on Chin history are collected under 21 headings.

Scholars of later times have not studied this History very much, and what few studies have been made are really not very well done.[11] Exactly one century after its compilation Ho Ch'ao 何超 prepared two chapters of *Yin-i* 音義, which are very brief and mostly concerned with the pronunciation of words.[12] Famous Ch'ing scholars like LU Wên-shao 盧文弨,[13] WANG Ming-shêng 王鳴盛,[14] CHAO I 趙翼,[15] CH'IEN Ta-hsin 錢大昕,[16] and LI Tz'ŭ-ming 李慈銘 [17] did comparatively little in the collation and annotation of the texts. This is especially true with the *Shih-huo chih* 食貨志 or treatise on economic affairs. For example, in the five chapters of collation on *Chin shu* by CH'IEN, there is only one note on the *Shih-huo chih*; in the ten chapters by WANG we find only two notes, in one of which he corrects one error but commits another. Other collators are hardly more helpful.[18]

The only commentary on the whole book available is the *Chin shu chiao-chu* (CSCC) 斠注 by WU Shih-chien 吳士鑑 and LIU Ch'êng-kan 劉承幹 printed in 1927. It is far from being comprehensive, and the work on the *Shih-huo chih* is very unsatisfactory. In some cases it fails even to utilize the most easily accessible references such as those in other dynastic histories. Thus evident errors are overlooked.

[11] The sole exception is the *ti-li chih* 地理 or treatise on geography. Cf. PI Yüan 畢沅: *Chin shu ti-li chih hsin pu-chêng* 新補正, FANG K'ai 方愷: *Hsin chiao Chin shu ti-li chih* 新校, HUNG Liang-chi 洪亮吉: *Tung Chin chiang-yü chih* 東晉疆域志 and *Shih-liu Kuo chiang-yü chih* 十六國 in *Erh-shih-wu shih pu-pien* 二十五史補編 3529-59, 3561-77, 3579-648, and 4083-209.

[12] Preface by his brother-in-law YANG Ch'i-hsüan 楊齊宣 in 747. The *Yin-i* is available at the end of the 1739 ed. of *Chin shu.*

[13] Lu's collation is confined to the annals, the *t'ien-wên chih* 天文, and the *li chih* 禮. It is in his *Ch'ün-shu shih-pu* 羣書拾補 (*Pao-ching t'ang ts'ung-shu* 抱經堂 *ts'ê* 67).

[14] *Shih-ch'i shih shang-ch'üeh* 43.1a-52.6a, especially 47.5a-b.

[15] *Nien-êrh shih ta-chi* 7.16a-8.18b.

[16] *Nien-êrh shih k'ao-i* 考異 (*Ch'ien-yen t'ang ch'üan-shu* 潛研堂全書 ed.) 18.1a-22.20a, esp. 20.17a; also *Chu-shih shih-i* 諸史拾遺 (*Ch'ien-yen t'ang ch'üan-shu* ed.) 1.11b-18b.

[17] *Chin shu cha-chi* 札記 1.1a-5b.

[18] Important ones like: HUNG I-hsüan 洪頤煊: *Chu-shih k'ao-i* 諸史考異 chapters 2 and 3 (*Kuang-ya ts'ung-shu*, *ts'ê* 341); CHOU Chia-lu 周家祿: *Chin shu chiao-k'an chi* 校勘記, 5 chaps. (ibid. *ts'ê* 219); LAO Ko 勞格: *Chin shu chiao-k'an chi*, 3 chaps. (ibid. *ts'ê* 220); TING Kuo-chün 丁國鈞: *Chin shu chiao-wên* 校文, 5 chaps. (*Ch'ang-shu Ting shih ts'ung-shu* 常熟 ed.).

Among the fifteen dynastic histories of China covering the long period from ancient times down to the fall of the Sui dynasty in 617 A. D., only five contain treatises or *chih* devoted to economic affairs. These are *Shih chi, Han shu, Chin shu, Wei shu*, and *Sui shu*.[19] The treatise in *Shih chi* called *P'ing-chun shu* 平準書 [20] is confined to the early part of the Han period, especially the reign of Emperor Wu (140-87 B. C.). The section on economic affairs in *Han shu* which begins the use of the title *Shih-huo chih* is more ambitious in scale.[21] It starts with the Three Dynasties back in the second millennium B. C. and ends with the gigantic reforms of WANG Mang at the beginning of the Christian era. The third in sequence of the time of compilation is the economic treatise in *Wei shu*, which naturally limits itself to affairs under the T'o-pa dynasty (386-550).[22] The chapters called *Shih-huo chih* in *Chin shu* and *Sui shu* were both compiled in the middle of the seventh century by official historians to supplement and continue the earlier works.

The ten treatises in *Sui shu* were designed to cover five dynasties, Liang, Ch'ên, Northern Ch'i, Chou, and Sui, and consequently were once well known as *Wu-tai shih chih* 五代史志.[23] The *Shih-huo chih* [24] is not an exception, and in parts it covers the Sung, the Southern Ch'i, and even the Eastern Chin (317-420). Its compilation was begun in 641, a few years before *Chin shu*

[19] The others are *Hou Han shu, San Kuo chih, Sung shu, (Nan) Ch'i shu, Liang shu, Ch'ên shu, Pei Ch'i shu, Chou shu, Nan shih* and *Pei shih*. The first, the third, and the fourth contain treatises but no *shih-huo chih*.

[20] Translated by Édouard CHAVANNES: *Les Memoires Historiques de Se-ma Ts'ien* 3. 538-604.

[21] Dr. Nancy Lee SWANN is preparing an annotated translation of this treatise, which is almost ready for publication. I have had the honor of reading her translation in an earlier stage.

[22] Working under the Northern Ch'i, WEI Shou 魏收 naturally took the rulers of the preceding Eastern Wei (534-550) as legitimate successors of the Northern Wei (386-534) and wrote annals for them. Cf. J. R. WARE: Notes on the History of the *Wei shu, JAOS 52* (1932) 35-45.

[23] *Shih t'ung* 12. 29a-b. Not to be confused with the Histories of the Five Dynasties after the T'ang.

[24] This chapter has been translated in an unpublished manuscript by Miss Rhea C. BLUE of the University of California. Cf. Woodbridge BINGHAM: *The Founding of the T'ang Dynasty* 13, note 11.

was started, but the finished chapters were not presented to the throne until 656, ten years after the completion of *Chin shu*.[25] Among the twenty-one known editors and compilers of *Chin shu* at least four worked also on the *Wu-tai shih chih*.[26] It was probably due to their effort that there is no overlapping in the treatises of the two histories. A peculiar result is that some records on the economic history of the Eastern Chin period are found in *Sui shu* but not in *Chin shu* as one would expect. As if in compensation the *Shih-huo chih* in *Chin shu* not only gives extensive accounts on the Western Chin (265-317) but also goes back to the Later Han dynasty (25-220), picking up the thread left by PAN Ku in *Han shu*. It is undoubtedly the most important document on the economic history of China during the second, third, and fourth centuries.

The term *shih-huo chih* has been translated as " treatise on economics," [27] " Monograph on food and commodities," [28] and " treatise on food and money." [29] The last is the most literal, because " medium of exchange " seems to have been the essence of PAN Ku's long definition of *huo* at the beginning of *Han shu* 24A, and all earlier treatises on economic affairs are distinctly divided into two parts, on food and money. The second translation then is wrong. The *Shih-huo chih* from the two T'ang histories down are divided into more sections because of the growing complexity of economic life in later periods.

The aim of the present thesis is to make a readable translation of this treatise with necessary annotations put in compact form. The basic text is the T'ung-wên shu-chü 同文書局 reproduction of the 1739 edition because it is one of the most popular. Collations are made with other editions with important differences indicated.

[25] The original postscript of the Sung (1026) ed. 宋本原跋 of *Sui shu*, which is also available at the end of the 1739 ed.

[26] *Hsin T'ang shu* 56.3a cites the names of the 21 historians. The four were LI Ch'un-fêng 李淳風, LI Yen-shou 李延壽, CHING Po 敬播 (*Chiu T'ang shu* 73.14b), and LING-HU Tê-fên 令狐德棻 (ibid. 73.12b).

[27] C. Martin WILBUR: *Slavery in China during the Former Han Dynasty*, 50.

[28] Woodbridge BINGHAM: ibid. 13.

[29] Used by Nancy Lee SWANN in her manuscript.

No attempt is made here to rewrite the economic history of the Chin dynasty. A few important features, however, are discussed in a historical introduction and the problems of the land system and land-tax system are summarized in two notes. References will be given in footnotes.[30] Unsolved problems will also be indicated in the hope that they will form the basis for more extensive studies.

2. Historical background and economic problems

From the end of the second century to the beginning of the fifth, Chinese history presented a series of great changes. Politically it saw the decline and fall of the Han empire, its division into Three Kingdoms (220-264), the short reunion under the Western Chin (265-317), the suicidal wars waged by the Chin royal princes against one another (300-310), the uprising and invasion of barbarian or semi-barbarian tribes inside and outside China Proper (from 304),[31] and the retreat of the Chinese Eastern Chin dynasty (317-420) to the south of the Yangtze river. The famous battle fought along the Fei 淝 river in modern Anhwei province in 383 crushed the attempt of the then most powerful non-Chinese ruler to conquer South China. On the other hand the rise of the T'o-pa Wei dynasty (386-543) and its unification of North China in the early part of the fifth century left little chance for the Chinese in the South to recover their lost empire after the last attempt failed in 418. For about two centuries China was to be ruled separately under Southern and Northern Dynasties until the reunion by conquest of the South in 589.

No less great were the cultural changes: Confucianism declined when its ethical teachings were openly discarded by rulers such as Ts'AO Ts'ao who welcomed people of talent but no virtue.[32]

[30] Date and place of publication are given only for a few modern works which are less well known to students of Chinese studies.

[31] Collectively known as the Five Barbarian Tribes 五胡: Hsiung-nu 匈奴, Hsien-pei 鮮卑, Ti 氐, Ch'iang 羌, and Chieh 羯. Roughly speaking, at the beginning of the fourth century the Hsiung-nu and the Chieh lived in Inner Mongolia and Northern Shansi, the Hsien-pei in Southern Manchuria and Northern Hopei, the Ch'iang and the Ti in Kansu and Shensi. Cf. WANG Yi-t'ung 王伊同; 五胡通考, *Bulletin of Chinese Studies* 3 (1943, Chengtu).57-79.

[32] *San Kuo chih* (SKC) 1.41b, commentary.

When the National University was reopened under the Wei (220-265) after the years of disturbances between 190 and 220, it became merely a refuge for incompetent students who wished to escape the burden of forced labor. The study of the Classics was limited to the meanings of words and to the methods of punctuation while the general principles were entirely overlooked.[33] Some attempts were made by Chinese and foreign [34] dynasties to improve the national education, but their achievements were small and scholarship was preserved only in some families and by private teachers. On the other hand Buddhism was beginning to become dominant throughout the whole of China. In a few centuries it became accepted not only by the masses but also by many intellectuals. Among its adherents were also those who sought exemption from levies and services under the protection of the Buddhist order.[35] Under the stimulation of the Indian teaching Taoism was revived as a philosophy and newly constituted as a religion. The extent of the influence exerted by these new beliefs and practices on Chinese culture is matched probably only by that of the introduction of modern Western civilization into China in the last one hundred years.

The social and economic changes with which we are here mainly concerned are also of paramount significance. First, we notice, according to the official accounts, an amazing decline of population. In 157 an official census put the population of China at 10,677,960 households and 56,486,856 individuals.[36] These were probably the highest figures ever reached in the Later Han period (25-220). In 280, when the Chin empire was at its peak, the population was 2,459,840 households and 16,163,863 individuals, only about ¼ of that of the Han.[37] The lowest point reached

[33] SKC 13.28b-29a.

[34] High respect for Chinese scholarship and civilization was shown by several semi-barbarian rulers. Cf. *Nien-êrh shih ta-chi* 8.5a-6a.

[35] J. R. WARE: WEI Shou on Buddhism, *TP* 30 (1933) 153, 178-9.

[36] *Chin shu* (CS) 14.10b-11a; *T'ung tien* (*Shih t'ung* 十通 ed.) 7.39b. The census of 156 (or 157) given in *Hou Han shu* (HHS) 29.3b at 16,070,906 households and 50,066,856 individuals has not been accepted by modern scholars. Cf. T'AO Yüan-chên 陶元珍: *San Kuo shih-huo chih* 三國食貨志 (1935, Shanghai) 1-2.

[37] CS 14.12a; *T'ung tien* 7.39c.

was probably during the thirty years from 190 to 220. People
at that time believed that only one-tenth of the Han population
was left.[38] The high peak of 280 probably continued for about
a dozen years, then the population again decreased because of
continual civil wars and barbarian invasions. In c. 363 the com-
mander-in-chief of the Eastern Chin troops said in a memorial
that the population in South China was even less than that of
a province under the Han.[39] This statement may have been an
exaggeration, because according to records the most populated
province under the Han had only about two and a half million
individuals;[40] nevertheless the emphasis put by contemporaries
on the population problem is significant.

The reasons for the decline of population were threefold: the
people either died, or migrated, or were not reported in the government records. The first was apparently the chief one. In the
years of disturbance around the end of the second and the third
centuries life was indeed very cheap. Plagues and poor harvests
helped to increase the toll of deaths exacted by wars. Cannibalism
appeared again and again. All these are clearly recorded in the
treatise on economic affairs in *Chin shu*. Successive migrations
to the south and the ‘ protection ’ of subordinates by powerful
people also account for the fall in official census figures. These
factors possess social-economic importance in themselves.

Migration of the Chinese from the northern and western regions
of China Proper to the central provinces of the lower Yellow river
valley and from there to the Yangtze valley began already under
the Eastern Han when the conquered Hsiung-nu people were
allowed to dwell inside the northern boundary and when the
Ch‘iang barbarians repeated their invasions from the west. It was
accelerated by the end of the second century because of disturbances in the central provinces. People migrated in groups of
hundreds and thousands. Their general direction was southward

---

[38] SKC 8.22a.   [39] CS 98.23b.

[40] According to *Han shu* 28A.21a, 22a, 27a the three most populated provinces in
2 A.D. were:

    Ju-nan (Southern Honan) .... 2,596,148 individuals
    Ying-ch‘uan (Southwestern Honan) 2,210,973   “
    P‘ei kuo (Northern Anhwei and Northern Kiangsu) 2,030,480   “

but in several cases southwestward to Szechuan and Yunnan, or northeastward to Hopei and Liaoning.[41] The largest migration however took place in the first quarter of the fourth century and especially after the revolt of the Hsiung-nu in Shansi in 304. It has been estimated that even during the first years (298-307) the number of people involved already reached two million,[42] that is, about one eighth of the population. It was said that from the fall of Lo-yang in 311 down to about 325 sixty to seventy percent of the upper classes had moved from the central provinces to south of the Yangtze river.[43] By the end of the fourth century about a million northerners had settled in their new homes in the south.[44]

In the Eastern Chin period the registration of the migrant families became a serious question. These families from the north still claimed to belong to their original provinces and did not share labor services as citizens of the provinces in which they now lived. It was only under two able generals in 364 and 412 that the government actually succeeded in carrying out the policy of t'u-tuan 土斷, " registration according to residence," i. e. to make the migrators register on the regular " Yellow Register."[45]

The practice of " protection " of subordinates by the powerful is traceable to Han times. When the central power of the empire had declined by the end of the second century, the ties between the local officials and their subordinates became reinforced. Government clerks considered themselves privately attached to their superiors and wore three years' mourning dress even for a former chief.[46] A similar linkage existed between students and their teacher. An influential teacher often could acquire corvée exemp-

[41] CH'ÊN Hsiao-chiang 陳嘯江: San Kuo ching-chi shih 三國經濟史 (1936, Canton) 101-2.

[42] LIU Shan-li 劉揅藜: 晉惠帝時代漢族之大流徙 Ch'êng ta shih-hsüeh tsa-chih 成大史學雜誌 1 (1929) 63-80, reprinted in Yü kung 禹貢 4.11 (1936) 11-23.

[43] CS 65. 2a.

[44] T'ANG Ch'i-hsiang 譚其驤: 晉永嘉喪亂後之民族遷徙 YCHP 15 (1934) 51-76.

[45] MASUMURA Hiroshi 增村宏: 黃白籍の新研究 Tōyōshi kenkyū 東洋史研究 2.4 (1937) 30-44.

[46] Nien-êrh shih ta-chi 3. 15b-16b.

tion for his students.[47] Both *ku-li* 故吏, " former subordinates," and *Mên-shêng* 門生, " private students," were important followers of officials and even generals in the second and third centuries.[48]

Members of a powerful clan usually lived together with a number of helpless families and individuals attached to it for livelihood and protection. These subordinates were called *k'o* 客 or " guests." Fighters privately attached to generals and powerful families were called *pu-ch'ü* 部曲,[49] whose status was as low as that of the *k'o*. Both *pu-ch'ü* and *k'o* were hereditarily owned and could be transferred as gifts to friends. The chief difference between them and the slaves 奴 was that they could not be sold. Under their masters they migrated and made new settlements or built strongholds in mountains during the period of turmoil.

K'o and slaves existed in considerable numbers under the Han,[50] but their number, especially that of the *k'o*, probably increased during the period of the Three Kingdoms and the Chin. The advantage of being a slave or *k'o* was exemption from public levies and services. The protection of *k'o* became institutionalized when the Wei rulers granted their officials the privilege of protecting various numbers of *k'o* households according to the official's rank.[51] The Western Chin regulation is minutely recorded in our text and a similar regulation of the Eastern Chin with more generous allowance may be found in *Sui shu* 24. 4a.

---

[47] CS 88. 5b-6a.

[48] Yang Lien-shêng: 東漢的豪族 *CHHP* 11.4 (1936) 1030-7. Chü Ch'ing-yüan 鞠清遠: 三國時代的客 *Shih-huo* 食貨 3.4 (1936) 15-9; 兩晉、南北朝的客、門生、故吏、義附、部曲 *Shih-huo* 2.12 (1935) 11-27.

[49] Ho Shih-chi 何士驥: 部曲考 *Kuo-hsüeh lun-ts'ung* 國學論叢 1.1 (1927) 123-62; Yang Chung-i 楊中一: 部曲沿革略考 *Shih-huo* 1.3 (1935) 21-31; Ho Tzŭ-ch'üan 何茲全: 三國時期國家的三種領民 *Shih-huo* 1.11 (1935) 1-5.

[50] C. M. Wilbur: *Slavery in China during the Former Han Dynasty* 166-77.

[51] CS 93. 3b has the following interesting paragraph: " The Wei dynasty granted [the privilege of] renting [government] cattle and [protecting] households as ' guests ' in different numbers to the dukes, ministers, and lower officials. Later many poor people who dreaded the corvée were glad to become ' guests.' Noble and powerful families usually had over a hundred of them. In prefectures like T'ai-yüan (central Shansi), Hsiung-nu barbarians were also made ' tenant-guests.' In the larger [establishments] their number reached several thousands."

The *k'o* were required to register under the household of their master,[52] although this rule was not always enforced. The generous allowance made by the Eastern Chin dynasty aimed probably to encourage the large families to have their protected vagrants registered as *k'o*, but the result was unsatisfactory.[53] The government, however, did not always protect the vested interests. On several occasions, especially during emergencies under the Eastern Chin, slaves and *k'o* were freed by imperial decrees and drafted as soldiers or transport laborers in spite of objection from powerful families.[54]

In view of these changes under the Three Kingdoms and the Chin, the government endeavored to induce people to settle down by encouragement of agriculture, creation and repair of water works, and establishment of agricultural colonies, civil and military. Of these activities we have plenty of records in our treatise. Changes in the land system and land-tax system will be discussed in the following sections.

From the third century there was a shrinkage in the use of metallic money.[55] High prices were often indicated by numbers of pieces of silk or cloth. Most levies were collected in kind. This was especially true in North China. In a few short periods during the third, fourth, and fifth centuries, copper coins were reported as being out of circulation.

Two problems which are almost untouched in the treatise are the improvement of technology and the condition of oversea trade. The third century witnessed the appearance of such inventive minds as MA Chün 馬鈞 and CHU-KO Liang. MA reduced the number of treadles 蹑 on the brocade loom from 50 and 60 to 12, so that complicated warp movements could be produced simply.[56]

---

[52] *Sui shu* 24. 4a.　　　　　　　　[53] *Nan Ch'i shu* 14. 10a.

[54] Slaves owned by dukes, princes, and others in Lo-yang were drafted in 302 (CS 4. 10b). Ten thousand slaves and *k'o* in southern Kiangsu were drafted in 321 (CS 6. 11b; 69. 8b-9a, 13b). Slaves in Hupei were drafted in 343 (CS 73. 20a; 77. 7b-8a; 94. 20a). Slaves in northern Chekiang who had been freed to be *k'o* were drafted in c. 399 (CS 64. 19a). These cases have been well summarized by SHIDA Fudōmaro 志田不動麿: 晉代の土地所有形態と農民問題 *SZ* 43. 2 (1932) 50-2.

[55] CH'ÜAN Han-shêng 全漢昇: 中古自然經濟 *CYYY* 10. 1 (1942) 75-176.

[56] SKC 29. 8b-10a.

He made the south-pointing cart based upon the mechanical principle of gear trains,[57] and was considered the most clever technician of his age. To CHU-KO Liang, famous statesman and general, was ascribed the invention of two types of transport vehicles called "the wooden oxen" and "the flowing horses," which were probably varieties of wheelbarrows.[58]

These inventions, however, may be likened to shooting-stars whose influences are hard to trace. More important is the fact that irrigation projects and the use of a crude sowing machine called the *lou*-plough 耬犁, which was invented probably at the beginning of the first century B. C., were spread to all corners of the empire, as indicated in our treatise. The *shui-tui* 水碓, or water-mill, known since the beginning of the Christian era,[59] became very popular in the third and fourth centuries when its ownership was mentioned along with the ownership of farms and slaves as great riches.[60]

Although land routes between China and the Western world had been traversed for millenia, oversea trade had comparatively less significance until the third and fourth centuries of our era. Coastal sailing must have been fairly common by the end of the Han. In 232-233 the Wu attempted to ally herself with the KUNG-SUN family, who ruled Liao-tung, to fight against the Wei. Missions were sent, in one case of seven to eight thousand people in

[57] A. C. MOULE: The Chinese South-pointing Carriage, *TP* 23 (1924) 83-98. HASHI-MOTO Masukichi 橋本增吉: 指南車考 *TYGH* 8.2 (1918) 249-66, 8.3 (1918) 325-89, 14.3 (1924) 412-29, 15.2 (1925) 219-35. WANG Chên-to 王振鐸: 指南車記里鼓車之考證及模製 *Shih-hsüeh chi-k'an* 史學集刊 3 (1937) 1-47.

[58] SKC, Shu 5.15b-16a. T'AO Yüan-chên: *San Kuo shih-huo chih* 80-2. L. Carrington GOODRICH: *A Short History of the Chinese People* 78.

[59] HUAN T'an's *Hsin Lun* 桓譚新論 in *Ch'üan Hou Han wên* 全後漢文 15.3b. Consequently it appeared in China some two centuries earlier than B. LAUFER suggests in his *Chinese Pottery of the Han Dynasty* 33-5. His translation (p. 34) of a paragraph on water-mills in *Wei shu* 66.18a contains several errors. A better rendering of the last few lines of the paragraph would read as follows: " He memorialized for the construction of several tens of water-mills to the east of CHANG Fang Bridge 張方橋 (the Bridge, located to the west of Loyang, is also mentioned in *Pei shih* 41.6b and *Lo-yang ch'ieh-lan chi* 洛陽伽藍記 *Ssǔ-pu ts'ung-k'an* ed., 4.9a, 19b) by damming up the Ku River 穀水. This device proved a tenfold advantage to the needs of the country."

[60] CS 33.23a; 43.12b.

about one hundred ships loaded with gifts to establish diplomatic and commercial relations.[61] To the South Seas the Wu sent envoys during the third century as far as southern Cambodia.[62] The products and laborers from Kwangtung, Kwangsi, Tonkin, and Annam proved of great help to the Wu.[63] It was probably not merely for political and military purposes that the Wei helped rebels in these regions against the Wu, and the Chin conquered this area before they attacked the lower Yangtze valley.

Trade with more distant areas was also noticeable. The Roman merchant who arrived at Annam in 226 and who was sent to the Wu ruler for investigation constituted the second case of early contact between China and the Roman world.[64] It is interesting to note that the famous monk Fa-hsien, after his long sojourn in India, sailed east from Ceylon in c. 414 with merchants.[65] The earliest extensive literature on Japan, found in *San Kuo chih*, probably resulted from the frequent communications between China and Japan in the third century.

3. The land system of the Chin dynasty

The land system of the Chin dynasty may best be grasped as a link between the land regulations of the Han dynasty and those

[61] SKC 8.13b-15b; Wu 2.20b-22a.

[62] Envoys K'ANG T'ai 康泰 and CHU Ying 朱應 were sent out c. 245-250. Cf. P. PELLIOT: Le Fou-nan, *BEFEO* 3 (1903) 248-303; La Théorie des Quatre Fils du Ciel, *TP* 22 (1923) 121-25. Fragments of records made by K'ANG and CHU have been collected in *Shih-hsüeh tsa-chih* 史學雜誌 1 (1929) 1-7 by Fo-t'o yeh-shê 佛馱耶舍 (penname of HSIANG Ta 向達).

T'ang-ming 堂明, one of the states visited by another group of envoys in c. 225-230 (SKC, Wu 15.8b), is not identified by PELLIOT (*BEFEO* 3.215). A question mark is put after the name by L. C. GOODRICH (*A Short History of the Chinese People* 74). However, HU San-hsing 胡三省 in his commentary to T'ung chien 通鑑 70.16b (*Ssŭ-pu pei-yao* ed.) says T'ang-ming is the same as Tao-ming 道明, located to the north of Chên-la (Cambodia). This is probably based upon *Hsin T'ang shu* 222B.5a. Tao-ming also appears twice in poems by SHÊN Ch'üan-ch'i 沈佺期 (*Ch'üan T'ang shih* 全唐詩, ts'ê 15, 2.8a, 3.10a-b, 1707 ed.) who was exiled to Huan-chou 驩州 in modern northern Annam from 705 to 707.

[63] SKC, Wu 3.10b, 4.10a, 8.8b.

[64] *Liang shu* 54.17a-b. The first was in 166 A.D.

[65] *TP* 30 (1933) 131-2. The *Fo-kuo chi* 佛國記 by Fa-hsien has been translated into English by BEAL, GILES, and LEGGE and into French by RÉMUSAT. A scholarly annotated edition is *Kōshō Hōken den* 考證法顯傳 by ADACHI Kiroku 足立喜六.

of the Northern Dynasties. The Han regulations, formulated but never enforced, were chiefly limitations set to the amounts of land to be owned by the rich and the powerful people. Their aim was to prevent exploitation of the poor and to check the growth of landed nobilities. The Northern Dynasties, turning to the lower classes, proclaimed a series of regulations to allot government owned land to the common folk. Their aim was to equalize ownership of land and to put the people to work. The Chin dynasty in between continued the limitation policy of the former and anticipated the allotment policy of the latter, thus attempting to work in both ways.

In the *Shih-huo chih* of *Chin shu* there are three paragraphs on the land system. The two dealing with regulations for the nobles and officials are comparatively easy to understand. The third paragraph which concerns the people, however, contains a few expressions with regard to which historians disagree in their interpretation.

The two easier paragraphs may be rendered as follows:

"After the Wu Kingdom was pacified [280], the officials again memorialized and the decree [read]: ' the princes and dukes having their domains as homes ought not to own additional houses or fields at the capital. At present, however, there being no time for the construction of official residences for them, they should be allowed to have stations in the city and " fields for hay-supply " in nearby suburbs. But let them now be restricted [as follows]: A prince, duke, or marquis may have one homestead in the capital; in the suburb the holder of a large fief may have fifteen *ch'ing* [66] of land, of a medium one ten *ch'ing*, and of a

---

[66] Weights and measures will be given in this thesis according to official standards of relevant dynasties. However, fluctuations must be allowed because these standards were not enforced all the time or in all places in China. References are made to H. H. DUBS: *The History of the Former Han Dynasty* 1.276-80 for Han times and to WU Ch'êng-lo 吳承洛: *Chung-kuo tu-liang-hêng shih* 中國度量衡史 (1937, Shanghai) 64-74 for other periods.

1 *ch'ing* = 100 *mu* 畝.
1 Han *mu* = 0.114 Eng. acre.
1 Chin *mu* = 0.121 Eng. acre.

small one seven *ch'ing*. Those without an abode in the city but having one outside may keep it.' " [67]

" Officials from the first to the ninth rank hold land 占田 according to their status: first rank, 50 *ch'ing*; second rank, 45; third, 40; fourth, 35; fifth, 30; sixth, 25; seventh, 20; eighth, 15; and ninth, 10." [68]

The regulations for the nobles were limited to fields and houses at the capital, whereas those for the officials were of a general character. At about the same time a discussion on the ownership of land and slaves took place at the court. According to a biography in *Chin shu* [69] " at that time T'IEN Ho 恬和, who was *t'ai-chung ta-fu* 太中大夫, offered advice in a petition. He cited the proposals by K'UNG Kuang 孔光 [and others] under the Han and Hsü Kan 徐幹 and others under the Wei to limit the number of slaves owned by princes, dukes, and others, and to forbid the people from selling their fields and houses. The Imperial Secretaries 中書 memorialized, ' Let the officials in charge formulate the regulations.' LI Chung 李重 said: ' . . . The proposals of both [K'UNG] Kuang and [Hsü] Kan mentioned by [T'IEN] Ho were to deal with troubles in an age of decay when people became extravagant. However, at the beginning of the glorious period of the Han no such regulations were discussed. [K'UNG] Kuang and others formulated the rules but did not put them into effect. [The problem] was not overlooked and neglected; but [the regulations] were not adopted in spite of their feasibility. Because the proper course to be followed by feudal lords has disappeared and the *ching-t'ien* 井田 system [70] had not been restored, the laws of the rulers should not restrict people's property. Since there are no restrictions on people's fields and houses, the number of slaves owned should not be regulated in particular. It is feared that laws would be formulated in vain and the actual cases would prove too minute to investigate. . . .' A decree followed his advice." Actually the

[67] CS 26.13a-b. [68] CS 26.13b-14a.

[69] 46.19a-20a. The time was somewhere between 277 and 290.

[70] A system of land allotment which according to tradition existed in ancient China. For important references on *ching-t'ien* cf. Henri MASPERO: *La Chine Antique* 109-10; *Tōyō rekishi daijiden* 東洋歷史大辭典 5.163-4.

dynasty adopted a mild policy of limitation as shown in the *Shih-huo chih*.

The establishment of private ownership of land has generally been dated as the middle of the fourth century B. C. when the Ch'in state began to abolish the so-called *ching-t'ien* system and permit the sale and purchase of land by the people.[71] This economic revolution in China was completed in a few centuries and large landlords began to appear. In c. 120 B. C. the famous Confucian scholar TUNG Chung-shu 董仲舒 first advocated the limitation of land-ownership but his proposal was not carried out.[72] In 7 B. C. a law was drafted that all people from the princes down should not own land beyond the limit of 30 *ch'ing*.[73] K'UNG Kuang, as prime minister, headed the memorial for its proclamation. Powerful families and court favorites however did not like the law, and it was not enforced. Then came the famous nationalization of land under WANG Mang in 9 A. D. and its abolition three years later.[74] The proposal of Hsü Kan is not recorded in *San Kuo chih*, but one made by SSŬ-MA Lang 朗 in c. 215 to restore the *ching-t'ien* system may have been related to it.[75] It was defeated also. Thus the limitation policy was never fully carried out.

Under the Chin dynasty public mountains and swamps were often enclosed by powerful families and as a consequence poor people were deprived of the privilege of gathering fuel or fishing there. The government proclaimed laws to forbid such enclosure; under the Eastern Chin a law issued in 336 made it subject to the death penalty.[76] The barbarian ruler SHIH Hu 石虎 in North China in c. 340 also decreed prohibition of enclosure by nobles and officials.[77] But " occupation of mountains " 占山 could not be stopped. In c. 457 the Sung dynasty in South China had to accept the fact and merely set proportional limits to enclosure of mountains and swamps by officials and others at three *ch'ing* or less.[78]

[71] *Han shu* 24A. 15a.
[72] *Han shu* 24A. 15b.
[73] *Han shu* 11. 3a; 24A. 18b-19a.
[74] *Han shu* 24A. 20a; 99B. 10a, 23b.
[75] SKC 15. 5b.
[76] *Sung shu* 54. 7a.
[77] CS 106. 10b.
[78] See note 76.

One thing worth noting is that these regulations, though not enforced, were based upon a traditional idea which favored government redress of evils even through interference with private ownership of land. Although LI Chung offered objection, the time-honored saying in the Classics that " under the whole heaven every spot is the sovereign's ground " [79] remained the guiding principle. In theory the government was free to adopt a limitation policy, whereas in practice vested interests oftentimes hindered its adoption.

The paragraph on the people's land in *Chin shu* 26.13b has been translated by CH'ÊN Huan-chang 陳煥章 [80] as follows:

> "Among all the people, each man was given seventy acres [*mu*] of land 占田, and each woman thirty acres. Besides these 其外, for the regular adults [16-60 years of age], the man was given fifty acres of taxed land which was required to pay the land tax 課田, the woman twenty acres; for the secondary adults [13-15 or 61-65 years], the man was given twenty-five acres of land, and the woman was given nothing."

According to his interpretation, which is probably based upon that in *Wên-hsien t'ung-k'ao* 文獻通考,[81] the expression *chan t'ien* was used to mean *shou t'ien* 授田 " to allot land " or " to be allotted land." Thus he says, " by this law, from sixteen to sixty years of age, every man got a hundred twenty acres of land and every woman fifty acres."

This traditional interpretation, followed by Mabel Ping-hua LEE,[82] has not been accepted by other modern scholars. In direct opposition to it, several Japanese scholars maintain that the whole paragraph was on limitations set to private ownership by the common people and no allotment was made at all.[83] Some others, however, support the Chinese traditional view in considering the regulations as bearing on allotments but make the modification that the 70 *mu* and 50 *mu* were not for the same adult. For

[79] *Book of Songs* and *Mencius,* LEGGE 2.228; 4.360.
[80] *The Economic Principles of Confucius and his School* (1911) 509.
[81] *Shih t'ung* ed. 2.38a.
[82] *The Economic History of China* (1921) 193.
[83] Names and works listed by SHIDA Fudōmaro, SZ 43.1.32.

example, SHIDA Fudōmaro suggests that the 70 were allotted to the head of a household while the 50 were allotted to each of the other male adults in the household.[84] Whose interpretation is correct?

It is to be noted that there are three key expressions in the paragraph, namely, *chan t'ien* " to occupy or take possession of land," *k'o t'ien* " to allot or assign land," and *ch'i wai* " besides." According to my view, each group of the Japanese scholars have grasped only half of the truth in understanding the first two expressions. Both have pushed their interpretation too far because they misunderstand *ch'i wai* by " other " instead of " besides." [85] The regulations were on both limitations and allotments.

The word *chan*, as illustrated in the preceding cases of *chan t'ien* and *chan shan* for officials and nobles, is used here as a technical term for occupation or holding. According to YEN Shih-ku 顔師古 [86] it was equivalent to the term *ming t'ien* 名田 " to own land " used under the Han. Similar use of *chan* may also be found in later times.[87] Thus a better way to render the first sentence in this paragraph may be: " A male may hold 70 *mu* of land and a female 30 *mu*." This part of the regulation apparently was not the main interest of the government because no age-groups are specified here. Actually this limitation may not always have been necessary because most of the people must have owned less.

The 50 *mu* per male adult and 20 *mu* per female adult probably constituted the allotments, or the amounts of land the government expected the people to work. Here the traditional interpretation seems to hold. " Because the great empire had only a sparse population, because landownership was either destroyed or changed, and because the land practically belonged to the government, Wu Ti was enabled to distribute the land to the people." [88] This summary by CH'ÊN Huan-chang is good except

[84] *Tōyō rekishi daijiden* 4.450.

[85] It is noteworthy that *T'ung tien* 1.12b omits the *wai*.

[86] *Han shu* 24A.15b, commentary.

[87] For example: *Wei shu* 53.11a, 110.14b; *Sung shu* 6.23b; *Liang shu* 3.19b; *T'ung tien* 2.15b.

[88] *The Economic Principles of Confucius and his School* 508-9.

that one must remember the limits in the enforcement of regulations. The description in *Chin shu* 26.3b that the land in all
corners of the empire was received by the people is certainly
exaggerated.

The expression *k'o t'ien* " to allot or assign land " is also a
technical term. The method of *k'o t'ien* can be traced back at
least to the first part of the third century. In a memorial offered
by a Chin official in 268,[89] we read:

" Formerly at the beginning of the Wei, the policy of land
assignments 課田 was intensive rather than extensive. As a
result, in dry fields the annual harvest reached as high as over
ten *hu* per *mu*,[90] while in water-fields, the harvest was scores
of *hu* per *mu*. Recently, however, the assigned acreage has been
increased day by day. This is especially true in the case of
agricultural soldiers. The cultivation can no longer be intensive
and the harvest becomes even less than a few *hu*, sometimes
not enough to pay for the seed."

This seems to suggest that the *k'o t'ien* method was used for
both agricultural soldiers and ordinary people, and their assignments were different. As we shall see in the next section levies
were imposed on ordinary citizens and government tenants at
different rates. The assignments specified in the *Shih-huo chih*
probably were for the ordinary citizens of the empire.

A Chinese scholar has offered the interpretation that the people
under the Chin dynasty were all made government tenants at
least in theory.[91] This is unlikely. But one has good reason to
assume that the method of *k'o t'ien* may have been first used in
military colonies and later extended to ordinary citizens. In his

[89] CS 47.3b.

[90] 1 *hu* or *shih* = 10 *tou* = 100 shêng.

    1 Han *hu* = 19968.753 cc.

              = 1218.5608 cu. in.

              = 0.565 U. S. bushel.

    1 Chin *hu* = 20234.92 cc.

              = 0.570 U. S. bushel.

[91] CH'IEN Mu 錢穆 in his *Kuo-shih ta-kang* 國史大綱 1.227 offers the interpretation that the 50 and 20 *mu* for each couple formed a part of the above 70 and
30 *mu*, and the product from the 50 and 20 *mu* was to go entirely to the government.

famous memorial for the establishment of agricultural colonies in 61 B. C., CHAO Ch'ung-kuo 趙充國 proposed to assign 20 *mu* to each soldier. The verb for " assign " used by him was *fu* 賦 a synonym of *k'o*.[92]

In a time of emergency under the Eastern Chin a petition was offered in c. 324 [93] to require local officials to be responsible for special assignments. According to the proposal a government-general 都督 was to get tenants for 20 *ch'ing* of land, a governor 10 *ch'ing*, a prefect 5 *ch'ing*, and a magistrate 3 *ch'ing*. The tenants were to be drawn from civil and military officers, physicians, and diviners, whereas the people should not be disturbed. Evidently this was a movement to increase the agricultural population.

To render *k'o t'ien* by " taxed land " is incorrect and to do so is to miss an important political ideal behind the expression. According to tradition to assign work is a part of the rôle of a good government. MENCIUS says, " Let the people be employed in the way which is intended to secure their ease, and though they toil, they will not murmur." [94] This means, the people should be put to work properly so that they could earn their livelihood. Good officials, like good teachers, were to assign works for those under them, encourage them, and supervise them. They were " to be an example to the people and to reward them." [95] Plenty of examples may be found in the biographies of model officials 循吏傳 in the dynastic histories. The assignments could be very specific and go into details like the amount of vegetables to be planted by each person and the number of household animals to be kept by each family.[96] From our text we learn how perfect YEN Fei in c. 223 assigned his people to learn the art of carpentry and to teach it to one another.[97] In the biography of CHÊNG Hun of the same period he is recorded, as a magistrate, to have seized his people's fishing and hunting tools and assigned them to works of agriculture and sericulture. As a prefect, he assigned his people

[92] *Han shu* 69. 12a.
[93] CS 70. 4b. [94] LEGGE 2. 454.
[95] The *Confucian Analects*. LEGGE's translation 1. 262 is not followed here.
[96] *Han shu* 89. 13b. [97] CS 26. 7a.

to grow fruits, and to plant elm trees in order to make fences.[98] These are only a few typical cases. The continuous effort made by emperors and officials of the Chin to encourage the farmers to give their best is clearly recorded in our text.[99]

The Chin land system has been considered the forerunner of a series of systems of land allotment developed under the Northern Dynasties, the Sui dynasty, and the T'ang. All these alike are known as the *chün t'ien* 均田 system. The regulations for the *chün t'ien* were not always the same in different periods, but can be generalized as follows: A male adult was to receive from the government a certain amount of arable land to work. This allotment was to be returned to the government when the recipient was old or dead. Besides, he could own a smaller amount of land as his household property. A female was to receive about half the allotment of the male. From 624 the allotment per adult male was increased to include that of his wife, and allotments to females were received only by widows.

Certainly the *chün t'ien* and *k'o t'ien* were similar in their objective of securing the people's service. Before launching the *chün t'ien* system in c. 485, the Northern Wei dynasty for over a century repeatedly issued decrees to emphasize assignment and supervision of agricultural work.[100] In a decree of 477 it is clearly stated that a male adult should work 40 *mu* of land and a secondary adult 20 *mu*.[101] Similar amounts were assigned according to the *chün t'ien* system. This policy probably was carried out to a limited extent when the government had large amounts of land on hand. On household registers of the eighth century discovered at Tun-huang, both the legal allotment and the actual holding are recorded for each household, although the people in most cases held only a small portion of what they were entitled to. That the registers from the later part of the ninth century contain no

[98] SKC 16.20b, 22b.

[99] CS 26.9a-10b, 14b-15b.

[100] *Wei shu* 2.2b; 4B.16a; 7A.3a, 18b, 22b; 110.2a. T'ao Hsi-shêng 陶希聖 and Wu Hsien-ch'ing 武仙卿: *Nan Pei Ch'ao ching-chi shih* 南北朝經濟史 (1937, Shanghai) 14-7.

[101] *Wei shu* 7A.10a.

139

record of such allotments shows that the *chün t'ien* system by that time had ceased to serve even in principle.[102]

4. The land-tax system of the Chin dynasty

The land-tax system of the Chin empire is only incompletely recorded. The fragmentary records which have come down to us are so obscure and sometimes so self-contradictory that a satisfactory interpretation of them is hardly feasible. The aim of this note is merely to indicate the problem and to make a few suggestions.

Approaching the end of the Han, Ts'ao Ts'ao in c. 204 A. D. levied a land-tax at the rate of four *shêng* per *mu*.[103] It is not clear whether this rate was applied to all grades of cultivated land or it was only an average. The land-tax through most of the Han period had been one-thirtieth of the product. If we take the average of production at three *hu* per *mu* as estimated by CHUNG-CHANG T'ung 仲長統 at the beginning of the third century, the tax probably amounted to ten *shêng* per *mu*.[104] The low rate fixed by Ts'ao Ts'ao perhaps was meant to afford relief to the people in hard times.

On the other hand, the Wei rulers had no need to pay much attention to the land-tax because their grain supply was assured by large numbers of military and civilian tenants who paid 50 to 60% of their product as rent to the government.[105] This rate was observed through most of the Chin period. Later it may have been changed to a fixed amount.

Among the histories of the Southern Dynasties *Sung shu* 92. 6a quotes a memorial offered by the prefect of Shih-hsing 始

[102] The literature on the *chün t'ien* system is too extensive to be listed here. A general account in English from the traditional point of view may be found in *The Economic Principles of Confucius and his School* 510-24. The T'ang household registers are reprinted in *Shih-huo* 4. 5 (1936) 1-38. Henri MASPERO's article " Les régimes fonciers en Chine," *Recueil de la Société Jean Bodin* (1937), 265-314, is comprehensive, although I do not agree with him in all his views.

[103] CS 26. 5a.

[104] HHS 79. 22b. The average yield, 1 to 1.5 *shih* per *mu*, estimated by W. EBERHARD (" Bermerkungen zu statistischen Angaben der Han-Zeit " *TP* 36, 1940, 4-5) seems too low for this period.

[105] CS 47. 5b.

與 [106] in 426. This memorial mentions that in the prefecture officers working on the great fields 大田武吏 [107] were taxed at the rate of 60 *hu* [108] per man reaching 16 years of age and 30 *hu* per boy from 13 to 15 years of age. The Northern Wei dynasty also, upon the suggestion of an official in 488, selected one-tenth of the people to be government tenants. They were given cattle and exempted from the regular levies, corvée, and military service. Each of them was to pay 60 *hu* per year.[109] The identical rate of 60 *hu* probably formed about 60 or 50% of the produce of one adult. This should not be confused with the ordinary land-tax.[110]

That the Chin levied some kind of land-tax from the beginning of the dynasty is unquestionable. The words *tsu* 租 and *t'ien-tsu* were used in decrees granting exemptions as early as the sixth (270) and the eighth (272) years of the first emperor.[111] Similar edicts were issued in 282, 283, and 304.[112] But in what form was the land-tax imposed? What was the rate? Was Ts'ao Ts'ao's rate at four *shêng* per *mu* adopted? Was there a levy payable in grain imposed upon the household or the individual as under some later dynasties?

As we shall see, although the term *t'ien-tsu* usually meant levy on land by the *mu*, the term *tsu* was used in the Chin and some later periods to mean grain payable either by the *mu*, or by the household or individual. The lack of precise nomenclature in taxation is comparable to that in the Later Roman Empire, when the term *capitatio* could mean a land-tax on defined fiscal units, a collateral tax assessed upon the human and animal power at work on the unit, or a poll-tax imposed upon all the cultivating classes.[113]

[106] Near Ch'ü-chiang 曲江 in northern Kwangtung.

[107] *Ta t'ien,* " great fields," is first used in the *Book of Songs,* LEGGE 3.380. Here it probably refers to the government farms.

[108] *T'ung tien* 4.27c reads 16 *hu,* which is obviously an error.

[109] *Wei shu* 110.9a.

[110] *Wên-hsien t'ung-k'ao* 10.108a-b, failing to compare the two cases under the Northern and Southern Dynasties, misunderstands the 60 *hu* in 426 as land-tax, and suggests that the amount might be the levy for more than a year.

[111] CS 3.11a, 12b.   [112] *Nan Pei Ch'ao ching-chi shih* 66.

[113] *The Cambridge Economic History of Europe from the Decline of the Roman Empire* 1.106-7.

Before discussing a bewildering document on the land-tax of the Western Chin (265-317), we may begin with the Eastern Chin (317-420), a period for which the land-tax has more records although they are not always clear. The tax system of the Eastern Chin is outlined in *Sui shu* 24. 4b:

" The levies on each adult male were

[1] 2 *chang* of cloth or silk, 3 *liang* of raw silk, 8 *liang* of floss; [114]
3 *ch'ih* of [woven] salary silk [i. e. silk for salaries of officials],
3.2 *liang* of salary floss; [115]

[2] 5 *shih* of *tsu* rice [or husked grain], and 2 *shih* of salary rice.

An adult female was to pay half these amounts. . . . The land was taxed at the rate of 2 *tou* [read: *shêng*] [116] per *mu*. It was probably like this in general."

It seems clear that grain imposts were levied on two different bases: as a kind of poll-tax at 5 *shih* plus 2 additional *shih* per adult male, and as a land-tax at 2 *shêng* per *mu*. However, the annals and *Shih-huo chih* of *Chin shu* both seem to suggest that the two ways were not employed simultaneously. According to *Chin shu* a tax of 3 *shêng* per *mu* was levied in 330, when fields of the people were surveyed for the first time. The rate was reduced to 2 *shêng* per *mu* in 362. The system of levying taxes in proportion to land measurement was abolished in 377, and 3 *hu* were collected from each person " from the princes and dukes down." Five *hu* were levied on each individual in 383.[117] Of the four rates only those of 362 and 383 agree with *Sui shu*.

A simple way to reconcile the two histories is probably to assume that the system recorded in *Sui shu* was the form in use after 383.

[114] 16 *liang* = 1 *chih*

1 [Chin dynasty] *liang* = 13.92 g.

[115] *Ts'ê-fu yüan-kuei* 册府元龜 504.30b considers these levies payable in silk and floss as of the Eastern Chin and all the Southern Dynasties 江左自晉至陳.

[116] *T'ung tien* 5.29c and *Ts'ê-fu yüan-kuei* 487.9a both have *shêng*. *Tou* probably is an error. In ancient texts the two characters *shêng* and *tou* are easily misread because of their resemblance in writing. Cf. Ku Yen-wu 顧炎武: *Chin-shih wên-tzŭ chi* 金石文字記 (亭林先生遺書彙輯 ed.) 3.4b-5b; Tschen Yin-koh 陳寅恪: 讀秦婦吟 CHHP 11.4 (1936) 964-6.

[117] CS 7.6a; 8.12a; 9.9a, 12a; 26.16a-b.

142

In *T'ung tien* 4.27c, 5.29c and *Wên-hsien t'ung-k'ao* 2.38a, 11. 119c these records from *Chin shu* and *Sui shu* are quoted only separately and thus no comment is made on their differences. However, MA Tuan-lin makes the following remark of alarm on the change in 377: [118]

"According to the Chin institution, an adult male received 70 *mu* of land. The levy on each individual would be 2.1 *hu* if the rate was 3 *shêng* per *mu*, and 1.4 *hu* if the rate was 2 *shêng* per *mu*. Now although the tax based on measured fields was abolished, the levy on each individual was fixed at 3 *hu* and even raised to 5 *hu*. The burden seems to be very heavy. Could it be that the phrase 'from the princes and dukes down' did not include the mass recipients of allotments [for cultivation]?"

T'AO Hsi-shêng and WU Hsien-ch'ing [119] disagree with MA's interpretation that the changes in 377 and 383 meant heavier taxes. They hold the opinion that taxes were reduced in 377 by combination of two levies payable in grain into one, and explain the prosperity in the last years of Emperor Hsiao-wu (373-396) as a result of the lighter burden on the people. Their assumption is that the tax-system recorded in *Sui shu* was adopted prior to 377 and probably from the beginning of the Eastern Chin. Thus a tax of 5 *shih* per adult male had been levied along with a land-tax at 2 or 3 *shêng* per *mu* until the two levies were combined and reduced to a tax at 3 *hu* per person in 377.

I agree with T'AO and WU in considering the change in 377 as a combination of two levies into one, but it does not necessarily follow that the tax system recorded in *Sui shu* was adopted prior to 377. We have records that a fixed amount of 4 *hu* was collected from each adult under the Western Chin. [120] It seems reasonable to assume that the same rate was also observed in the early part of the Eastern Chin period up to 377. Accordingly during the period between 362 and 377 there may have been a double levy of grain at the rate of 4 *hu* per adult male and 3 or 2 *shêng* per *mu*. The low rate of 3 *hu* per individual in 377 was probably to facili-

[118] *Wên-hsien t'ung-k'ao* 2.38a-b.
[119] *Nan Pei Ch'ao ching-chi shih* 51-2.
[120] See below, text following footnote 125.

tate the inclusion of the nobles and officials who were usually exempted from the payment.

Examples of occasional double levy of grain can also be found under later dynasties. That the people paid both the *tsu* (2 *shih* per person) and the *ti-shui* 地稅 (2 *shêng* per *mu* of cultivated land) simultaneously through a great part of the first half of the T'ang period has been pointed out.[121] For earlier periods the tax system is not always clear. Unless the system of the Eastern Chin described in *Sui shu* was followed by the Southern Dynasties as suggested in *Ts'ê-fu yüan-kuei* 504.30b, very little about the taxation of the latter is known. This suggestion is supported by a decree in 580 under the Ch'ên dynasty, which mentions separately the *t'ien-shui* (land-tax) and *ting-tsu* (grain payable per adult).[122] Under the Northern Dynasties grain was first levied per household and later per married couple, but a land-tax of 5 *shêng* per *mu* was collected on fields near the capital Lo-yang in 526.[123] It is not improbable that a double levy of grain was imposed simultaneously at least during some period of the Eastern Chin.

As for the Western Chin there is no record of the rate of imperial land-tax in *Chin shu*. The only information is the following paragraph from the T'ang encyclopaedia *Ch'u-hsüeh chi* 初學記 [124] which quotes the *Chin ku-shih* 晉故事: [125]

[121] HAMAGUCHI Shigekuni 濱口重國: 唐の地稅に就いて *TG* 20.1 (1932) 138-48; T'AO Hsi-shêng and CHÜ Ch'ing-yüan: *T'ang tai ching-chi shih* 唐代經濟史 (1936, Shanghai) 143-6. BALÁZS: Beiträge zur Wirtschaftsgeschichte der T'ang-Zeit, *MSOS* 34 (1931) overlooks this point and thus finds no satisfactory interpretation of Tu Yu's revenue estimation of both *tsu* and *ti-shui* (*T'ung tien* 6.36a) on p. 34 and misidentifies *ti-shui* with *tsu* on p. 83 in his translation of a decree in 763. His punctuation of the decree is also incorrect. It should read 一戶之中、三丁放一丁庸調、地稅依舊每畝稅二升 "In one household the *yung* (commutation for corvée) and *tiao* (levies payable in terms of silk or cloth, etc.) of one out of every three adults should be exempted. The *ti-shui* should be collected at the usual rate of 2 *shêng* per *mu*."

[122] *Ch'ên shu* 5.22b.

[123] *Wei shu* 110.13b.

[124] Ku-hsiang chai 古香齋 ed. 27.19b.

[125] *Sui shu* 33.1a mentions *Chin ku-shih* in 43 chapters. The work is now preserved only in fragments. This paragraph is not seen in other encyclopaedias and is not well known to students of Chinese economic history.

" Each adult is assigned [or expected to work] 50 *mu* of land. [From him] are collected 4 *hu* [of grain] as *tsu*, [and from the household] 3 *p'i* of silk and 3 *chin* of floss. If [he and his household] belong to a noble, the *tsu* grain shall be reduced by 1 *tou* [read: *shêng*] per *mu*.[126] The deduction shall be translated into silk for the noble at the rate of 1 *p'i* per household. The silk is to be the salary (*chih* 秩) of the noble. Also 2 *hu* of the *tsu* from each household shall be transferred as the provision (*fêng* 奉) of the noble.[127] The remaining *tsu* and the old [established] levies of 3 *p'i* of silk and 3 *chin* of floss from every [omit the " two "][128] household are to be recorded as state imposts. In keeping with the harmonious relationship among the nine grades [of households] 九品相通, the payments shall be made to the government following the old institutions."

This paragraph throws light on a few questions but it raises more. The assignment of 50 *mu* per adult male, and the levies of 3 *p'i* of silk and 3 *chin* of floss agree with the institution of the Western Chin in *Chin shu* 26. 13b. Thus we have good reason to assume that this paragraph deals with regulations of that period.

[126] *Tou* is in apparent contradiction to the deduction rate stated below when the farmer belonged to a noble.

[127] This would be a valuable indication of the official rate of exchange between silk and grain at this time if we knew the number of adults which constituted a household. A few examples from the T'ang period may help us to understand the fluctuations of the ratio. The official rate for paying cloth for the grain levy *tsu* varied with the grades of the households in favor of taxpayers in lower graded households. The average was about 3 *tuan* 端 (1 *tuan* = 5 *chang*) to 2 *shih* (*T'ung tien* 6. 34a). A *tuan* of cloth was supposed to be the equivalent of a *p'i* of silk in tax payment under the Sui and T'ang dynasties. Thus, the rate was about one *p'i* of silk to two-thirds of a *shih* of grain. In 780 one *p'i* of silk was valued at two *shih* of grain. In about 810 the rate was one *p'i* to four *shih,* and in about 820 it was one *p'i* to 1.6 *shih* (*Ch'üan T'ang wên* 634. 3b, 8a-b). If we take one *p'i* to two *shih* as the Chin average rate, it would require four adults in one household to make the total deducation of their land-tax (4 × 50 × 1 *shêng* = 200 *shêng* = 2 *shih*) the equivalent of one *p'i* of silk per household for the noble. The noble's share was probably about one-third of the original levies in accordance with CS 14. 12a. Prof. J. R. WARE considers this a very clever method to make the noble responsible for the size of households in his district: he would not allow them to become too large and include too many adults.

[128] The mention of two households does not fit in very well with the so-called old levies and the deduction rate. The number " two " appears like an interpolation.

The record of 4 *hu* tax is valuable because no other statement of the rate is known. It has been suggested that these 4 *hu* were levied on the 70 *mu* to which each adult male was entitled and on the 30 *mu* for his wife, so the rate was exactly 4 *shêng* per *mu* identical with that of Ts'ao Ts'ao.[129] However, there seems no justification for setting aside the 50 specified in our text and substituting for them the 70 and 30 from another text.

How the nine grades of households were distinguished is not known, yet the Ch'üan-nung fu 勸農賦 written by Shu Hsi 束皙 in the Western Chin period [130] may be giving us a description, satirical to be sure, of the procedure whereby the government periodically determined these categories: " The established officials of a district are various and enjoy different functions, but if we study these lowly positions in government, we shall find that none is more fair than that of the officer who encourages the farmers. His power is absolute over the whole village and everybody in it. When the green banners [131] [are erected to] restrict wanderers and idlers, and when taxes on land are being assigned by acreage, the size of the assessment is determined by himself alone and full say regarding the quality of the land is his. The winning of his favor depends upon [gifts of] rich meat, and the securing of his support upon good wine. When the harvest work is finished and the levies are to be made, and he gathers the head men of the village and summons the chiefs of the hamlets to register holdings and name, —chickens and pigs fight their way to him and bottles and containers of wine arrive from all directions. Then it is that a ' one ' can become a ' ten ' or a ' five ' a ' two.' I suppose this is because hot food is twisting his belly and Bacchus obstructing his stomach!"

Under the Northern Wei, a decree in 435 ordered the local officers to adjust the levies according to the people's property by

[129] Ch'üan Han-shêng: *CYYY* 10.1 (1943) 120-1.

[130] *Ch'üan Chin wên* 全晉文 87.2a-b. The *ch'üan-nung* officer is also mentioned in HHS 38.6a.

[131] It was a practice under the Han to erect green banners outside the city gate from the first day of Spring to encourage production by sympathetic magic. Toward the end of the Han officers even carried banners on their shoulders. Cf. HHS 14.2a; *Yen-t'ieh lun* 鹽鐵論 (*Ssŭ-pu ts'ung-k'an* ed.) 6.18b (not trans. yet); Wang Ts'an's 王粲 *Wu-pên lun* 務本論 in *Ch'üan Hou Han wên* 91.5b.

nine grades 九品混通.[132] This *hun-t'ung* is certainly synonymous with *hsiang-t'ung*. The adjustment was in force until about 485 when the famous *chün-t'ien* system was introduced. The nine grades of the Northern Wei may have been copied from the Chin.[133]

The system of taxation adopted by two self-styled rulers toward the end of the Western Chin may have reference value. The barbarian leader SHIH Lo in North China levied 2 *p'i* of cloth or silk and 2 *shih* of grain per household in 313.[134] LI Hsiung 李雄, a leader of rebel vagrants in Szechuan, taxed 3 *hu* from each adult male and 1.5 *hu* from each adult female. Each household was to pay a few *chang* of silk and a few *liang* of floss. These were considered low rates.

With the limited information available we have to be satisfied with the few general remarks made by MA Tuan-lin in relation to the land-tax system of the Chin:

(1) " In the Han and previous periods the land-tax and levies on the household or individual were separated from each other. It seems that they have been mixed together only since the Wei and Chin times." [136]

(2) " The levies on the household became very heavy from the time of the Wei and Chin. This tendency was continued through the Northern Dynasties to the Sui and the T'ang. In general, many regulations applied to levies on the household and only a few to levies on land." [137]

[132] *Wei shu* 4A. 18a, 110. 4b. T'AO and WU in their *Nan Pei Ch'ao ching-chi shih* 70 explain the term *chiu-p'in hun-t'ung* as a levy of equal amount upon each household in disregard of the nine grades.

[133] A peculiar mistake appears on the two pages 18b and 19a of *Ch'u-hsüeh chi*, which contains various quotations relative to silk. On p. 18b before the paragraph from *Chin ku-shih* about one line is quoted from the Han work *Ssŭ-min yüeh-ling*, before which again there is the bare title *Hou Wei shu* (i. e. *Wei shu*) without any quotation. However, on p. 19a after a paragraph quoted from *Chin ling* 晉令, there are about three lines which record an old regulation on width and length of silk and cloth and the later disregard of the regulation. The words are almost identical with those in *Wei shu* 110. 4b. The title *Hou Wei shu* probably should be moved here according to the chronological order of the quotations.

[134] CS 104. 20a.

[135] CS 121. 6a. *T'ung chien* 89. 2b-3a records this in 314.

[136] *Wên-hsien t'ung-k'ao* 10. 108a-b.   [137] *Ibid.* 3. 48b.

MA's interpretation is that under these dynasties each household was supposed to have received an allotment of land from the government, so that land-tax could be collected as a part of the levies on household. This may have been true. But two other reasons may also be suggested. First, a light land-tax or no land-tax would encourage cultivation of land when large amounts of it had become waste as a result of frequent disturbances. Secondly, to secure an adequate revenue a land-tax requires survey and registration of the holdings, which always proves a tremendous task for an empire, especially when it is declining.

Translation of *Chin shu* 26

[(1) Introduction]

[1a] In ancient times the early kings measured and surveyed the land in order to form towns and settle the people.[1] The duties of the people were regulated in accordance with the Three Primordial Forces 三才.[2] Regard was paid to the four seasons so that the work of the people could be completed. After inspecting folk songs and local customs, [The kings] established law and order. The fundamental occupations of agriculture and the raising of silkworms were encouraged. The profit of fishery and the salt industry was promoted. People climbed rich mountains to mine jade and sailed over great seas to net pearls. Midday was made the market hour, and in their market were gathered the folk of the world.[3] First cloth and silk were introduced [as media of exchange] and coined money followed in use. The people traded what they had for what they had not, and every one acquired what he desired.

According to *Chou li* in the first moon when the weather began to become pleasant, instructions were proclaimed on the imperial city gate 象魏 [4] regarding the adult farmer, homesteads of ten *mu*,[5] the three days' corvée,[6] and taxes adjusted according to the nine grades of land.[7] Rites based on the *yang* principle were practised to raise the spirit of humility.[8] Spring sacrifice to the god of the soil was ordered to be offered to encourage the cultivation of the land.

---

[1] LEGGE: *Lî kî* (*SBE* 27) 1.230. [2] Heaven, earth, and man.

[3] The two sentences were based upon *I ching* (LEGGE: *Yi king* 383) and *Han shu* 24A.1b where we have 致天下之民、聚天下之貨. *Li* 隸 probably was used here to take the place of *min* 民, which was a T'ang taboo.

[4] BIOT: *Tcheou li* 1.210.

[5] It is not clear how many families lived on these ten *mu*. Mencius mentions twice 'homesteads with their five *mu*' probably for one family (LEGGE: *Chinese Classics* 2.149, 461). *Han shu* 24A.2b records twenty *mu* for eight households. The *Book of Songs* describes mulberry-planters 'among their ten *mu*' (LEGGE: ibid. 4.169). LEGGE suggests that the ten *mu* may have been reduced from the original twenty.

[6] LEGGE: *Lî kî* 1.227.

[7] BIOT: 1.199. [8] BIOT: 1.196.

[1b] What heaven values is the human being. What the wise seek is learning.[9] To study the classics and to join the officials are the ways of the gentleman. The *Book of Songs* reads, " In the days of [our] third month, they take their ploughs in hand; in the days of [our] fourth month, they take their way to the field." [10] Hence the officials in charge of agriculture and the inspector of marshes 澤虞 [11] each had their proper duty. People readily learned the trades of their fathers and elder brothers.[12] When a boy reached the age of fifteen,[13] he entered his trade and began to be able to wear the dress [of the grown man]. No idlers were found in the country side; neither was time wasted in the town. This is what is meant by " In the beginning each person had his own task." Therefore, T'ai-kung 太公 [14] by facilitating the exchange of commodities in the market succeeded in making Ch'i 齊 a great power. Ch'ih-i 鴟夷,[15] being skilled at storing and selling at the proper times, expanded his extensive business at T'ao 陶, the central place [of China].[16]

The ancient ruler Chin-t'ien 金天 [17] was industrious in his people's affairs. He ordered his official called the Spring Bird to take care of tilling and farming, and summoned the Summer Bird to be in charge of weeding and spading. The Autumn Bird was intrusted with harvesting and collecting, and the Winter Bird with covering and storing. The *Book of History* relates [the ancient ruler Yao ordered his officials] " to calculate and delineate the movements and appearances of the sun, the moon, the stars, and the zodiacal spaces; and so to deliver respectfully the seasons to

[9] CSCC 26.1b suggests that *ming* 明 probably was substituted for *min* 民. But *Ch'ien-fu lun* 潛夫論 (*Ssŭ-pu pei-yao* ed.) 1a has 天地之所貴者人也...明智之所求者學問也.

[10] LEGGE: *Chinese Classics* 4.226. For the Classics Legge's translation is adopted unless it is erroneous.

[11] BIOT 1.374-5.

[12] *Kuo yü* (*Ssŭ-pu ts'ung-k'an* ed.) 6.3b-5a; *Kuan tzŭ* 管子 (*Ssŭ-pu ts'ung-k'an* ed.) 8.6a-b.

[13] BIOT 1.242.

[14] CHIANG T'ai-kung or CHIANG Shang 姜尚, biog. *Shih chi* 32.1a-4a; GILES 343.

[15] Name assumed by FAN Li 范蠡, biog. *Shih chi* 129.4a-b; GILES 540.

[16] Near the present Ting-t'ao 定陶 in the southwestern part of Shantung.

[17] Better known as Shao-hao 少昊. His officials named after birds are fully described in *Tso chuan*, LEGGE 5.667.

the people." [18] Our tradition says, " Yü 禹 and Chi 稷 personally wrought at the toils of husbandry, and they became possessors of the kingdom." [19]

When the nine provinces had been laid out [by Yü], the four classes of people 四民 [20] all received the instructions [of their rulers]. Wu 吳 in the east [21] was abundant in ivory and horns; Shu 蜀 in the west [22] was rich in cinnabar. Yen 兖 and Yü 豫 [23] were storehouses of varnish and silk; Yen 燕 and Ch'i 齊 [24] were the home of precious stones. In Ch'in 秦 and Pin 邠 [25] there were streamers and plumes, and also good jade from adjacent areas. [2a] In Ching 荊 and Ying 郢 [26] there were cassia groves,[27] and bamboos and other materials to make arrows nearby. Along the Yangtze river one found oranges and pummeloes, and to the other side of the Yellow river 河外 [28] boats and wagons. To the west of the Liao river were villages rich in manufacture of felt. To the right [i. e. to the west] of the Ts'ung-ling 葱嶺 were steeds like *P'u-shao* 蒲梢.[29] Of all kinds of curious and miscellaneous things produced there was nothing one could not find [in China].

[The ancient rulers] took heavenly lessons from the movements of the stars and other astronomical phenomena, while their less elevated thoughts were centred upon their boundless empire. They made use of the benefits given by heaven and earth, and gathered riches from the mountains and the seas. Each farmer was allotted one hundred *mu* of land, from which ten per cent of

---

[18] LEGGE 3.18.

[19] From the *Confucian Analects,* LEGGE 1.277.

[20] Officials, agriculturalists, artisans, and traders. *Kuo yü* 6.3b; *Han shu* 24A.2a.

[21] Roughly modern Kiangsu province.

[22] Szechuan.

[23] Honan and western Shantung.   [25] Shensi.

[24] Hopei and eastern Shantung.   [26] Hupei.

[27] Kuei-lin 桂林, ' cassia groves,' may be a place name, roughly the modern Kuangsi. It is sometimes used to mean the precious things produced there. For example, *Yen-t'ieh lun* has the statements, " Pearls and ivory are produced in Kuei-lin," and " In Ching [and] Yang there is the fertile land [rather ' riches ' or ' wealth '] of Kuei-lin to the south " (Esson M. GALE: *Discourses on Salt and Iron* 15, 19).

[28] The term *Ho-wai* was used on different occasions to mean Shensi, Shansi, or Honan. It is not clear which side of the Yellow river was meant here.

[29] Steed acquired by Emperor Wu of the Han from Ta-yüan 大宛. *Shih-chi* 24.3b. CHAVANNES 3.237.

the product was taken as taxes. After nine years of (personal) farming there would be a storage of food enough for three years. This surplus could be used to bring up children and to provide for the aged. Revenue was received from the people and used for the nation. Palaces were built according to regulation; flags and insignia were made for different ranks. Court-visits were carried out with proper ceremony; banquets were given in accordance with instituted custom. Families became rich and the nation prosperous. People from afar were attracted to come and those nearby lived in peace. Disasters of flood and drought were relieved and the world's defects were taken care of. Only then would the ruler enjoy at intervals the playing of calabash organs and bells during his every-day meals. The rise of the Shang and the Chou dynasties was because of the adoption of this course.

[The last ruler of the Shang, Shou] Hin 受辛, or Chou 紂, was tyrannous and paid no attention to his regular expenditure. His palace Ch'ing Kung 傾宮, [decorated] with gold and carvings, stretched for one hundred li.[30] His jade [adorned] terrace Lu T'ai 鹿臺 had a height of one thousand jên 仞.[31] In his palaces there were nine markets each under a female director. The king levied heavy taxes to accumulate money on the Lu Terrace, and collected vast amounts of grain to increase the store in the granary called Chü Ch'iao 鉅橋. He sent for glamorous and charming girls to fill the Ch'ing Palace with beauties, and gathered from far and near precious curios to provide for his entertainments at Sha-ch'iu 沙丘. [2b] Meat was hung like a forest and liquor was accumulated to form a pond. In and about the forest and pond naked men and women were ordered to chase one another. Those who crawled to the wine pond to drink like cattle numbered over three thousand. In his palace seats were made of brocade, and mats of silk gauze.[32]

After the Chou king had Chou executed, he saluted respectfully the old site of the Yin, and ordered that all the money in the Lu

[30] The description here is apparently exaggerated.

[31] An ancient measure, traditionally equivalent to eight ch'ih.

[32] This long description of the life of Chou was largely based upon Shih chi 3. 10b-11a (CHAVANNES 1. 199-201). Other versions are collected in MA Su's 馬驌 I shih 繹史 (1889 P'u's 浦氏 ed.) 19. 12a-b.

Terrace and all the grain in the Chü Ch'iao should be granted for relief. With this good fortune from heaven the Yin people were greatly pleased.

Approaching the end of the Chou, King Nuan 赧 removed the capital to Hsi Chou 西周.[33] The nine tripods were all lost.[34] [The old tradition described in] the first two chapters of the *Book of Songs*[35] had passed to decay. The King borrowed from his subjects but had nothing to pay back. Then he climbed a storied terrace to avoid meeting his creditors, so that the Chou people called the king's residence Debt-refuge Terrace.

Formerly [at the beginning of the Chou] the Duke of Chou formulated the six codes of administration. The official *chih-fang shih* 職方氏, or director of regions,[36] made reports on the nine kinds of tribute.[37] Supplies were handled by the imperial treasury. This was to be a permanent measure. [Later] when the judicial and executive administration declined, the tribute three-ribbed rush 菁茅 rarely arrived.[38] The Marquis of Lu began to tax land by the *mu*.[39] The ruler of Ch'in levied taxes amounting to two-thirds of the people's income.[40] Nothing of the good pattern of the former kings was left.

The official historian says, PAN Ku 班固 wrote the *ch'ih-* [*shih-*] *huo chih* 殖, which, covering the period from the Three Dynasties to the execution of WANG Mang 王莽, gives complete details from the old records.

[33] The city was called Wang-ch'êng 王城, to the northwest of the present Lo-yang.

[34] According to *Shih chi* 4.39a (CHAVANNES 1.317) the nine tripods were lost to the Ch'in only after the death of King Nuan.

[35] *Êrh nan* 二南, i.e. *Chou nan* 周 and *Shao nan* 召.

[36] BIOT 2.263-79.   [37] BIOT 1.31-2.

[38] According to *Tso chuan*, Duke Huan of the Ch'i 齊桓公 in 656 B.C. asked the Ch'u 楚 to resume their tribute rush to the Chou. LEGGE 5.140.

[39] *Han shu* 24A.6a.

[40] *Han shu* 24A.7b. According to WEI Chao 韋昭 (*Shih chi* 7.28b, commentary) *t'ai-pan* 太半 means 'two-thirds' and *shao-pan* 少 'one-third.' These terms also appear several times in the Han mathematical work *Chiu-chang suan-shu* 九章算術 (Wei-po Hsieh 微波榭 ed.) 2.5a, 7b, 8a; 3.12a. It is interesting to note that *t'ai-pan* and *shao-pan* are regularly abbreviated to *t'ai* (written as *ta*) and *shao* in the Han wooden documents discovered in Western Kansu (LAO Kan 勞榦: *Chü-yen Han chien k'ao-shih*, shih-wên 居延漢簡考釋、釋文 2.30b-79a). That *t'ai* means two-thirds and *shao* one-third can be verified by simple calculations.

Emperor Kuang-wu 光武 [25-57 A. D.], being generous and kind, respectfully carried out heaven's punishment. After the fall of WANG Mang the bandits called the Red Eyebrows were anew defeated. [3a] Although the Emperor devoted all his days to his duties, the provinces were still in a very poor condition. When the Lung 隴 area [41] had been conquered [34 A. D.] and the conquest of Shu was anticipated, the people began to settle down. After that the coinage of five-*shu* 五銖 pieces was gradually resumed.[42] The land-tax was one thirtieth of the produce.[43] A subject who had a son born was excused from the poll tax for three years.[44]

When Hsien-tsung 顯宗 [, or Emperor Ming 明 58-75], came to the throne, the empire was peaceful. The people suffered no unreasonable corvée. Harvests were plentiful year after year. In the fifth year of Yung-p'ing 永平 [62] a Ch'ang-man Ts'ang 常滿倉, or Ever-full Granary, was built. A grain market was established to the east of the capital.[45] A *hu* 斛 [46] of unhusked grain was valued at twenty coins.[47] Plants and trees were in abundance. Cattle and sheep were seen everywhere. Tribute was levied on a very low scale, yet stores accumulated in treasuries and granaries. No wickedness or evil was practised; good etiquette and righteousness alone ruled. At that time, at the dawn of morning, the officials went to the court. Imperial inlaws and other nobles competed to display [their splendid means of transportation].

[41] Kansu and northern Shensi.

[42] In 40 A. D. HHS 1B. 12b.   [43] In 30 A. D. HHS 1A. 3a.

[44] This is quoted in a decree issued in 85 A. D. as from the administrative code. HHS 3. 13b.

[45] According to *T'ung tien* 12. 69c the granary was a ch'ang-p'ing ts'ang 常平倉. Also cf. *Yü hai* 184. 7b. However *Lo-yang ch'ieh-lan chi* 2. 1b mentions a Ch'ang-man Ts'ang to the east of Lo-yang in the Western Chin period.

[46] A Han *hu* = 0.565 U. S. bushel.

[47] HHS 2. 15a gives 30 coins per *hu* in 69 A. D. According to LAO Kan's study (*Chü-yen Han chien k'ao-shih*, k'ao-chêng 考證 1. 20a-23a) the normal price of unhusked grain was about 70 to 80 coins per *hu* under the Western Han and about 100 coins per *hu* under the Eastern Han. The word *su* 粟 in its narrower sense means unhusked millet, but in our text it seems to be used to mean unhusked grain (*ku* 穀) in general. The ratio between husked (*mi* 米) and unhusked grain (*ku* or *su*) was fixed at 10 to 6 under the Han. It is mentioned in *Chiu-chang suan-shu* 2. 1a and also in Han wooden documents (LAO Kan: ibid. 1. 23a).

Vehicles proceeded in succession like a running stream. Mettled horses swept by like flying dragons. Brilliance shining on the eaves of carts was reflected on the carriages in front.

Our tradition says, according to the *san-t'ung* 三統 calendar in a whole period [of 4617 years] there are disastrous years in a whole period [of 4617 years] there are disastrous years called *yin-chiu* 陰九 and *yang-chiu* 陽九.[48] These are probably appointments of destiny in the universe. In the third year of Yung-ch'u 永初 [109] under Emperor An 安 [107-125] the empire suffered drought and flood. There was cannibalism. The Emperor loaned the imperial land at Hung-pei 鴻陂[49] to the paupers. Because of the inadequacy of revenue the Three Highest Officials 三公 also petitioned for permission to allow officials and others to purchase the title *kuan-nei hou* 關內侯 in return for money and grain.

In the first year of Yung-hsing 永興 [153] [3b] under Emperor Huan 桓 [147-167] one-third[50] of the prefectures and principalities suffered a plague of locusts. The Yellow river flooded over several thousand *li*. The people of over 100,000 households became vagrants. [It was ordered that] everywhere they should be fed and supplied.

In the early years of Chien-ning 建寧 [168] [*read*: Yung-ch'u 永初 (107)] and Yung-ho 永和 [136] the western Ch'iang revolted for over twenty years. Troops were kept in service until exhausted. Military expenses amounted to over 32,000,000,000 coins.[51] The

[48] The *san-t'ung* calendar is described in detail in *Han shu* 21AB, and also by W. EBERHARD and R. HENSELING: Beiträge zur Astronomie der Han-Zeit 1, 2 *SBAW* phil.-hist. Kl. (1933) 209-29; 937-56. A *yüan* 元 was composed of 4617 years and divided into three *t'ung* of 1539 years each. A superstition believed that following the first 106 years of a *yüan* there were to be nine years, which would suffer *yang* disasters or droughts, called *yang-chiu*. Following the next 374 years there were to be nine years, which would suffer *yin* disasters or floods, called *yin-chiu*. Following the next 480 years there were again to be nine disastrous years called *yang-chiu*. In the whole period of 4617 years there were to be 4560 normal years and 57 bad years. *Han shu* 21A. 23a-4b; EBERHARD and HENSELING 220-1.

[49] HHS 5. 6b has Hung-ch'ih 鴻池 instead of Hung-pei. The place was about twenty *li* to the east of Lo-yang.

[50] See note on *t'ai pan*, CS 26. 2b.

[51] HHS 117. 20b gives the expenses from 107 to 118 for expeditions against the Ch'iang barbarians as over 24,000,000,000; 117. 25b records the expenses from 136 to 145 as over 8,000,000,000. The amount 32,000,000,000 was certainly the sum of the two. Therefore the first year title should be Yung-ch'u instead of Chien-ning.

treasury became empty. Even the inner prefectures were involved in suffering.

Emperors Ch'ung 沖 [145] and Chih 質 [146] had only short reigns. Emperors Huan and Ling 靈 [168-189] ruled in disregard of the established principles of government. In the second year of Chung-p'ing 中平 [185] the southern palaces caught fire. The flame spread to the northern gate. Thereupon again ten coins were collected from each *mu* of land in the empire to rebuild the palaces.[52] The Emperor was from the family of a marquis [53] and had lived in poverty. After coming to the throne he often remarked, " Emperor Huan did not know how to take care of a household. He had not even private savings." Hence he ordered a Wan-chin T'ang 萬金堂, or Ten Thousand Gold Hall, to be built in his Western Garden, and used it as a private treasury. In addition he deposited private money in the houses of some small eunuchs. The sum in each house reached scores of millions.[54] Thereupon placards were hung on the palace gate Hung-tu 鴻都 to initiate the sale of offices. The prices were graded from dukes and ministers down to lower positions.[55] Ts'UI Lieh 崔烈, who was *t'ing-wei* 廷尉 or chief judge, sent in 5,000,000 coins to buy the post of *ssŭ-t'u* 司徒 or Grand Minister of Civil Affairs. All governors and prefects when appointed or promoted were compelled to contribute money for palace-building. Those of large prefectures sometimes had to pay as much as 20,000,000 coins. Some who could not fulfill [the requirement] committed suicide.

Emperor Hsien 獻 [190-220] [*read* Ling] [56] made five-*shu* coins on which were four lines connecting [radially the perforation] with [4a] the edge. Some wise men disliked them and said, " Would it not mean that the capital is going to be destroyed and the coins

---

[52] Emperor Huan first levied coins from each *mu* in 165. HHS 7. 16a.

[53] The Emperor's grandfather, father, and himself held in succession the title of *Hsieh-tu t'ing-hou* 解瀆亭侯. HHS 8. 1a.

[54] *T'ung chien°* 224. 9a, commentary defines *chü-i* as *i* times *i*. The number seems to be unreasonably large. It may be used to mean a large number of *i*, or vaguely a very large number. Here I follow HHS 108. 24a where we have 數千萬.

[55] According to HHS 8. 8a-b this office-selling was launched in 178, several years prior to the fire in 185.

[56] According to HHS 8. 13b Emperor Ling minted the *ssŭ-ch'u-wên* 四出文 coins in 184. The attribution to Emperor Hsien was a mistake. CSCC 26. 4a.

will spread out in the four directions [like the four lines]? " Later
when Tung Cho 董卓 rose in arms and set fire to the palaces, he
kidnapped Emperor [Hsien] and carried him west to Ch'ang-an
[190]. He had all the five-*shu* coins destroyed and reminted into
small coins. All the bronze human figures, the spiritual beasts
called *fei-lien* 飛廉,[57] and other bronzes in Ch'ang-an and Lo-yang
were collected for coinage. His coins had no raised edge and bore
no characters, which proved to be inconvenient. According to
people of that time the bronze human figures were made by the
First Emperor of the Ch'in when a giant was seen at Lin-t'ao
臨洮.[58] Now Tung Cho [who destroyed them] was from Lin-t'ao.
Though there is a difference between construction and destruction,
the evil [59] was similar in both cases.

When Tung Cho received his punishment and was killed [192],
[two of his generals] Li Chüeh 李傕 and Kuo Fan 郭汜 attacked
each other inside the city of Ch'ang-an, which they made their
battlefield [195]. During that time a *hu* of grain cost 500,000
coins, and of beans or wheat 200,000. There was cannibalism. The
landscape was white with piles of bones. Corpses rotted in the
streets. The Emperor ordered Hou Wên 侯汶, who was *shih-yü-shih* 侍御史 (attendant censor), to bring out grain and beans
from the T'ai Ts'ang 太倉 or Imperial Granary to make congee
for the hungry people. It was given for several days, but still
more perished. The Emperor then began to suspect that the
officials in charge stole the provisions. So he had the relief granted
in his presence.[60] The hungry people all wept and said, " Only
now do we begin to get it."

When the Emperor returned to the east [195], [4b] Li Chüeh,
Kuo Fan, and their followers pursued and defeated the imperial
guards at Ts'ao-yang 曹陽.[61] The Emperor crossed the Yellow

[57] The *fei-lien* were supposed to have a deer's body, a bird's head with horns, a
snake's tail, and a panther's skin. Their bronze figures were made in 109 B.C. at
Ch'ang-an. *Han shu* 6.23b.

[58] Min-hsien 岷, southwestern Kansu.

[59] HHS 102.6b gives *hsiung-pao* 凶暴 instead of our *hsiung-o* 訛.

[60] According to HHS 9.6b the Emperor made the test by having congee made in
front of him, and not by watching the relief personally.

[61] To the west of Shan-hsien 陝, western Honan.

river secretly at night. All the imperial consorts went afoot. While walking out of the camp and railing, the Empress had a few *p'i* of thick levantine in her hand. TUNG Ch'êng 董承 sent SUN Hui 孫徽, who was *fu-chieh ling* 符節令 or official in charge of credentials, to threaten her with a sword and steal the pieces.[62] SUN killed an attendant at the side of the Empress, the blood splashing over her dress.

Having arrived at An-i 安邑,[63] the Emperor, with his clothes all torn, had only wild jujubes and garden vegetables as provisions. From this time on the city of Ch'ang-an became entirely empty. People scattered in all directions. For two or three years no travellers were found in Kuan-chung, or inside the [Han-ku][64] pass.

In the first year of Chien-an [196], the Emperor arrived at Lo-yang. The palaces were destroyed utterly. The officials cleared away thorn-bushes to get a place to dwell in. The provincial leaders each kept in hand large military forces, but no supplies for the Emperor arrived. The imperial secretaries went out in person to pick wild rice[65] for themselves. Some lacked strength to return and perished [from hunger] in the streets or among the ruins.

When [Ts'AO Ts'ao, posthumously named] Emperor Wu of the Wei, first came to power, the nine provinces were in disorder like disturbed clouds. To attack cities and to seize land, and to protect these and to pacify the people, military expenses were met by temporary levies. At that time, all the troops under YÜAN Shao 袁紹 were fed with mulberries and jujubes; those under YÜAN Shu 術[66] with oysters and clams. Ts'AO Ts'ao then called free citizens to colonize the region near Hsü 許 [196].[67] In addition agricultural officials were appointed in the provinces and prefectures. Each year there were collected some scores of millions of *hu*, which were earmarked for military expenses.

[62] This episode, although based upon HHS 10B.15a, may be unfounded. TUNG Ch'êng seems to have been a very loyal minister. CSCC 26.4b.

[63] An-i, southwestern Shansi.

[64] Or Hsien-ku.

[65] HHS 9.8b, where the character 梹 is correctly read 稆.

[66] The two YÜANS were cousins, and both were rivals of Ts'AO Ts'ao.

[67] Near Hsü-ch'ang 許昌, central Honan.

[5a] When the YÜANS were first conquered and Yeh 鄴,[68] capital [of Chi chou], was pacified [204], the land-tax was fixed at four *shêng* of unhusked grain per *mu*. Each household was to contribute two *p'i* of silk and two *chin* of floss. No other levies were to be arbitrarily made; nor were the rich to be passed by and [only] the poor be taxed.

In the second year of Huang-ch'u 黃初 [221] under Emperor Wên 文 [220-226], the five-*shu* coins were first abolished on account of the high price of grain.[69] At that time the empire was not yet united. Military forces were in action every year. Confucius has said, " Let it [a state] be suffering from invading arms, then there will ensue a famine in corn and in all vegetables."[70] This means that when men engage in disastrous wars, the forces of nature respond in a similar discord.

At that time the people of the three sides [Wei, Shu, and Wu] aimed at conquering one another. Battles were fought and won, and places attacked and seized, so that farmers abandoned their ploughs. In the region along the Yangtze and Huai rivers the amount of grain stored was especially insufficient. Lu Hsün 陸遜, Generalissimo 上大將軍 of the Wu,[71] sent up a memorial suggesting that the generals be permitted to extend their fields. [Sun] Ch'üan 孫權 replied, " Splendid! Now I myself and my sons shall personally receive fields. To go with the carts there should be eight cattle for four pairs to plough together.[72] Although unable to equal the ancients, we do wish to share the toil of the common folk." From this began the devotion of the Wu to agriculture and [particularly] to the raising of grain.

[68] West to Lin-chang 臨漳, northern Honan.

[69] TUNG Cho's small coins were abolished and the five-*shu* revived when Ts'AO Ts'ao became prime minister in 208. Cf. SKC 2.17b, 18b; CS 26.18b; *T'ung tien* 8.48c. According to SKC 2.17b the five-*shu* coins were revived in the third moon of 221 and again abolished in the tenth moon of the same year.

[70] These were really words of Tzŭ-lu 子路, disciple of Confucius, recorded in the *Analects*. LEGGE 1.247.

[71] The memorial was dated 226 (SKC, Wu 2.17a) but LU was not made Generalissimo until 231 (SKC, Wu 13.7a).

[72] The Wu ruler perhaps had in mind the eight farmers who were supposed to work on a *ching* 井 of land according to the *ching-t'ien* system in ancient times. It is interesting to note that the standard plough team in medieval England was also of eight oxen.

Emperor Ming of the Wei [227-239] was not reverent, and was extravagant in building palaces. The officials were drafted as laborers. The people in the empire had no opportunity to carry on farming. Afterwards the region to the east of the [Han-ku] pass suffered from flood, and the people lost their estates. Moreover, troops were raised [to fight] to the north of the Liao river, and [5b] mailed soldiers were stationed along the Yangtze valley. The two expeditions exhausted the regular budget utterly.

In the first year of T'ai-k'ang 太康 [280] under Emperor Wu or Shih-tsu 世祖武皇帝 [280-290], SUN Hao 皓 [last ruler of the Wu] was conquered and millions of cash were taken over so that the resources of the Three Wu regions [73] were emptied. The revenues from Shu in the west were also put under control, after one thousand years' [development of the place]. Weapons were stored in arsenals. [War]ships were destroyed in the rivers.[74] River banks, seashores, the Three Hills,[75] and the Eight Marshes,[76] which ploughs and hoes had never touched, were all received by the people [as allotments]. When the stars called *nung-hsiang* 農祥 were in the middle of the morning sky [i. e. at the beginning of spring],[77] it was time "to adjust and arrange the labors of the spring."[78] Those who carried spades on their shoulders and brought their own provisions spread [over the fields] like clouds.

Thus regard was paid to the courses of the Five Planets 五緯 in heaven, and the use of the Five Materials 五才 [79] was promoted

[73] Probably Wu-hsing 吳興, Tan-yang 丹陽, and Wu-chün 吳郡. Another tradition gives Kuei-chi 會稽 instead of Tan-yang. Cf. *Shih-ch'i shih shang-ch'üeh* 45. 2b-5a.

[74] Nothing is mentioned in CS annals on the destruction of warships after the conquest. WANG Tsun 王濬 was accused of burning 135 Wu ships after the pardon of 280. This episode may be referred to here (CS 42. 15b). Or perhaps these statements were merely rhetorical expressions inspired by the description of the disarmament in the twelfth century B. C. after the conquest of Shang in *Shu ching* (LEGGE 3. 308-9).

[75] Same as *San Shan* 三山, i. e. P'êng-lai 蓬萊, Fang-chang 方丈, and Ying-chou 瀛洲. *Wên hsüan* 文選 (*Ssŭ-pu pei-yao* ed.) 15. 4b.

[76] *Han shu* 64A. 7b.

[77] This phrase is from *Kuo yü* 1. 7a. *Nung-hsiang* refers to the *fang* constellation 房星.

[78] LEGGE 3. 19.

[79] 才 is probably the same as 材 (*Tz'ŭ t'ung* 辭通 425). For the Five Materials

on earth. The generation enjoyed a period of peace. Supplies flowed into granaries and treasuries. Palaces had additional adornments; dresses and playthings sparkled brightly. Thus people like WANG [K‘ai 王愷 *tzǔ*] Chün-fu 君夫,[80] [WANG Chi 濟 *tzǔ*] Wu-tzǔ 武子,[81] and SHIH Ch‘ung 石崇 [82] vied with one another in displaying [their riches]. Their carts, dresses, and food utensils were comparable in elegance to those of the imperial family. A racecourse was paved with coins.[83] A coral tree was broken into small pieces [without pity].[84]

That things decay after flourishing is merely normal. At the beginning of the Yung-ning 永寧 period [301] there were still [in the imperial treasury] in Lo-yang four million [*p‘i*] of brocade and silk, and over one hundred *hu* of jewels, gold, and silver. When Emperor Hui 惠 [290-306] went on an expedition to the north [303], he returned after reaching T‘ang-yin 蕩陰 [85] [and being defeated]. He was given some cold peaches to eat, and [later] only a single chicken was provided. Two cloth coverlets and three thousand coins in a bag were all the Emperor's means of living.[86]

[6a] When Emperor Huai 懷 [307-312] was besieged by LIU Yao 劉曜 [87] in Lo-yang [311], the imperial army suffered successive defeats. The treasury was already empty; the officials were starving. No [cooking] smoke arose from the houses. The hungry people ate human flesh.

When Emperor Min 愍 [313-316] moved west [to Ch‘ang-an], there were many famines. A *tou* of husked grain cost two units of gold. Two-thirds of the people perished. When LIU Yao took up arms [again], the capital was cut off from the outside, only ten

---

Chou li gives metal, wood, leather, jade, and earth (BIOT 2.457), whereas *Tso chuan* has metal, wood, water, fire, and earth (LEGGE 5.534).

[80] Biog. CS 93.4a; GILES 2189.

[81] Biog. CS 42.5a-7a.

[82] Biog. CS 33.18b-23a; GILES 1709.

[83] Owned by WANG Chi. CS 42.6a.

[84] SHIH Ch‘ung broke a two-feet high coral tree of WANG K‘ai, and produced several three or four feet in height. CS 33.21b.

[85] T‘ang-yin 湯陰, northern Honan.

[86] CS 4.12a. Both the coverlets and the money were borrowed from attendant eunuchs.

[87] A barbarian leader. Biog. CS 103.1a-23b. GILES 1365.

cakes of leaven were powdered [to make congee] to feed the Emperor. The Emperor and the officials looked at each other and no one could refrain from weeping.[88]

When Emperor Yüan 元 [317-322] crossed the Yangtze river, due to the military emergency [the government organization] was in a rough state. The taxes in cloth from the barbarian regions were not regularly received. The store in the central treasury consisted of no more than four thousand *p'i* of cloth. At that time SHIH LO 石勒,[89] being brave and valorous, made trouble as far as to the south of the Yangtze river. The Emperor greatly fearing his invasion gave direction to the governors that whoever cut off SHIH LO's head should be rewarded with one thousand *p'i* of cloth.[90]

[88] CS 5.14b-15a.

[89] A barbarian leader. Biog. CS 104.1a-105.18a; GILES 1720.

[90] CS 6.6b cites a decree issued in the sixth moon of 317, which gives only the reward for beheading SHIH HU 石虎 (mentioned in *Chin shu* by his *tzŭ* Chi-lung 季龍 because *hu* was a T'ang taboo), nephew and general of SHIH LO, as two thousand *p'i* of cloth and other things. However, a decree in the third moon of the same year (*Ch'üan Chin wên* 8.10a) gives the reward for the execution of SHIH LO as five thousand *p'i* of silk and other items proportionally more than those for SHIH HU.

[(2) On Food]

Under the Han after the disturbance of TUNG Cho the people were driven from their homes and became vagrants. The price of a *hu* of grain came to exceed 500,000 coins. There was much cannibalism. Having conquered the Yellow Turbans, Ts'AO Ts'ao wished to reduce the empire to order, but was handicapped by an insufficiency of food for soldiers. TSAO Chih 棗祇 from Ying-ch'uan 潁川,[1] who was the commander of the *yü-lin* guards 羽林監, suggested the establishment of military agricultural colonies. Ts'AO Ts'ao thereupon issued an order saying, " The way to pacify a state is to have a strong army and sufficient food. [6b] The Ch'in unified the world through their devotion to agriculture; Emperor Wu [of the Han] conquered the Western Regions by establishing military agricultural colonies. These are good examples set by earlier generations." Thereupon JÊN Tsun 任峻 [2] was appointed *tien-nung chung-lang-chiang* 典農中郎將, commander in charge of agriculture.[3] People were called to colonize the fields around Hsü.[4] The yield amounted to 1,000,000 *hu* of grain. Agricultural officials were established in prefectures and principalities. Within a few years grain was stored everywhere. Granaries all became full. After the death of [TSAO] Chih, Ts'AO Ts'ao called to mind his achievements and bestowed a title of nobility upon his son.

[1] Prefecture in southern Honan. Biog. of TSAO Chih SKC 16.1b-2a, commentary, where the character 祇 is written 祗.

[2] Biog. SKC 16.1a-2b.

[3] HHS 36.2a commentary gives the salary of this newly created post as 2000 *shih*, the same as that of a prefect. Under it were agricultural officials called *tien-nung tu-wei* 都尉 with a salary corresponding to that of a district magistrate. For small prefectures a *tien-nung hsiao-wei* 校尉 was appointed instead of a *tien-nung chung-lang-chiang*. The *tien-nung* officials were all under the *Ta ssŭ-nung* 大司農, Minister of Public Finance, and formed an administrative system independent to that of the prefects and magistrates. Cf. YÜ Chêng-hsieh 俞正燮: *Kuei-ssŭ lei-kao* 癸巳類稿 (*Anhwei ts'ung-shu* ed.) 11.41a-2a; OKAZAKI Fumio 岡崎文夫: *Nambokuchō ni okeru shakai keizai seido* 南北朝に於ける社會經濟制度 185-93; CHÜ Ch'ing-yüan: 曹魏的屯田 *Shih-huo* 3.3 (1936) 39-45; T'AO Yüan-chên: *San Kuo shih-huo chih* 41-6.

[4] Near Hsü-ch'ang, central Honan.

Early in the Chien-an period [196-220], over 100,000 households of the people fled from Kuan-chung to Ching-chou 荆州.[5] Later, when they heard that their native places had become peaceful and quiet, they all hoped to return, but could find no occupation for themselves. Then WEI Ch'i 衛覬[6] offered his opinion[7] that salt was a treasure of the state. It has become scattered since the hard times set in. Now officials should be appointed to supervise its sale as in former times. The profit [from the monopoly] should be used to purchase more ploughs and cattle to supply to the returning people. They could cultivate the land industriously and accumulate grain to enrich Kuan-chung. People from afar on receiving the news would certainly hurry back in great numbers. Then Ts'AO Ts'ao sent the *Yeh-chê p'u-yeh* 謁者僕射, head of imperial ushers, to supervise the salt officials. The *Ssŭ-li hsiao-wei* 司隸校尉, inspector of [seven] prefectures near the capital, was moved to be stationed at Hung-nung 弘農.[8] The wanderers returned as expected and Kuan-chung became prosperous.

Later LIU Fu 劉馥[9] from P'ei 沛[10] was made governor of Yang-chou 揚[11] and was stationed at Ho-fei 合肥.[12] [7a] He extended the military agricultural colonies and repaired the dams and dikes of reservoirs like Shao Pei 芍陂,[13] Ju Pei 茹陂,[14] Ch'i-mên 七門,[15] and Wu-t'ang 吳塘[16] to water rice-fields. Both the government and the people [thus] had stores, which benefited later generations.

[5] Hupei.

[6] Biog. SKC 21.11b-14b.

[7] *T'ung-tien* 10.59a reads 以爲.

[8] Prefecture in western Honan. According to SKC 21.12a the people after returning were often made *pu-ch'ü* by military leaders. The policy of WEI Ch'i was to attract people to be citizens owing direct allegiance to the government.

[9] Biog. SKC 15.1a-b.

[10] Principality in northern Kiangsu.

[11] Northern and central Anhwei.   [12] District in central Anhwei.

[13] To the south of Shou-hsien 壽, northwestern Anhwei. *Tu shih fang-yü chi-yao* (TSFYCY) 讀史方輿紀要 21.26a-27a.

[14] To the southeast of Ku-shih 固始, southeastern Honan. TSFYCY 50.44b.

[15] To the southwest of Shu-ch'êng 舒城, central Anhwei. TSFYCY 26.9b. According to *Wên-hsien t'ung-k'ao* 6.67a-b this water work was originally built in the early part of the 2nd cent. B.C.

[16] To the west of Ch'ien-shan 潛山, southeastern Anhwei. TSFYCY 26.35a-b.

When CHIA K'uei 賈逵 [17] governed Yü-chou 豫, [18] which was bounded to the south by territory of the Wu, he built military works for both offence and defence. He dammed the Ju river 汝 to form a Hsin Pei 新, or New Reservoir. [19] Also a transportation canal of over 300 [or 200] li [20] was cut and became known as CHIA-hou Ch'ü 賈侯渠, or Marquis CHIA's Canal. [21]

In the middle years of Huang-ch'u [220-226] the area of cultivation under the prefects increased yet more and therefore government revenue was abundant. At that time YEN Fei 顏斐 [22] of Chi-pei 濟北 [23] was prefect of Ching-chao 京兆. [24] The people there had not devoted themselves to agriculture since the revolt of MA Ch'ao 馬超 [25] [211-214], and they had neither carts nor cattle. YEN Fei assigned [some of] the people to take the materials and make carts in the idle months, thus to teach in turn the art of carpentry to one another. Those who had no cattle were instructed to raise pigs [26] and, when the price was high, sell them to purchase cattle. At first they all considered the procedure troublesome. In a couple of years all households had carts and

[17] Biog. SKC 15.16a-21a; GILES 323.

[18] Eastern Honan and northwestern Kiangsu.

[19] SKC 15.19a says CHIA K'uei damned both the Yen 鄢 and Ju rivers to construct reservoirs. The reservoirs are not identified, probably in southeastern Honan.

[20] CS pai-na ed. 26.4a, SKC 15.19a, and Shui-ching chu 水經注 (Ssŭ-pu pei-yao ed.) 22.32a all give ' over 200 li.' The canal passed to the west of Huai-yang 淮陽 and the east of Ju-nan 汝南, both in eastern Honan. Its exact course was not identifiable even in the early part of the 6th century when Shui-ching chu was prepared. TSFYCY 47.36a-b, 50.20b-21a.

[21] CHIA K'uei held the title kuan-nei hou 關內侯. CHI Ch'ao-ting 冀朝鼎 in his book, Key Economic Areas in Chinese History 102, gives an unsatisfactory interpretation of the significance of CHIA K'uei's works. From 220 to 222, the years in which these water-works were probably built, the Wu, being fully occupied by a war against the Shu, made a temporary pretence of subjection to the Wei. The armed peace was soon ended, and a war broke out between the Wei and the Wu in the winter of 222. Ignoring these facts, CHI superficially labels the Chia-hou Canal " a monument of Wei-Wu friendship." His statement that CHIA K'uei " utilized tools which had been prepared for military purposes " to construct these works is also fanciful.

[22] Biog. SKC 16.23b, commentary.

[23] Central Shantung.

[24] Central Shensi.

[25] Biog. SKC, Shu 6.6a-9a.

[26] SKC 16.23b commentary mentions ' pigs and dogs.'

cattle. Farming became less laborious, and the people had enough. In this way Ching-chao became prosperous.

CHÊNG Hun 鄭渾 [27] was prefect of P'ei 沛. The prefecture was located in a low and wet region, which suffered from floods, so that the people were poor and hungry. [CHÊNG] Hun [planned to] construct dams and reservoirs in the two districts of Hsiao 蕭 [28] and Hsiang 相 [29] and to lay out rice-fields. No people in the prefecture considered it practical. [CHÊNG] Hun, convinced of the [7b] eventual benefit, in person led the people to start the works, which were all completed in one winter. Harvests were abundant in successive years; and the area of cultivation increased year by year. The land-tax collected was double that of normal times. The people in the prefecture were benefited. They had a eulogy for him inscribed on a stone, and named the reservoir CHÊNG'S Reservoir.[30]

In the reign of Emperor Ming of the Wei [227-239], Hsü Miao 徐邈 [31] was governor of Liang-chou 涼.[32] The region had little rain and often suffered from insufficiency of grain. [Hsü] Miao suggested the repair of the salt ponds in Wu-wei 武威 and Chiu-ch'üan 酒泉 [33] in order that grain might be purchased from the barbarians. Also he opened extensive water-fields and engaged poor people to work on them as tenants. Every household had abundance. Granaries became full and overflowed. He made arrangements to use the surplus from military expenditures in the province to purchase gold, brocade, dogs, and horses ? to provide generally for home consumption in China?. That the people from the Western Regions came to offer tribute and that money and merchandise circulated were both due to [Hsü] Miao.

Afterwards HUANG-FU Lung 皇甫隆 [34] was prefect of Tun-huang. The people there did not have the custom of making lou-

---

[27] Biog. SKC 16.19a-22a.

[28] Hsiao-hsien, northwestern Kiangsu.

[29] Northwest of Su-hsien 宿, northern Anhwei.

[30] TSFYCY 29.13a. These were probably all in Emperor Wên's reign (220-226).

[31] Biog. SKC 27.1a-3a.

[32] Western Kansu.   [33] Both in western Kansu.

[34] SKC 16.23a commentary mentions the time he went to Tun-huang (or more properly T'un-huang) as around 251.

ploughs 耰犁.[35] Neither was irrigation known to them. Altho much labor of men and cattle was expended, the yield of grain was inferior. [Huang-fu] Lung arrived and taught them to make *lou*-ploughs and to irrigate. At the end of the year, a general accounting revealed that over half of the labor was saved and the grain product increased by fifty per cent. Therefore the western region prospered.

In the fourth year of Chia-p'ing 嘉平 [252][36] Kuan-chung suffered from famine. [Ssŭ-ma I 懿 posthumously named] Emperor Hsüan 宣 of the Chin, petitioned for the removal of 5000 farmers from Chi-chou 冀 to till Shang-kuei 上邽.[37] The salt ponds in Ching-chao 京兆, [8a] T'ien-shui 天水,[38] and Nan-an 南安[39] were developed to increase military resources. In the first year of Ch'ing-lung 青龍 [233] the Ch'êng-kuo Canal 成國[40] was dug from Ch'ên-ts'ang 陳倉[41] to Huai-li 槐里.[42] The Lin-chin Reservoir 臨晉[43] was built. Water was led from the Ch'ien 汧[44] and Lo 洛 rivers to irrigate over 3000 *ch'ing* of alkali land. Thus the state was enriched.

In the fourth year of Chêng-shih 正始 [243] Ssŭ-ma I again commanded troops to attack the Wu general Chu-ko K'o 諸葛恪[45] and burned his stores. [Chu-ko] K'o abandoned his city and fled. Thereupon Ssŭ-ma I wished to extend tillage and accumulate a store of grain in preparation for wars of conquest. Têng Ai

---

[35] A rough kind of sowing machine attached to a plough, also known as *lou-ch'ê* 車. It was probably invented by Chao Kuo 趙過 in c. 100 B.C. Cf. *Ch'i-min yao-shu* 齊民要術 (*Lung-hsi ching-shê ts'ung-shu* 龍谿精舍 ed.) 1.6b-7a; T'ao Yüan-chên: *San Kuo shih-huo chih* 54-5. The Ming work *San-ts'ai t'u-hui* 三才圖會 (pub. 1609) 10.49a-b contains the picture and description of a contrivance bearing the same name.

[36] This is an error. CS 1.2b-3a gives the fourth year of T'ai-ho (230).

[37] Western Shensi. According to CS 37.3a the removal of farmers was planned by Ssŭ-ma Fu 孚, younger brother of Ssŭ-ma I.

[38] Western Shensi.

[39] Southern Kansu.

[40] TSFYCY 53.41a, 54.36a, 55.14b.

[41] Pao-chi 寶雞, western Shensi.

[42] Southeast of Hsing-p'ing 興平, central Shensi.

[43] Probably in central Shensi.

[44] In western Shensi.   [45] Biog. SKC, Wu 19.1a-15.

鄧艾 [46] was sent to examine the region from Ch'ên 陳 [47] and Hsiang 項 [48] east to Shou-ch'un 壽春.[49] [TÊNG] Ai was of the opinion that the fields there were excellent, but that there was not enough water to permit full use of them. Canals should be dug so that military supplies could be accumulated in large quantities and water transportation could also be facilitated. Thereupon he prepared an essay, called the *Chi ho lun* 濟河論 to explain his idea. He also declared, " Formerly, when the Yellow Turbans had been destroyed, military agricultural colonies were opened to accumulate grain at the capital Hsü to permit control of the country in all directions. Now, three of the four corners have already been pacified. The [only] problem lies at the south of the Huai river. Whenever great forces are raised for an expedition, the quartermaster corps forms over half of the army. The expense is counted in hundreds of millions [50] and it is considered an enormous burden. Now in the region between Ch'ên 陳 and Ts'ai 蔡 [51] the land is low and the fields are excellent. The rice-fields around Hsü-ch'ang should be abandoned and the rivers there should be led to flow downward to the east. Twenty thousand troops [should be stationed] to the north and thirty thousand to the south of the Huai river. While having furloughs in turn, [8b] they should both cultivate the land and defend [the territory].[52] When water becomes abundant, the average harvest will be three times that of the west. After allowing for all expenses, there would be 5,000,000 *hu* per year for military supply. Within six or seven years there would be a store of over 30,000,000 *hu* in the Huai valley,[53] enough

[46] Biog. SKC 28.16b-26a.
[47] Huai-yang 淮陽, eastern Honan.
[48] Hsiang-ch'êng 項城, eastern Honan.
[49] Shou-hsien, northwestern Anhwei.
[50] See note on *chü-i*, CS 26.3b.
[51] Two states in the Ch'un-ch'iu period in southeastern Honan.
[52] According to SKC 28.17b, every 20 per cent were to have furloughs in turn so that there would always be 40,000 on duty. Some editions of SKC, for example the *Ssŭ-pu pei-yao* edition, read 4000 instead of 40,000. This is obviously an error. However, it may be noticed that CH'ÊN Hsiao-chiang has made some calculation on the rate of production based upon the wrong data in his *San Kuo ching-chi shih* 67, 85.
[53] The *pei* 北 in our text is probably a corruption of *shang* 上. CS *pai-na* ed. 26.5a, SKC 28.17b, and *T'ung tien* 2.19a all read *shang*. CSCC 26.10a reads *t'u* 土.

to feed 100,000 troops for five years.[54] With such resources at hand, when one takes advantage of the enemy one will never fail to conquer."

Ssŭ-ma I approved this project and carried it out completely in accordance with [Têng] Ai's plan.[55] Thereupon along the southern bank of the Huai river, starting at Chung-li 鍾離 [56] and going south [west] to the Pi river 泚 [57] west of Hêng-shih 橫石,[58] camps each containing sixty people were established five *li* apart for over 400 *li* to cultivate the land and to defend [the territory]. Two canals, Huai-yang 淮陽 and Pai-ch'ih 百尺 [59] were also repaired and widened. Water was led from the Yellow river downwards to the Huai and Ying rivers. It was regulated [60] on a large scale by reservoirs.[61] A canal of over 300 *li* in length was dug to the north and south of the Ying river, which watered 20,000 [or 30,000] [62] *ch'ing* of fields. Thus [the lands] south and north of the Huai river were united. From Shou-ch'un to the capital [63] the cries of chickens and dogs [could be heard] from field to field in the military colonies under agricultural officials. In times of military emergency in the southeast, when a large army went on

---

[54] The average is about 5 *hu* per person per month. It may have been a very rough estimation. According to Han wooden documents one officer or soldier was allowed 2 *hu* of husked grain or 3.333 *hu* of unhusked grain per month. Cf. Lao Kan: *Chü-yen Han chien k'ao-shih, shih-wên* 2.30a-79b.

[55] CS 1.13b-14a mentions the works in 242 and 243, but SKC 28.17b says they were begun in 241.

[56] Northeast of Fêng-yang 鳳陽, northeastern Anhwei.

[57] *T'ung tien* 2.19a gives the pronunciation as 旁脂反. Instead of 泚, CSCC 26.10a reads 沘, which is preferred by Li Tz'ŭ-ming in his *Chin shu cha-chi* 2.15b. TSFYCY 46.30b identifies the river with the Pi river 淠 in Anhwei.

[58] TSFYCY 46.30b identifies it with Chia-shih 硤石, northwest of Shou-hsien, northwestern Anhwei.

[59] TSFYCY 46.30b identifies the former with the Chia-hou Canal. The latter was also near Huai-yang, eastern Honan.

[60] Being a T'ang taboo, the character *ch'ih* or *chih* 治 is read *li* 理 in *T'ung tien* 2.19a. Li Tz'ŭ-ming considers *ch'ih* as a later alteration or restoration. *Chin shu cha-chi* 2.15b.

[61] The logical relationship of the last three sentences is not clear.

[62] *T'ung tien* 2.19a gives 30,000.

[63] Lo-yang or Hsü-ch'ang? Although Lo-yang was the capital, both Lo-yang and Hsü-ch'ang were among the five capitals of the Wei (SKC 2.17a, commentary) and the emperors often travelled between palaces in the two cities.

an expedition, they reached the Yangtze and Huai rivers by boat. Provisions were stored and flood disasters were avoided. These were all the work of [TÊNG] Ai.[64]

When the Chin received the Mandate of Heaven [i. e. became the ruling dynasty], Emperor Wu wished to pacify and unify the territory south of the Yangtze. At that time grain was cheap, but cloth and silk were expensive. [9a] The Emperor wanted to establish the *p'ing-ti* 平糴 method [65] of purchasing grain with cloth and silk to provide a store of provision. Advisers said that the military supply was still insufficient, so it was not proper to exchange what was dear for what was cheap. In the second year of T'ai-shih 泰始 [266] the Emperor issued an edict saying, "That the people spend lavishly in productive years and in time of famine become poor and exhausted is normal. Accordingly the ancient people estimated the government expenditure, purchased the surplus [in good years] and released the stores [in bad years]. Thus they had the methods of *ch'ing-chung* 輕重 [66] and *p'ing-ti*, the state finances were in order, and relief was granted equitably. To bestow grace without spending too much money is the highest form of government. However, these measures have long been abandoned, and few people are familiar with their propriety. In addition, the government stores have not become large. Advisers hold different opinions on economics and are unable to comprehend thoroughly these institutions. Further, in years of abundance the national treasures are left dispersed and are not collected by the government. The poor and weak suffer in famine years but the state is unprepared. Powerful people and rich merchants hold mobile capital and hoard heavy stores with a view to profit. Therefore, while farmers suffer at their occupation, less essential

[64] CHI Ch'ao-ting paraphrases part of the two paragraphs and translates the rest, but he has made several slips (*Key Economic Areas in Chinese History* 103-4).

[65] It is for the government to purchase grain when cheap and to sell it when dear, thus keeping the price of grain around an established fair price called the *p'ing-chia* 平買. The measure was introduced in the state of Wei in the period of Warring States and practised in the empire under the Han. Cf. *Han shu* 24A. 6a-7b; LAO Kan: *Chü-yen Han chien k'ao-shih*, k'ao-chêng 1. 20a-23a.

[66] Government control of prices by participation in purchases and sale or by other measures. It is discussed at length in chapters 80-86 of *Kuan tzŭ*. Also cf. Esson M. GALE: *Discourses on Salt and Iron* 12, note 2; 85, note 1.

workers cannot be restricted. Now forced labor is reduced to put emphasis on the essential occupation [i. e. agriculture]. Efforts are concentrated on cultivation. The hope is to have better agricultural results and the farmers more encouraged. Yet occasionally [the general price] jumps so high that the farmers all suffer. Now the government shall make a practice of purchasing the surplus grain in preparation for years of famine. The officials in charge shall discuss and draft the regulations." [9b] However, the measure was not carried out after all.

At that time the country to the south of the Yangtze river was not yet pacified. The government exerted itself to promote agriculture. On the day *ting-hai* in the first moon of the fourth year [268], the Emperformed the ceremony of personally ploughing the imperial fields. On the day *kêng-yin* an edict said, " If the people in the empire are to abandon non-essential occupations in favor of the essential and devote themselves emulously to farming, those who can follow and publish my will, and cause the people to take pleasure in their work and to enjoy their occupations, are, possibly, only the leading officials in prefectures and districts. [Successfully] " to be an example to the people and to reward them " depends upon " not growing weary." [67] I am constantly mindful that in their administration of affairs they are indeed industrious. Let one brood mare [68] of the officials in charge of the central and left pastures 中左典牧 [69] be bestowed upon each of the magistrates of large and small districts, ministers of principalities, and chief assistants of provinces and principalities." In this same year [268] [70] the *ch'ang-p'ing* granary was established. In years of abundance grain was purchased and in years of famine it was sold to benefit the people.

On the day *kuei-ssŭ* in the first moon of the fifth year [269], an imperial mandate warned the report-bearers from prefectures and principalities: " The prefects, ministers of principalities, and magistrates of large and small districts shall take full advantage of the

---

[67] From the *Confucian Analects*. LEGGE 1.262.

[68] *Ts'ao ma*, 草馬 or 騳草馬, ' female horse.'

[69] CS 24.15b mentions *tso, yu,* and *chung tien-mu,* three offices, each headed by a *tu-wei* 都尉.

[70] CS 3.16a gives 276, which is considered correct in CSCC 26.11a.

land, and prohibit wandering people and travelling traders. People on vacation [or furlough] [71] are commanded to share the toil with their fathers and elder brothers. The mighty are not allowed to purchase or hold titles [on land] privately 私相置名 while exploiting the helpless and weak."

In the tenth moon, a decree was issued concerning WANG Hung 王宏,[72] prefect of Chi 汲,[73] who had been reported by SHIH Chien 石鑒, the *Ssŭ-li hsiao-wei*, as "industrious in pitying the people and able in leading and influencing them.[74] He supervised and encouraged the cultivation of over 500 *ch'ing* of waste land. [10a] When there was a general famine, his prefecture alone suffered no insufficiency. He may be designated as one who is competent in getting the people to give of their best and one whose accomplishments have been extraordinary although the odds have been even. Let 1000 *hu* of grain be bestowed upon him, and let the fact be published in the empire."

In the eighth year [272] SHIH Pao 石苞, Minister of Civil Affairs 司徒, reported that there was not yet a system for grading [accomplishment in] agriculture and the raising of mulberry trees in provinces and prefectures.[75] Subordinate officials and clerks should be increased [in the ministry] so that they could be sent out to inspect. The Emperor approved his suggestion. The whole story is in SHIH Pao's biography.[76] As [SHIH] Pao was wise in [devising methods for] urging the people to the performance of their service, they felt secure in his proposals.

In the tenth year [274] HSIA-HOU Ho 夏侯和, who was the *Kuang-lu hsün* 光祿勳,[77] petitioned for the repair of the three

[71] The Chin officials were allowed to be absent for five days in a month or sixty days in a year. The T'ang officials enjoyed a 'farming vacation" 田假 of fifteen days in the fifth moon to be spent in work on the land and another fifteen days in the ninth moon. *T'ai-p'ing yü-lan* 太平御覽 (Hsüeh-hai T'ang 學海堂 ed.) 634. 5a; NIIDA Noboru 仁井田陞: *Tōryō shūi* 唐令拾遺 733, 736.

[72] Biog. CS 90. 6b-7b.   [73] Southwest of Chi-hsien, northern Honan.

[74] CS *pai-na* ed. 26. 5b reads 導.

[75] The practice of grading local officials by agricultural achievements can be traced back at least to the Han times. *Hsi Han hui-yao* 西漢會要 (Kiangsu shu-chü ed.) 39. 6b-8b.

[76] CS 33. 17a-b.

[77] Commander of imperial guards and workmen, one of the *chiu ch'ing* 九卿. CS 24. 15b.

reservoirs, Hsin-ch'ü 新渠, Fu-shou 富壽, and Yu-yei 遊陂,[78] which irrigated 1500 *ch'ing* of fields.

In the twelfth moon of the first year of Hsin-ning 咸寧 [275], a decree read: "Although it has been common from ancient times for people to go out to fight and to come back to tilling, up until the campaign is ended we must be ever mindful of [our need for] warriors. Today let male and female slaves under the *Hsi-kuan* 奚官 [79] in Yeh be stationed at Hsin-ch'êng 新城 [80] to replace the cultivating soldiers in raising rice. Fifty male or female slaves shall form a camp, each headed by a *Ssŭ-ma* 司馬. Let everything follow the rules used in the military agricultural colonies."

In the third year [277] [81] again a decree read, "This year has had too much rain and in addition has suffered from plagues of locusts. In Ying-ch'uan 潁川 and Hsiang-ch'êng 襄城 [82] practically nothing has been sown since the spring. We are greatly worried. What can be done by the officials for the people? [10b] Take care of this matter quickly!" Tu Yü 杜預 [83] offered a memorial saying, "Your subject would give particular thought [to this problem]. At present the flood disaster is especially bad in the southeast. Not only has none of the five crops been harvested, but also the houses and other properties of the people have been injured. Those low fields have all become muddy and clogged up, while much of the high land is poor and lean. This means that the people will suffer from poverty immediately in the coming year. Although decrees earnestly warn the magistrates and prefects to plan for them, no comprehensive scheme has been laid down to determine the proper course to take. It is feared that empty words would hardly be beneficial. Even during the present summer and fall, which are vegetable-eating seasons, some people are already unable to get enough food. When the winter and spring come, the fields will lack green grass, so the people will certainly

[78] None of the three is identified.

[79] An office in charge of government slaves. It was under *Shao-fu* 少府, one of the *chiu ch'ing*. CS 24.16b.

[80] To the south of Lo-yang.

[81] CS 34.17a gives 278, which is followed by *T'ung chien* 80.14b.

[82] Both were prefectures in the central part of Honan.

[83] Biog. CS 34.14a-22b; GILES 2072.

look to the public granary for their food. This is a great problem special to one region, which has to be considered before [the crisis arrives].

"According to the humble opinion of your subject, since the people are suffering from flood, they might rely upon fish-food 魚菜,[84] water snails, and clams. However, because of the over-flowing flood, these are after all unobtainable for the poor and the weak. Now the reservoirs at the eastern boundary of the provinces Yen 兗 and Yü 豫 should be destroyed on a large scale. The water should be permitted to take its natural course. In this way the hungry can be benefited by the abundance of water products. The people will find food outside their doors in the morning and evening without leaving their homes. This will be beneficial for a time in providing a sufficient daily supply. [11a]

"After the water has gone the muddy and reclaimed fields will yield several *chung* 鍾 [85] per *mu*. When the spring comes, the five grains can be planted intensively and the harvests will be plentiful. This will be a benefit next year.

" Your subject formerly petitioned, ' The brood cows under the officials in charge of pastures are not used for ploughing or pulling carts. Cows which become old without having their noses bored, being of no use, represent only a waste of officials, soldiers, grain, and hay. Very few are sent in yearly for cart-pulling, and these are not well trained. They should be sold in large numbers in exchange for grain and used for payments.' Your Majesty decreed, ' Things for breeding should not be reduced in number or scattered.' So the question was put aside. According to information from the officials in charge, at present there are altogether over 45,000 large and small brood cows under the head warden of the parks and ponds 典虞, and the official in charge of the right pasture 右典牧.[86] Unless they are utilized, despite their great number, they will be a continually increasing expense. In ancient times the horses and the cattle contributed by the people on a plot of land [87]

---

[84] *Nan Ch'i shu* 5.3b and *Nan shih* 5.7b both mention *chêng yü-ts'ai* 蒸 ' steamed fish dish.'

[85] An ancient measure, the equivalent of 6.4 *hu*.

[86] Both under *T'ai-p'u* 太僕, one of the *chiu ch'ing*. CS 24.15b.

[87] LEGGE 5.337, 828. The requirement was three horses and one head of cattle.

174

were used inside [the country] for agriculture and outside for campaigns. They are unlike pigs or sheep. Now being kept to no purpose, these useful cows will eventually become a useless waste. It is a great mistake.

" In the southeast people work on water-fields, and have neither cattle nor calves. Now after the reservoirs are destroyed, 35,000 brood cows may be distributed among the officers, soldiers, and others in the two provinces so that the cows can be used for cultivation in the spring. [11b] When the grain is harvested, 300 [read 200] [88] *hu* can be charged per cow. This is to make use of a useless waste. When the grain is transported to the river valley, 7,000,00 *hu* can be collected. This will be another benefit after a few years.

" In addition, after the people come down from the high land and dwell on the plain, the future prosperity of the government and the people will be unlimited. The retained 10,000 good cows can be kept by those under the head of the right pasture 右典牧 都尉. When there are more people and less animals, the pasture land can also be cultivated. The results should be properly supervised. This [pasture land] is in the near-by imperial domain of the Three Wei regions.[89] An annual income of several hundred thousand *hu* [90] of grain would be received in addition. The cows should also be well trained so that they can be harnessed. These are the things that can be completed today."

[Tu] Yü also said, " Those who wish to cultivate water-fields all consider it convenient ' to till the land with fire and hoe it with water ' 火耕水耨.[91] It is not untrue. But this method is to be limited to newly opened land which is isolated from the dwellings of the people. In the previous periods when the territory of the southeast began to be exploited, the population there was sparse, therefore the people received the benefit of the method of fire

[88] 35,000 × 200 = 7,000,000. CSCC 26.13a.

[89] According to *T'ung chien* 96, 21a, commentary, San Wei were Wei-chün, Yang-p'ing 陽平, and Kuang-p'ing 廣平. Also cf. *Shui-ching chu* 10.7a.

[90] The text 數千萬斛 ' scores of millions of *hu* ' is probably erroneous. CSCC 26. 13a has 數十萬斛, which is followed in our translation.

[91] "A primitive form of agriculture, cultivating more or less virgin soil by burning down the overgrowth, flooding the land, and at about the same time seeding rice." CHI: *Key Economic Areas in Chinese History* 98.

farming. Recently since the population has increased every day, reservoirs and dikes [or dams] have been drained each year, so that good fields have been growing weeds and the people living in swamps. Both the water and the land are being misused; pasturage has stopped; trees stand dry.[92] This is all due to the harm done by reservoirs.

[12a] " When there are too many reservoirs, the soil will become poor, and streams shallow. The puddles made by rain will not give the benefit of moistening the soil.[93]   Therefore, whenever there is rain, the water will overflow, causing flood, and even reach the dry fields. The advisers not thinking of the reason consequently remark, ' This land cannot be sown dry.' Your subject has studied the Han population and discovered by verification that the region at present occupied by reservoirs was entirely cultivated dry. The few old reservoirs and dikes are solidly built, unlike those which today are called ' harmful to people.'

" Your subject formerly read the memorial offered by Imperial secretary Hᴜ Wei 尚書胡威,[94] requesting the destruction of reservoirs. His words were earnest and to the point.   Your subject more recently also read the petition by Yɪɴɢ Tsun, Minister to the Marquis of Sung 宋侯相應遵,[95] for the destruction of the Ssŭ Reservoir 泗陂 and a shifting of the route of transportation. At that time the *tu-tu* 都督 or governor-general [96] and the *tu-chih* 度支 or imperial secretary in charge of state finance [97] were commanded to hold a joint discussion. Each of the two held his own views and Yɪɴɢ Tsun's proposal was not followed.

[92] Mabel Ping-hua Lᴇᴇ (*The Economic History of China* 196-7) gives a translation of about a quarter of these two (or one) long memorials, which is followed in general here. For these two clauses 放牧絕種、樹木立枯 her version is " the pasture works have put an end to the raising of grains; and the trees and woods all become dry at once."

[93] 潦不下潤 similar to 水不潤下, which is an expression frequently seen in the *Wu-hsing chih* of the dynastic histories.

[94] Biog. CS 90.3b-5a.

[95] Sung was a district to the north of T'ai-ho 太和, northwestern Anhwei.

[96] Commander of troops in provinces or prefectures. These troops were often assigned to agricultural colonies.

[97] Or *to-chih*. The full title was *tu-chih shang-shu* 尚書. CS 24.9a-10a. Tᴜ Yü himself once served as *tu-chih shang-shu*.

" Your subject would speak as follows: as far as [YING] Tsun's petition is concerned, it is true that a route of transportation goes east to Shou-ch'un via an old canal, so that it is possible to dispense with the Ssŭ Reservoir. The Ssŭ Reservoir, located in the region under [YING] Tsun, occupies over 13,000 *ch'ing* of land and [thus] damages cultivated fields. In [YING] Tsun's district the government tenants [97a] are only 2600, which may be considered a very small number, and yet, suffering from a shortage of land, they cannot fully utilize their labor. This damage is all done by the water. They should be pitied by all. However, the *tu-tu* and *tu-chih* keep insisting on their own differing opinions. It is not that [individual] opinions [12b] are in error 難直; [but rather] that the differences impede a reasonable [settlement]. Since people's personal opinions vary, one and the same thing can be advantageous to some while harmful to others. The military colonies against the prefectures and districts, the upper classes against the common folk—between them there is no unanimity of opinion. All of them consider only one-sidedly their own benefit, but forget the harm [to others]. This is why, when reasonableness does not fully prevail, there is much trouble in affairs.

" Your subject also noticed that within the boundary of Yü-chou, as far as the tenants under the two *tu-chih* [98] are concerned, the regular and miscellaneous troops belonging to the prefectures and provinces used, altogether, only 7500 *ch'ing* of water-fields. A storage of three years' water supply does not require much over 20,000 *ch'ing*. Normal reasoning finds no benefit in the accumulation of much useless water, particularly given that the stored water is now flooding and causing great trouble. According to your subject it is better to let the water flow off than keep it improperly. An edict should be issued to the effect that the governors and prefects should see to it that all the old reservoirs and dikes built up by the Han dynasty, and also small ponds in mountains and valleys built by private families, be repaired and fixed so as

---

[97a] The *hapax legomenon* " ying tien " looks like a textual corruption. Accordingly I do not translate the " ying."

[98] Probably assistants to the *tu-chih shang-shu*. *T'ung tien* 2.17c gives 荆河州界中度支 instead of 豫州界二度支. Accordingly the *tu-chih* may have meant only one official, .i e. the *shang-shu*.

to store the water; and that those reservoirs which have been built since the Wei dynasty and those like P'u-wei [Pei] 蒲葦 and Ma-ch'ang Pei 馬腸陂 [99] which overflow when it rains be all drained off. The prefects and magistrates should supervise the work in person. [13a] The work of the laborers should be temporarily recorded, so that when the marsh becomes dry it can be allotted to the laborers who have contributed to the work. The old reservoirs and dikes which need repair should be examined minutely as called for by the Han tradition. The plan should be worked out in sections and submitted in advance. When winter comes and the troops in the southeast are to be replaced, let them be retained for one month to help in [the work].

" Rivers and streams have their normal courses; the configuration of places is definite. Under the Han dynasty, although the population was large and the people suffered no disaster. Now, because of the trouble which reservoirs are causing, they should be drained. When the tracing of history throws light on the modern situation, the general principles being perfectly clear, it is possible to discuss [problems] successfully from an armchair. Your subject cannot refrain from thinking that his humble suggestion is a genuine benefit for today."

The government followed it.

After the Wu Kingdom was pacified [280], the officials again memorialized and the decree [read]: [100] " The princes and dukes having their domains as homes ought not own additional houses or fields at the capital. At present, however, there being no time for the construction of official residences 邸 for them,[101] they should be allowed to have stations in the city and ' fields for hay-supply ' [102] in near-by suburbs. But let them now be restricted

---

[99] Unidentified.

[100] It is possible that the whole passage was a memorial in which a former decree was quoted. *T'ung tien* 1.12b cites the paragraph in full but lacks the two characters 詔書 for decree.

[101] Under the Han there were official stations in the capital for the chiefs of provinces and principalities (*Han shu* 19A. 8a). Emperor Wu of the Han also ordered such stations for feudal lords to be built at the foot of the holy mountain T'ai Shan and near the Kan-ch'üan Palace outside Chang-an (*Han shu* 25A. 32b, 25B. 3b). According to a tradition (*Shih chi* 58. 8b) under the Western Han a prince or marquis was allowed to stay in the capital for not more than twenty days during a court visit.

[102] In fact for supply in general.

as follows: A prince, duke, or marquis may have one homestead in the capital; in the suburb the holder of a large fief [103] may have [13b] fifteen *ch'ing* of land, of a medium fief ten *ch'ing*, and of a small one seven *ch'ing*. Those without an abode in the city but having one outside may keep it.''

The system of *hu-tiao* 戶調 or 'household levies' [104] was also established. A household headed by a regular male adult [105] paid annually three *p'i* of silk and three *chin* of floss.[106] A household headed by a female or secondary male adult was to pay one half of the taxes. For prefectures along the boundary the levies were sometimes reduced to two-thirds, and for the farthest ones to one-third. Barbarians contributed taxes in cloth at the rate of one *p'i* per household, and those farthest away sometimes only one *chang* [per household].

A male may hold 70 *mu* of land, and a female 30 *mu*. Besides, a regular male adult [may be expected] to work 50 *mu*, a regular female 20 *mu*, and a secondary male adult 25 *mu*; a secondary female adult none. Males and females between 16 and 60 years of age are regular adults; between 13 and 15 or between 61 and 65, secondary adults. Those under 12 or over 66 are 'the old' or 'the young,' [106a] and [are expected] not to work.[107] Barbarians

---

[103] The grades of fiefs were defined in 265, and revised in 277 when practically all the nobles were sent to their domains. CS 24.23a-4a; *T'ung tien* 31.179b-c.

[104] The *hu-tiao* system was probably first instituted by Ts'ao Ts'ao in 204 or earlier. SKC 23.13a mentions *hu-tiao* payable in silk and floss in about 200.

[105] These terms are defined in the next paragraph.

[106] 1 *p'i* = 4 *chang* = 40 *ch'ih*; 1 *chin* = 16 *liang*.

1 Chin *ch'ih* = 0.241 metre = 0.788 ft.

1 Chin *liang* = 13.92 grams.

[106a] The categories, adult male 丁男, secondary male 次男, and young male 小男, appear on a fragment of a local household register dated 416 which was discovered in Tun-huang. The age classification of males in the register, with a few exceptions, seems to agree with the regulations mentioned here, but females are recorded only in one group, 女口. Cf. Lionel GILES: A Census of Tun-huang, *TP* 16 (1915) 468-88; and NIIDA Noboru: *Tō Sō hōritsu bunsho no kenkyū* 唐宋法律文書の研究 668-73. GILES is probably wrong in rendering *tz'ŭ nan* by "younger (adult) sons." The expression seems to be used in the register to mean over-aged males or even the "old." NIIDA, overlooking GILES' note on the word 散 which indicates a status or profession (*TP* 16.474), mistakes it for a surname (p. 668).

[107] For a discussion on this paragraph see Introduction. 1 Chin *mu* = 0.121 Eng. acre.

179

in remote districts [108] who do not work land are to pay *i-mi* 義米 or 'voluntarily contributed husked grain' at the rate of three *hu* per household; those in farther regions five *tou* [i. e. half a *hu*]; and those in the farthest region twenty-eight coins per individual.

Officials from the first to the ninth rank hold land according to their status: first rank, 50 *ch'ing*; [14a] second rank, 45; third, 40; fourth, 35; fifth, 30; sixth, 25; seventh, 20; eighth, 15; and ninth, 10. They are also allowed in proportion to their ranks, to 'protect' [i. e. to acquire exemption from taxes and corvée for] their relatives, the maximum as many as nine generations [or families],[109] the minimum three generations. Imperial agnates, 'national guests,' [110] and descendants of early sages, and sons and grandsons of scholars also share the privilege [of protecting their relatives].

There was also a privilege of protecting *i-shih-k'o* 衣食客 lit. 'clothing-food-guests' and *tien-k'o* 佃客 lit. 'tenant-guests.' [111] Officials of the sixth rank and above were each allowed to have three *i-shih-k'o*; those of the seventh and eighth rank, two; those of the ninth rank and imperial attendants called the *chü-nien* 舉輦 [lit. carriers of the imperial chair] and *chi-ch'in* 跡禽, guards 司馬 in three groups called the *ch'ien-ch'ü* 前驅 [heralds], *yu-chi* [marksmen like YANG Yu-chi 養由基 in the sixth century B. C.], and *ch'iang-nu* 強弩 [strong crossbow men], gentlemen of the *yü-lin* guards 羽林郎, foot-guards freely attending in palaces 殿中宂從武賁,[112] foot-guards in palaces 殿中武賁, foot-guards and horse-guards with maces and axes 持椎斧武騎武賁, freely attending foot-

---

[108] OKAZKI Fumio in his *Nambokucho ni okeru shakai keizai seido* 162-3 omits in a quotation the two characters *yüan-i* 遠夷 'barbarians in remote districts' and thus misinterprets the whole sentence as a regulation for the secondary female adult.

[109] There have been two interpretations of the term *chiu-tsu* 九族, the one referring to the nine generations of one's own clan, the other referring to four generations of one's own clan, three of his mother's, and two of his wife's.

[110] Representative descendants of the former dynasties. In 265 three princes of the Chou, Han and Wei dynasties were made the *san k'o* 三恪 or 'Three Respectables' following an ancient tradition. *T'ung tien* 74.405b-c.

[111] See Introduction, paragraph following footnote 48.

[112] *Jung-ts'ung* or *san-ts'ung* 散從 means to attend but have no definite duties (*T'ung tien* 21.123a note on *san-chi ch'ang-shih* 散騎常侍; 28.163b note on *jung-ts'ung p'u-yeh* 宂從僕射). *Wu-pên* was originally *hu-pên* 虎, here changed because *hu* was a T'ang taboo. *Ts'ê-fu yüan-kuei* 505.8b gives *hu-pên*.

guards with short spears 持鈒宂從武賁, and marksman guards on foot or on horseback 命中武騎武賁,[113] one.

Those who were allowed to have 'tenant-guests' should not have more than fifty households if holding the first or the second rank; ten households if the third rank; seven if the fourth; five if the fifth; three if the sixth; [14b] two if the seventh; and one if the eighth or the ninth.

At that time the empire was peaceful; taxes were equitably levied; and the people, secure in their livelihoods, enjoyed their work. After the reign of Emperor Hui both administration and culture declined. By the Yung-chia period [307-312] trouble and disturbances were very wide-spread. From Yung-chou 雍[114] eastward many suffered from hunger and poverty. People were sold [as slaves]. Vagrants became countless. In the six provinces of Yu 幽, Ping 幷, Ssŭ 司, Chi 冀, Ch'in 秦, and Yung[115] there was a bad plague of locusts. Grass, trees, and hair of cattle and horses were all eaten up [by the locusts]. Further virulent disease accompanied the famine. Also the people were murdered by bandits. The rivers were filled with floating corpses; bleached bones covered the fields. During Liu Yao's invasion [311] the court discussed the desirability of moving the capital to Ts'ang-yüan 倉垣.[116] There was much cannibalism. Famine and pestilence came hand in hand. Eighty to ninety per cent of the officials fled and became vagrants.

When Emperor Yüan was the Prince of Chin [317], he assigned and supervised agricultural work. A decree was issued that the prefects and magistrates were to be graded by the amount of grain yielded [in their prefectures and districts]. Soldiers unless on the important duty of guarding the imperial palace should all join in the work of cultivation. Each army should work in the fields and use the harvest as their stores.

In the first year of T'ai-hsing 太興 [318] a decree said, " In the two provinces of Hsü 徐 and Yang 揚[117] the land is suited to the

[113] Most of these officers can be found in CS 24. 20a-b.
[114] Shensi.
[115] Northern Hopei, Shansi, Honan, southern Hopei, Kansu, and Shensi.
[116] To the northeast of Kaifeng, Honan.
[117] Kiangsu and western Anhwei.

planting of three kinds of wheat and barley 三麥.[118] The people should be ordered to plant these in dry land at the approach of autumn. The crop ripened by summer can be used to fill the gap [15a] between the old and the new [grain]. [The people] will be relieved by it, and the benefit will be very great. Formerly the Han sent FAN Shêng-chih 氾勝之,[119] messenger travelling in a light cart 輕車使者, to supervise wheat and barley plantation in the three prefectures near the capital, with the result that the Kuan-chung region had rich harvests. [Now], do not let the people be late!" For many years after, although wheat and barley suffered from frequent droughts and plagues of locusts, the benefits [of this plan] were still many.

In the second year [319] the Three Wu regions suffered a serious famine. People perished in hundreds.[120] TÊNG Yu 鄧攸,[121] prefect of Wu, opened the granaries on his own responsibility to give relief. Emperor Wu [read Yüan] [122] sent Yü Fei 虞騑斐 and HUAN I 桓彝,[123] who were both attending secretaries inside the imperial yellow gate 黃門侍郎, to open granaries to give relief. Corvées were reduced. The officials were asked to offer memorials. YING Shan 應詹,[124] who was the general of the hou-chün 後軍, petitioned, "When one person fails to cultivate, the consequent starvation will certainly be suffered by somebody in the empire.[125] Since the beginning of the military emergency huge sums have already been spent on expeditions, transportation, the imperial court, the ances-

[118] The term san mai, also mentioned in CS 27.11a, is rarely seen in other places, and its meaning is not very clear. It may have referred to ta-mai 大 'barley,' hsiao-mai 小 'wheat,' and kung-mai 穬 'a kind of bare barley?,' which are often mentioned together in Ts'ui Shih's 崔寔 Ssŭ-min yüeh-ling 四民月令 (Ch'üan Hou Han wên 47.4a, b, 6a). Kung-mai also appears many times on Han wooden documents (LAO Kan: Chü-yen Han chien k'ao-shih, shih-wên 2.31a-73a).

[119] Famous agriculturalist in the first century B.C. Fragments of his work on agriculture have been collected in MA Kuo-han's 馬國翰 Yü-han shan-fang chi-i-shu 玉函山房輯佚書 ts'ê 69.

[120] CSCC 26.17a questions the 'in hundreds,' but the same expression is in CS 6.9b.

[121] Biog. CS 90.12a-4b; GILES 1907.

[122] "Wu" is evidently an error. CSCC 26.17a.

[123] Biog. CS 76.17a; 74.1a-3.

[124] Biog. CS 70.1a-6a.

[125] An old saying quoted by many thinkers. Kuan tzŭ 23.7b; Lü-shih ch'un-ch'iu 呂氏春秋 (Ssŭ-pu ts'ung-k'an ed.) 21.8a; Han shu 24A.8b.

tral temples, and the officials. Of the lower classes, craftsmen, merchants, vagrants, servants, and slaves, those who wander about and consume without working on farms or on silk culture, amount to several hundred thousand. Is it not difficult to hope for a prosperous country and well-fed people when no thought is being given to the winning of the fairest of profits?

" The ancients said, ' When starvation and cold arrive, even [sage rulers like] Yao and Shun would not be able to prevent the growth of banditry in the country. When there is a monopoly of both poverty and wealth, even [wise judges like] Kao-yao 皋 陶 126 cannot check the insults given by the powerful to the weak.' 127 [15b] Therefore do rulers of a state ever fail to devote themselves to agriculture and the planting of grain? Recently Emperor Wu of the Wei adopted the proposal of TSAO Chih and HAN Hao 韓浩,128 and established military agricultural colonies on a large scale. And even during campaigns, armed soldiers were sent to cultivate the fields at proper occasions. So without overworking the lower people, great achievements were made.

" Meanwhile, vagrants went to Wu in the east. Now, however, since Wu suffers from dearth, they have already returned. The fertile fields to the west of the Yangtze river 江西 129 have been abandoned for years. It should be comparatively easy to apply the method of ' fire plowing and water cultivating. People should be selected from the vagrants [to work on the fields] and the agricultural officials should be restored.130 Rewards to achievements

126 Biog. GILES 965.

127 Probably not exactly a quotation. A similar idea may be found in *Han shu* 23.21b and some earlier works as collected in WANG Chi-p'ei's 汪繼培 commentary on *Ch'ien-fu lun* 3.7b-8a.

128 Biog. SKC 9.3a-b.

129 According to HU San-hsing (*T'ung chien* 66.15b, commentary) the region from Li-yang 歷陽 (Ho-hsien 和, eastern Anhwei) to Ju-hsü k'ou 濡須口 (near Ch'ao-hsien, 巢 central Anhwei) was generally called Chiang-hsi.

130 The agricultural officials were abolished and reappointed as prefects and magistrates in 264 (SKC 4.35a) or 266 (CS 3.7a). Yü Chêng-hsieh (*Kuei-ssǔ lei-kao* 11.41b) questions the thoroughness of the abolition in 264, but fails to mention the abolition in 266. The two cases of agricultural officials which he cites as still acting (FU Hsien 傅咸, CS 47.1a and Ho Tsêng 何曾, CS 33.8a) were in fact both before 264.

should be given according to the tradition of the Wei dynasty: in the first year the whole income goes to the people; in the second year it is divided equally between them and the government; and from the third year they are subject to levies and corvée.[131] When the government and the people are both benefited, the days can be counted when the granaries will be full and stores abundant."

[YING Shan] also said, " Formerly Emperor Kao-tsu 高祖 [of the Han] appointed HSIAO Ho 蕭何 [132] to govern Kuan-chung; Emperor Kuang-wu sent K'OU Hsün 寇恂 [133] to govern Ho-nei 河內; [134] Emperor Wu of the Wei intrusted affairs in the west [i. e. in Shensi] to CHUNG Yu 鍾繇.[135] Therefore rebels in all directions were conquered and the empire was pacified. Now the central provinces [i. e. Honan] are in depression and the land there has not been properly laid out, so that the people are still yearning. Shou-ch'un is the capital of an area not far from Honan. A governor-general of civil and military talent should be selected [and stationed there] [16a] in order that the military situation in the far Yellow and Lo valleys may be improved, and the near provinces of Hsü and Yü protected. The governor-general should collect and soothe the vagrants and give them protection. He should be given sole charge of the agricultural work so that affairs will be conducted to a definite aim. [Formerly] CHAO Ch'ung-kuo 趙充國 [136] conquered the Hsi-ling 西零 barbarians [137] through the foundation of military agricultural colonies in Chin-ch'êng 金城; [138] CHU-KO Liang 亮[139] managed to fight against a superior nation by the cultivation of fields in the Wei river valley.[140] Now the troops, except those facing the enemy, should all work [at agriculture]."

---

[131] The Wei system of sharing profits with civil or military tenants is recorded in CS 47.4a-b and 109.9a. The tenant received 40 per cent of the product if he used the government's cattle, and 50 per cent if he used his own. According to SKC 16.2a commentary it was TS'AO Chih who convinced Ts'AO Ts'ao that he should adopt the profit-sharing system instead of collecting rent in terms of a fixed amount of grain.

[132] Biog. *Han shu* 39.1a-7a; GILES 702.

[133] Biog. HHS 46.17b-23a.   [135] Biog. SKC 13.1a-8b; GILES 521.

[134] Northern Honan.   [136] Biog. *Han shu* 69.1a-18a.

[137] Better known as Hsien-ling or Hsien-lien 先零, a Ch'iang tribe.

[138] Prefecture in central Kansu.

[139] Biog. SKC, Shu 5; GILES 459.

[140] In both cases soldiers did the farming work.

In the fifth year of Hsien-ho 咸和 [330] Emperor Ch'êng 成 [326-342] for the first time [141] had the people's fields measured, and one-tenth [of the product] was taken as taxes, the average being three *shêng* of husked grain per *mu*.[142] In the sixth year [331] water transportation of supplies was discontinued because of raids made by pirates. Over a thousand adults [143] were summoned from the families of princes and dukes down. Each was to transport six *hu* of husked grain.

Afterwards floods, droughts, and plagues of locusts came year after year, and no crops arrived [to the central government]. In the first years of Hsien-k'ang 咸康 [335-342] an account was rendered on the husked grain taxed by acreage 算度田稅米.[144] The uncollected amount was over 500,000 *hu*. Imperial secretary CH'U [*read* HSIEH] P'ou 褚(謝)裒 [145] and some officials of lower ranks were discharged.

In the reign of Emperor Mu 穆 [345-361] large levies of troops were raised so frequently that the grain-transport broken down. A decree commanded the loan of one person from every thirteen households belonging to the princes and dukes down to help the *tu-chih* in transportation.

In the first years of Shêng-p'ing 升平 [357-361] HsÜN Hsien 荀 羨 [146] was governor-general of the northern provinces and was stationed at Hsia-p'ei 下邳.[147] He had fields established at Shih-

[141] This should not be understood as the first time that land-taxes were collected under the Chin. It has been pointed out by T'AO Hsi-shêng and WU Hsien-ch'ing (*Nan Pei Ch'ao ching-chi shih* 66, note 6) that edicts granted regional or partial exemptions from land-taxes in disastrous years in 282, 283, and 305 (CS 3.21b, 22a, 4.13b).

[142] If three *shêng* formed one-tenth of the product, the average rate of production would be thirty *shêng* or three *tou* of husked grain (or five *tou* of unhusked grain) per *mu*, which seems too low. An average rate at three *hu* (thirty *tou*) in the second century is given in HHS 79.22b. The rice-fields in south China produced even more in the third and fourth centuries. Cf. T'AO Yüan-chên: *San Kuo shih-huo chih* 56-8.

[143] CS 7.6b reads 千餘丁.

[144] According to CS 7.9b, in 336 "an account was rendered on husked grain taxed for military supplies" 算軍用稅米.

[145] "CH'U" is an error. CSCC 26.18a.

[146] Biog. CS 75.22b-23b.

[147] To the east of P'ei-hsien, northern Kiangsu. This was in 357.

pieh 石鼈 in Tung-yang 東陽,[148] of which both the government and the people received the benefit.

When Emperor Ai 哀 [362-365] came to the throne, the land-tax was reduced to two *shêng* per *mu* [362]. [16b] In the second year of T'ai-yüan 太元 [377] under Emperor Hsiao-wu 孝武 [373-396] the method of collecting tax by acreage was abolished.[149] Every one from a prince or duke down was to pay three *hu*, with the only exemption granted to those who were on corvée 在役之 身.[150] In the eighth year [383] the tax payable in husked grain was raised to five *shih* [or *hu*] per person. In the last years of the reign the empire suffered from no disturbances. The time was peaceful and harvests were plentiful. The people enjoyed their occupations. Grain and silk were in abundance. Almost every household and every person had a sufficiency.

[148] To the west of Pao-ying 寶應, central Kiangsu. CS 75.23a mentions the establishment before he was stationed at Hsia-p'ei and when he was at Huai-yang 淮陽 in central Kiangsu. CSCC 26.18a-9b.

[149] CS 9.9a gives 376.

[150] Perhaps also people in military service.

(3) On Money

Formerly the Han used the five-*shu* coins as currency. After the reform of WANG Mang[1] the people all found [his new coins] inconvenient. When KUNG-SUN Shu 公孫述[2] arrogated the imperial title in Shu, there was a ballad saying, " When yellow cattle become white-bellied, the five-*shu* coins will be resumed." [3] Those who were interested in superstitions remarked secretly, " WANG Mang has declared yellow as his color. [KUNG-SUN] Shu wishes to succeed him and therefore declares white (belly)[4] as his. The five-*shu* coins were the Han currency. [This ballad] means that the Han will reunite the empire." When Emperor Kuang-wu refounded the [Han] dynasty, the *huo-ch'üan* 貨泉 coins[5] issued by [WANG] Mang were abolished.[6] In the sixteenth year of Chien-wu 建武 [40 A.D.] MA Yüan 馬援[7] again[8] offered a memorial saying, " The fundamental measure to enrich the state lies

[1] Homer H. DUBS: " WANG Mang and his economic reforms," *TP* 35 (1940).234-40, deals with the complicated series of new currency issued by WANG Mang.

[2] Biog. HHS 43.15a-24b.

[3] This ballad is recorded in HHS 23.13b as in 30 A.D. KUNG-SUN Shu styled himself emperor in 25 A.D.

[4] No ' belly' is mentioned in the interpretation of the ballad in HHS 23.13b. The character *fu* 腹 is probably an interpolation, which is replaced by *ti* 帝 ' emperor' in CSCC 26.19a. KUNG-SUN considered himself to have the white virtue and thus made white his imperial color, based upon the so-called mutual productive theory of the five virtues. Cf. HHS 43.17b, 19a-b.

[5] WANG Mang issued the *huo-ch'üan* coins to replace the others in 14 A.D. However, the expression *huo-ch'üan* is possibly used here to mean coins in general as in CS 26.1a.

[6] A mold of *huo-ch'üan* coins dated 26 A.D. recorded in *Chin-shih ch'i* 金石契 (a Ch'ing work by CHANG Yen-ch'ang 張燕昌 which I have not seen) shows that the *huo-ch'üan* were continued at least for a period after Kuang-wu came to the throne in 25 A.D. Cf. TING Fu-pao 丁福保: *Ku-ch'ien ta tz'ŭ-tien* 古錢大辭典 (1938, Shanghai) 下 359b-361b.

Since writing this note, my friend Mr. WANG Yü-ch'üan has informed me that no such mold is found in CHANG's work (1778 ed.).

[7] Biog. HHS 54.1a-19b; GILES 1490.

[8] MA Yüan had made a similar proposal two years previously. It was rejected after a discussion headed by the Three Highest Officials. MA Yüan then secured a copy of their unfavorable report and disputed all the thirteen points in it. Thus the Emperor was convinced by him.

in food and currency. The five-*shu* coins should be reminted as in former times." The proposal was approved by the emperor. Thereupon five-*shu* coins were minted again and the empire found them convenient.

In the reign of Emperor Chang 章 [75-88] the prices of grain and silk became high. The government [9] [17a] income was not sufficient, wherefore the imperial court was worried. Imperial secretary CHANG Lin 張林 remarked: " Now it is not only grain that is expensive; everything is expensive. The simple reason is that money has become cheap. The people in the empire should be ordered to pay their taxes in cloth and in silk, which should also be used exclusively as the media of exchange. Let the coins all be sealed [in the treasury] and not allowed to go out. In this way there will be less money and the goods will all become cheap. Moreover, salt is an essential item of food. The government may assume for itself the sale [10] of salt. . . .[11] This was practised under the name of *chün-shu* 均輸 [12] in the reign of Emperor Wu [140-87 B. C.]." Thereupon the affair was referred to a general discussion of the imperial secretaries. Imperial secretary CHU Hui 朱暉 [13] argued: "According to Royal Regulations 王制 [14] the Son of Heaven does not discuss possessions or non-possessions; a lord does not discuss quantities; the one who receives a salary does not

[9] The expression *hsien-kuan* 縣官 was used in the Han period to mean the government or the emperor.

[10] For the character *mai* 賣 HHS 73.4a reads *chu* 鬻 (not *yü* 鬻), which means ' boiling,' i. e. ' manufacture.'

[11] According to HHS 73.4a there should be inserted here the statement: "Also we should take advantage of the trips of the report-bearers from Annam and Western Szechuan to purchase jewels and to make profit out of them."

[12] This term refers to a practice of the government of collecting the levies and freight together and using the total to purchase profitable local products to ship to the capital. The measure originated in 115 B. C. It was supposed to bring about equitable division of labor and facilitate transportation of tribute, but actually it was for profit and to make trade in commodities. Cf. *Shih chi* 30.17b-8a (CHAVANNES 3.579); *Han shu* 19A.8b, commentary; HHS 73.4a, commentary; *Chiu-chang suan-shu* 2a-6b; and especially GALE, *Discourses on Salt and Iron 2*, 9-11.

[13] Biog. HHS 73.1a-4b.

[14] This statement is not in the *Wang-chih* chapter of either *Li chi* or *Hsün tzŭ* 荀子. A very similar passage is in the *Ta-lüeh* 大略 chapter of *Hsün tzŭ* (*Ssŭ-pu pei-yao* ed.) 19.14a, which DUBS omits in his translation. It is interesting to note that the last clause is included in the T'ang code. Cf. NIIDA Noboru: *Tōryō shūi* 244-5.

compete with the people for profit. The *chün-shu* measure is no different from [ordinary] trade and retail. To make taxes payable in cloth and silk would cause much corruption of the officers. Government sale of salt means to compete with the subjects for profit. These are not measures fit for wise rulers." The Emperor, already in favor of [CHANG] Lin's opinion, became angry upon the reception of [CHU] Hui's discussion. Consequently [CHANG] Lin's proposal was adopted, but soon again abolished.[15]

In the reign of Emperor Ho 和 [89-105][16] a memorial was presented saying, " The people have become poor and suffered on account of the light and thin coins. These should be reminted to make large coins." The affair was referred to the officials in the Four Offices 四府 [17] and scholars in the Imperial University who were able to offer an opinion. LIU T'ao 劉陶,[18] who was a *hsiao-lien* 孝廉,[19] presented a memorial: [17b] " Your subject in all humility has studied the decree on coinage and the proposal to adjust the weight [of coins]. Your Majesty wishes to extend the consultation to the insignificant and not to overlook [the opinion of] the poor and humble. Thus even a person fed on greens [like me] is referred to by over-extension.

[15] According to HHS 73.4a CHANG's proposal was first put aside on account of the objection from CHU and others. This memorial of CHU was offered when the proposal was made again and a favorable decision had been made by the Emperor in about 85 A.D. According to HHS 66.7a-b the famous scholar CHÊNG Chung 鄭衆 also offered strong objection to a proposal to restore government sale of salt and iron in about 81 A.D. The Confucian scholars still held their position against government monopoly as they did during the celebrated discussions on salt and iron in 81 B.C.

[16] According to the biog. of LIU T'ao, HHS 87.4a-11a, this was in the reign of Emperor Huan (147-167). *T'ung chien* 54.1a-2a records the discussion in 157.

[17] Offices of the Three Highest Officials and the Generalissimo 大將軍. HHS 87.6a, commentary.

[18] *Ch'üan Hou Han wên* 33.6b cites a fragment of a memorial by LIU T'ao-t'u 劉駒騊, the wording of which is almost identical with this one by LIU T'ao. LIU T'ao-t'u is mentioned in HHS 110A.15a as an imperial collator in c.110, but nothing is recorded about his opposition to the proposal of coinage. Probably the memorial was attributed to him by mistake because of the similarity of the two names.

[19] *Hsiao* and *lien*, " filial " and " incorrupt," were founded in 134 B.C. as two separate degrees, each gained by the best man in every prefecture at an annual competition. The two gradually became one degree in the course of the next two centuries. According to HHS 87.8b, LIU T'ao was only a member of the Imperial University, but was made *hsiao-lien* after the offer of the memorial.

" Probably the present worry should not be about money but about the hunger of the people. Thus the ancient kings observed the astronomical phenomena in order to [promote] the production of things. They delivered respectfully the calendar to the people, so that no man should flee the farm and no woman should leave the loom. Therefore, the proper relation between the ruler and the ruled was kept and the royal instructions were carried out. Reasoning it in this way, [one finds] that food is the treasure of the owner of a state and the most precious thing for the people. According to [your subject's] private opinion, in recent years excellent [grain] sprouts have been eaten up by locusts, and the loom has been emptied by public and private levies.[20] What [the people] worry about has been their daily pittance; what has given them concern has been the [imperial] business which is not to be performed slackly.[21] How can one say that [the problem lies] in the thickness and weight of coins? At present, even if sand and gravel were transformed into metals as precious as those of the south,[22] and tiles and stone became jade as excellent as that owned by the Ho 和 clan,[23] while the people were left neither food nor drink to assuage their hunger and thirst, even if [the ruler has] the pure virtue of The Emperor 皇 and [Fu-] hsi 羲 [24] and the high civilization of Yao and Shun, he would not be able to protect even the area ' within the screen of his own court.' [25]

" It is probable that the people could live for a hundred years without money, but not for a single day in starvation. Thus food is extremely important. Advisers do [18a] not grasp the fundamentals of agricultural production, and talk much about the convenience of coinage. Some [even] wish to cheat with it in order to purchase the state's wealth. When the state's wealth is about to be exhausted, competitors will struggle over it, and there grows the need of [more] coinage. Probably the fact is: when one person seizes upon [the coins], even ten thousand minters will not be

[20] LEGGE 4.353.   [21] LEGGE 4.183, 247-8, 260, 266, 360.
[22] LEGGE 4.620.
[23] *Han Fei tzŭ* 韓非子 (*Ssŭ-pu ts'ung-k'an* ed.) 4. 6b-7a.
[24] According to *T'ung chien* 54. 1b, commentary, Huang refers to the legendary ruler T'ien Huang 天皇.
[25] LEGGE 1.309.

able to supply him; how much the less, today, when only one person [i. e. the ruler] mints and ten thousand people seize upon [the coins]? Even if the *yin* and *yang* elements were the charcoal and all creation the copper, even if the people employed took no food and the overseers knew no hunger, yet the coins would not be enough to satisfy a boundless demand.

" Now the way to enrich the people lies chiefly in the stoppage of forced labor [26] and the prohibition of illegal use of the people's time, so that the people will have sufficient without [too much] toil. Your Majesty with holy virtue, pitying the worry and the difficulties of the people in the empire, wishes to mint coins and to unify the currency in order to relieve them. This is like rearing fish in a tripod of boiling water or nesting birds on live coals. Wood and water are what fish and birds usually live on or in. But when these are not used in their proper time they will certainly result in burning and thorough cooking. It is desired that Your Majesty will relax the prohibition of chipping coins and postpone the discussion of coinage." The Emperor finally did not mint coins.

When in the Ch'u-p'ing 初平 [190-193] era under Emperor Hsien TUNG Cho recast [the five-*shu* coins] into small coins, money becoming cheap, good became expensive, so that one *hu* of grain cost several millions of cash. [18b] When Ts'AO became prime minister these [small coins] were abolished and the five-*shu* coins were restored. At that time coinage had long been suspended; the currency, of modest volume from the beginning, had not been increased; thus grain became cheaper and cheaper.

In the second year of Huang-ch'u 黄初 [221] Emperor Wên of the Wei abolished the five-*shu* coins and had the people use grain and silk as media of exchange. By the reign of Emperor Ming 明 [227-239] coins had long been abolished and grain used [as the medium of exchange]. Counterfeiting gradually increased among the people. They competed in wetting grain to make profit [27] and produced thin silk for exchange. Even severe punishments could not stop them. SSǓ-MA Chih 芝 [28] and others led a general dis-

[26] The repeated *i* 役 is superfluous.
[27] This is probably done in order to increase the size of the grains.
[28] Biog. SKC 12. 18b-22a.

cussion at court. According to them " the use of coins not only enriches the state but also diminishes the infliction of punishment. Now if the five-*shu* coins are minted again, the state will become rich and punishments diminished, so that the general welfare will be benefited." Thus Emperor Ming of the Wei restored [29] the five-*shu* coins, which, as far as we know, were used until the Chin without change.

In the fifth year of Chia-p'ing 嘉平 [-ho 禾 236] [30] under SUN Ch'üan large coins were minted, each equivalent to 500 [cash]. In the first year of Ch'ih-wu 赤烏 [238] coins equivalent to 1000 [cash] were also minted. [31] Therefore when Lü Mêng 呂蒙 [32] conquered Ching-chou 荊, [33] SUN Ch'üan bestowed upon him one hundred million coins. [34] Since the coins were valued too highly, their denominations were only empty names, so that the people suffered. [35] SUN Ch'üan, hearing that the people did not consider them convenient, [ordered:] "Abolish them and cast utensils and things. [19a] Let the government not issue them any more. Let the private families which own them turn them over to the treasury. Let payment be made at a fair price so that none may be wronged." [36]

Under the Chin, after disturbances arose in Central China and

[29] OKAZAKI Fumio (*Nambokuchō ni okeru shakai keizai seido* 124) suggests that coins were merely restored, but no new coins were minted in this period, because no Wei coins have been recorded in works on Chinese numismatics.

[30] Chia-p'ing (253) is evidently an error. Cf. CSCC 26.21b. According to *T'ung tien* 8.48a this coin had a diameter of 1.3 *ts'un* and weighed 12 *shu*.

[31] According to *T'ung tien* this coin had a diameter of 1.4 *ts'ung* and weighed 16 *shu*. Illustrations of these large coins may be found in works on Chinese numismatics like *Ku-ch'üan hui* 古泉匯、利 5.5a-6a and *Ku-ch'ien ta tz'ŭ-tien* 上 184a-b.

[32] Biog. SKC, Wu 9.14a-22a; GILES 1452.

[33] Hupei.

[34] OKUHIRA Masahiro 奥平昌洪 in his *Tō A sen-shi* 東亞錢志 8.20b-21a points out an error: The conquest of Ching-chou was in 219 and Lü Mêng died immediately afterwards. These large coins were only minted 17 and 20 years after his death.

[35] A large coin of the denomination of 5000 cash was excavated in 1912 in Shang-yü 上虞, northern Chekiang. It has been identified as coined under the Wu, although there is no written record of it in the dynastic histories. A coin of the denomination of 2000 cash recorded in Sung numismatic works may also belong to the same period. Cf. OKUHIRA: ibid. 8.22a; *Ku-ch'ien ta tz'ŭ-tien* 上 184b-5a, 下 82b, 509b-10a.

[36] According to SKC, Wu 2.30b the decree was issued in 246.

Emperor Yüan crossed the Yangtze river, the old coins issued by the SUN family were used. They varied in weight: the large ones were called *pi-lun* 比輪 [37] and the medium ones *ssŭ-wên* 四文. SHÊN Ch'ung 沈充 [38] from Wu-hsing 吳興 [39] also minted small coins, which were called Mr. Shên's coins 沈郎錢. Since coins were not too many, they became rather dear.

In the third year of T'ai-yüan [378], under Emperor Hsiao-wu, a decree read: " Coins are an important treasure of the state. The folk tempted by profit have destroyed them continuously. The officials who have the duty of supervision 監司 should take note of this. The barbarians in Kuang-chou 廣 set a high value on bronze drums [40] but no copper is produced in that province. We hear that traders, backed by officials or otherwise,[41] tempted by the comparatively heavier weight of the *pi-lun* coins, export these to Kuang-chou and sell them to the barbarians for melting down and casting into drums. Let this be severely prohibited. Those who are caught shall be punished."

In the years of Yüan-hsing 元興 [402-404], under Emperor An 安, when Huan Hsüan 桓玄 [42] was the prime minister, he proposed the abolition of coins and the adoption of grain and silk [as mediums of exchange]. K'UNG Lin-chih 孔琳之 [43] argued as fol-

[37] Lit. " comparable to wheels." The expression " even though the shell-money had at times been as large as wheels " 貝或如輪 is found in *Sung shu* 56.9b. The character *shu* 輸 in our text is an error. CS *pai-na* ed. 26.10b-11a, Chi-ku ko 汲古閣 ed. 26.13b, and *T'ung tien* 8.48a all read *lun*.

[38] Biog. CS 98.15a-16a.

[39] Prefecture in northern Chekiang.

[40] Kuang-chou refers to modern Kwangtung and Kwangsi. Bronze drums have played a very important part in the social and religious life of many tribes in Southeastern Asia. Their use can be traced back to the beginning of the Christian era, and is still found in modern time in some backward tribes, for example the Miao tribes in Kwangsi and Kweichow. Cf. F. HEGER: *Alte Metalltrommeln aus Südost-Asien* (Leipzig, 1902; TORII Ryūzō 鳥居龍藏 *Myōzoku chōsa hōkoku* 苗族調査報告 (1903), Chinese translation (1936) 300-42; H. PARMENTIER: Anciens tambours de bronze, *BEFEO* 18(1918).1-30.

[41] Officials have been deeply interested in commerce since the Ch'in and Han times in spite of government restriction. Cf. T'AO and WU: *Nan Pei Ch'ao ching-chi shih* 106-12. The three characters 於此下 in our text seem to be an interpolation. Cf. CSCC 26.22a.

[42] Biog. CS 99.1a-21a; GILES 837.

[43] Biog. *Sung shu* 56.3a-9a; *Nan shih* 27.6b-9b. The discussion probably took place

lows: "Among the *Hung-fan's* 洪範 [44] eight items in government, money is listed immediately after food. Is it not because money, being the medium of exchange, is of most important use? If the people devoted their energy to making coins, their livelihood would be hindered, [19b] and it would be proper to prohibit [coinage]. Now, however, the farmers are naturally occupied with the production of grain, and the craftsmen with the production of tools or utensils. Each clinging to his own trade, when [45] have they devoted themselves to coinage?

"Therefore the sage kings instituted currency, [otherwise] useless, to serve as a medium of exchange for useful wealth. Not only is the waste from destruction avoided, but also the difficulty in transportation is avoided. That is why coins have succeeded to the function of tortoise [shells] and cowries [46] and have never been abolished through the dynasties.

"Grain and silk are treasures fundamentally for food and clothing. If part of them is set off to be used as currency, the accruing disadvantage will be great. Also they will be found bothersome [47] to the hands of the traders, and will be diminished and wasted when used in cut [pieces]. This defect is well known from the past. Thus CHUNG Yu 鍾繇 said, 'Those who are clever in counterfeiting compete in wetting grain [48] to make profit and produce thin silk to augment their wealth.' The Wei dynasty prohibited the practice with severe punishment, but could not stop it. Therefore SSŬ-MA Chih considered that the use of coins would not merely enrich the state but also result in fewer punishments.

"Automatic abolition of coins may result from a continuation of military disturbances, as toward the end of the Han dynasty. Now, however, coins are in use; if abolished, the people will imme-

---

in 402. In the twelfth moon of the year, HUAN Hsüan usurped the throne. He was defeated and executed in 404. A collation of this long discussion has been made in CSCC 26.22b-23a with *T'ung tien* 8.48a-b, but, curiously enough, not with the two biographies of K'UNG.

[44] A chapter in *Shu ching*, LEGGE 3.320-44.

[45] *Ho-tang* 何當 means "when," but here is probably a corruption of *ho-ch'ang* 曷嘗.

[46] Used as money in ancient times.

[47] *Nan shih* 27.7a reads *fan* 煩 instead of *hui* 毀.

[48] *Sung shu* 56.3b has "compete in storing wet grain" 競蘊濕穀.

diately lose their profit.[49] Today, if we were to put together [50] the grain in the world to provide food for all, [we should find that] some have full and overflowing granaries [20a] while others have not even a peck of stock.[51] If they are to provide for one another 以相資通, then the poor will be beholden to the rich. The way to acquire riches is indeed based upon coins. If they are suddenly abolished they will become waste. That means that those who own coins but not grain will all helplessly suffer starvation.[52] Accordingly its [money's] abolition will also create trouble.

"Moreover, to consider the present situation, places where money is used have not been impoverished and places where grain is used [as currency] have not been enriched. In addition, the people, long accustomed to coins, certainly would be confused by the abolition. The proverb says, 'Unless there are a hundred advantages, one is not to change his course.' How much the more when coins are more convenient than grain!

" By the reign of Emperor Ming of the Wei, coins had long been abolished [53] and grain adopted [as the medium of exchange]; yet, since the people found it inconvenient, the whole court held a grand discussion. The scholars of superior talent and expertness in government all considered it fitting to restore coins. The people had no different feeling and in the court there was no different advice. That they chose to give up grain and silk in order to use money is enough to show that the error of using grain and silk has already been warned against.[54]

"People sometimes say that the Wei dynasty, during the long period of the abolition of coins, had stored hundreds of millions and thus wished to put them to use in order to benefit the govern-

---

[49] *Sung shu* 56.3b and *Nan shih* 27.7a both give " their wealth " 財.

[50] *T'ung tien* 8.48a has " estimate " 計度.

[51] *Sung shu* 56.3b and *T'ung tien* 8.48b both read *tou* 斗 instead of *ping* 幷.

[52] *Yin* 因 is an error for *k'un* 困. *Sung shu* 56.3b, *Nan shih* 27.7b, *T'ung tien* 8.48b, and CS *pai-na* ed. 26.11b all have *k'un*.

[53] *Sung shu* 56.3b gives " it had been thirty years " but *Nan shih* 27.7b and *T'ung tien* 8.48b give " it had been forty years." Both seem to be incorrect because there were only less than twenty years from the abolition of coins in 221 to the end of Emperor Ming's reign in 239.

[54] *Sung shu* 56.3b, *Nan shih* 27.7b, and *T'ung tien* 8.48b all have " already tested."

ment and enrich the state. This is probably incorrect. Duke Wên of the Chin state, regarding as secondary the tactfulness of Uncle Fan 舅犯, put first the honesty of Ch'êng-chi 成季. He considered that although [the former's scheme] had temporary success, it was not so good as [the latter's principle], which was a permanent benefit.[55] At that time [under the Wei] celebrated wise men were among the officials and the court was filled with [20b] gentlemen of virtue. They were laying broad plans for the benefit of the empire and determining devices critical to national organization. If grain was, in fact, more convenient than coins, it is certain that actuated by principle, they would not have been blinded by an immediate advantage to give up a general course of permanent utility.[56] It is indeed nothing but a reform and new course caused by straitened circumstances.

" Recently, in the last years of Emperor Hsiao-wu, the empire suffered from no disturbances. The time was peaceful and the harvests were plentiful. The people enjoyed their occupations. Grain and silk were in abundance. Almost every household and every person had a sufficiency. Upon studying the facts of this function in affairs, [one learns that] coins are not a hindrance to people.

" Most recently, campaigns have been frequent and poor harvests have come in succession. This is indeed the reason why the cold and starved have not yet been relieved. Since you, the minister, have already given a hand to them, it is known that great reforms are under way. Instruction emphasizing the essential occupations is spread; rules to promote agriculture are pro-

[55] This story has several versions. The earliest is in *Lü shih ch'un-ch'iu* 14. 11b-12a: Before the famous campaign at Ch'êng-p'u 城濮 (south of P'u-hsien, western Shantung) against the state of Ch'u in 632 B.C., Duke Wên of the Chin state discussed strategy with Uncle Fan and then with Ch'êng-chi. Uncle Fan suggested the use of deceptive tactics, whereas Ch'êng-chi was against him. Duke Wên adopted Uncle Fan's policy and won the war. However, when he came to give bounties, the first prize went to Ch'êng-chi who stood for principle. Uncle Fan, also written 咎犯, had the name HU Yen 狐偃 (GILES 825); and Ch'êng-chi, also known as Yung-chi 雍季, had the name CHAO Ts'ui 趙衰 (GILES 188).

[56] CS Chi-ku ko ed. 26. 14b, *Sung shu* 56. 4a, and *T'ung tien* 8. 48b read *yung* 永 instead of *ch'iu* 求.

claimed. The calendar is respectfully delivered to the people, so that each of them will pursue his own trade. The wanderers having learnt to return [home] and those who devote themselves to less essential works having desisted, they both, therefore, are working together in the fields and no land is left waste any longer. If this is continued, an age of peace and prosperity will certainly come. Why worry about food and clothing? In my humble opinion, the device for curing the defects does not lie in the abolition of coins."

The opinion of the court tended to agree with [K'UNG] Lin-chih, therefore [HUAN] Hsüan's proposal was not put into effect.

BUDDHIST MONASTERIES AND FOUR MONEY-RAISING INSTITUTIONS IN CHINESE HISTORY

LIEN-SHENG YANG
HARVARD UNIVERSITY

In Chinese history there are four money-raising institutions which either originated in or had close connections with Buddhist temples and monasteries.[1] These four are the pawnshop, the mutual financing association, the auction sale, and the sale of lottery tickets. Pawnshops owned by and opened in Buddhist monasteries can be traced back to the fifth century. Mutual financing associations were closely connected with monasteries in the T'ang period if not earlier. Personal belongings of deceased monks were auctioned in monasteries under the T'ang, Sung, and Yüan dynasties, and perhaps also in earlier times, Lottery tickets were issued by monasteries to raise funds under the Yüan.

Pawnbroking and mutual financing have become general practices outside of monastic communities and have served as important means for those needing money to raise funds. The other two institutions, however, do not seem to have had such a notable and continuous record. Although various forms of drawing lots have appeared throughout Chinese history, they have been used chiefly for gambling and divination. In the farming out of taxes,[2]

---

[1] Buddhist temples and monasteries are scarcely separable in China. In this article, the word "monasteries" is used for both, including also nunneries.

[2] Tax farming can be traced back at least to the fifth century. In 486, Prince Ching-ling 竟陵王, i. e., HSIAO Tzŭ-liang 蕭子良 (460-494) said in a memorial, "Moreover, from ancient times the important post of superintendent of markets 司市 has been considered difficult to fill. Recently appointment to this office has been made not on the basis of talent, but merely by listing a large sum [of taxes to be collected] and permitting people to bid for the post. An incumbent will increase his estimate [of collections] seeking to hold on to the post, while a candidate will augment the tax [quota] in his bid to replace the former" 前人增估求俠, 後人加稅請代 (Nan-Ch'i shu 40.6b). For more instances of bidding for similar posts, see Nan-Ch'i shu 46.9a and Liang shu 10.3a-b.

From Sung times on, the term for bidding by a tax farmer is mai-p'u 買撲 or p'u-mai 撲買. Under the Yüan dynasty, in spite of strong objection from the

which is again a time-honored practice in China, competitive bidding has been featured prominently; however, it is not really an auction sale. Auction sales and the sale of lottery tickets apparently were discontinued as means of raising cash from Ming times onward, even in the monasteries. Their reappearance in the nineteenth century is probably a reintroduction from the West.

The Buddhist origin of pawnbroking in China has been noted by several Chinese and Japanese scholars. The celebrated Sung poet Lu Yu 陸游 (1125-1210) in his *Lao-hsüeh-an pi-chi* 老學庵筆記 [3] mentions pawnshops known as *ch'ang-shêng k'u* 長生庫, lit. "long-life treasuries," in Buddhist monasteries of his time and traces the practice back to the end of the fifth century when a certain CHÊN Pin 甄彬 [4] pawned a bolt of hemp cloth 束苧 in the treasury of a monastery. Later, having redeemed it, he found in it five taels of gold, which he promptly returned. The eighteenth century scholar CHAI HAO 翟顥 in his *T'ung-su pien* 通俗編 [5] quotes the note by Lu Yu and gives additional references to various names used for pawnshops under different dynasties. He concludes that prior to the T'ang, pawnbroking was limited to

wise statesman YEH-LÜ Ch'u-ts'ai 耶律楚材, certain taxes were raised from 1,100,000 taels of silver in 1238 to double this sum as a result of bids from tax farmers. (*Yüan shih* 146.9a). In the *Ch'ing-shih kao* 清史稿 129.18b-19a we find the term *p'u-hu* 樸戶 for tax farmers, in which the character *p'u* 樸 is either a misprint or a variation of *p'u* 撲. The term *chiu p'ai-hu* 酒拍戶 is found in the *I-chien chih* 夷堅志 (Han-fên-lou 涵芬樓 ed.), *pu* 補 7.3a. It refers to a tax farmer in wine, which was under government monopoly in Sung times (see *Sung hui-yao kao* 宋會要稿, *ts'ê* 130, "Shih-huo" 食貨 19.1a-19a). *P'ai* 拍 is a variant form of *p'u* 撲 in *p'u-mai* which appears in the same passage. The text refers to the early years of the Ch'un-hsi 淳熙 period (1174-1189). For related meaning of the character *p'u*, see notes 50 and 53 below.

Nankai Social and Economic Quarterly 8.4 (1936).824-852 contains a useful article by C. M. CHANG 張純明, "Tax farming in North China, a case study of the system of auctioned revenue collection made in Ching-hai Hsien, Hopei Province." Mr. CHANG is, however, incorrect in saying "References to tax farming do not go beyond the Manchu dynasty" (p. 826).

[3] Han-fên-lou ed., 6.1b.

[4] *Nan-shih* 70.10b. No date is given for the story, but the history says Emperor Wu of the Liang dynasty heard about it when he himself was still a commoner. CHÊN Pin was appointed to a government post after the Emperor came to the throne, which was in 502.

[5] Wu-pu-i-chai 無不宜齋 ed. (preface 1751), 23.15b-16b.

Buddhist monasteries. The Japanese authority on the history of legal institutions, MIYAZAKI Michisaburō 宮崎道三郎 (1855-1926),[6] has made a thorough study of the early history of pawn-broking in both China and Japan. He agrees with CHAI Hao as to its Buddhist origin and suggests that Japanese monks in the Kamakura period or earlier introduced pawnbroking from China. He also makes the interesting remark that pawnshop proprietors under the Sung wore black gowns, which may have been influenced by the black robes worn by Buddhist monks. MIYAZAKI, however, does not over-stress this point, because black gowns were also worn by the *shih ta-fu* 士大夫, or literati, under the Sung.

The story of the honest CHÊN Pin, however, is not the only early reference to pawnbroking in Buddhist monasteries. The *Nan Ch'i shu* 23.8b says that after the death of the prime minister CH'U Yüan 褚淵 in 482, his younger brother Ch'êng 澄 redeemed from the Chao-t'i ssŭ 招提寺 a white fur cushion, a cap pin made of rhinoceros horn,[7] and a yellow cow, which had been pawned by the prime minister. The white fur cushion was a gift from the late Emperor to the prime minister. The younger brother had the fur cut up to make other articles for himself. For this he was impeached and dismissed in 483. Through these few references, we can trace pawnbroking to the late fifth century.[8]

It appears that the term *ch'ang-shêng k'u* originally referred to monastery treasuries in general and not necessarily to their pawnbroking functions. In this sense it is synonymous with *wu-chin tsang* 無盡藏, lit. "inexhaustible treasury," which is also discussed by MIYAZAKI.[9] The most famous *wu-chin tsang* in

[6] His lecture on pawnshops 質屋の話, delivered in 1899, was published the next year and is included in his collected essays on the history of legal institutions, *Miyazaki sensei hōseishi ronshū* 宮崎先生法制史論集 compiled by NAKADA Kaoru 中田薫, Tōkyō, 1929, pp. 11-44.

[7] According to *Nan-Ch'i shu* 2.8b, jade pins were the fashion in the second half of the fifth century.

[8] This reference is quoted in the *Tōyō rekishi daijiten* 東洋歷史大辭典 3.471 and in the article 質庫源流考 by FANG Tê-hsiu 方德修 in the *Ch'ün-ya* 羣雅 1.3 (1940).14a-15b.

[9] *Miyazaki sensei hōseishi ronshū*, pp. 15-19.

200

Chinese history was that in the Hua-tu ssŭ 化度寺 in Ch'ang-an, headquarters of the San-chieh Sect 三階教 [10] founded by the monk Hsin-hsing 信行 (540-594) under the Sui dynasty. The tremendous amount of donated wealth in the monastery was used for the repair of temples and monasteries all over the country in the early T'ang period, until the treasury was confiscated by imperial order in 713. In its heyday, loans were made from this " inexhaustable treasury " even without written documents.[11] Probably most borrowers did pay back the loans for fear of divine retribution.[12]

The term *wu-chin*, or *mujin* in Japanese, was borrowed by the Japanese along with the institution of pawnbroking. In Japanese, the expression *mujinkō* means either a lottery or a mutual financing association. These extended meanings become clear when we find that the latter was also closely connected with Buddhist monasteries and that drawing lots may be used as a means of determining which member receives the loan from the association (see below).

It is certain that under the T'ang dynasty laymen were also in the pawnbroking business. For example, Princess T'ai-p'ing 太平公主,[13] daughter of Kao-tsung and Wu-hou, and her protégés (including a barbarian monk) are reported to have owned farms, gardens and *chih-k'u* 質庫, i. e., pawnshops. A T'ang story mentions a pawnshop (*chi-fu p'u* 寄附鋪) owned by a layman in

---

[10] For a thorough study of the San-chieh Sect and a collection of related materials from Tun-huang and Japan, see *Sankaikyō no kenkyū* 三階教の研究 by YABUKI Keiki 矢吹慶輝, Tōkyō, 1927.

[11] Like laymen, monastic moneylenders ordinarily would also require loan contracts signed by borrowers, guarantors, and witnesses. For examples of such contracts, see NIIDA Noboru 仁井田陞, *Tōsō hōritsu bunsho no kenkyū* 唐宋法律文書の研究, Tōkyō, 1937, pp. 225-390.

An article by NABA Toshisada 那波利貞 on moneylending and other profit-making activities in Buddhist monasteries in the middle and late T'ang period, based on Tun-huang documents, in *SG* 10.3 (mentioned in *SZ* 54.2.150) is unfortunately not available.

[12] Stories about retribution to those who failed to pay such debts were common in both China and Japan.

[13] *Chiu T'ang shu* 183.19b.

the Western Market in the city of Ch'ang-an.[14]   Under the
Southern Sung dynasty, there were wealthy laymen who formed
partnerships to open pawnshops in Buddhist monasteries. Their
main purpose was to evade a kind of property tax known as
ho-mai 和買,[15] from which monasteries were exempted. According
to a memorial of 1201,[16] it was common practice for ten people
to form a partnership known as *chü* 局 to back a pawnshop in a
monastery. The partnership was usually organized to last ten
years. At the end of each year, one of the partners would take
out of the partnership the year's profit as his share but would
leave his capital. Thus the total amount of capital would remain
the same at the end of each year. Following a suggestion in the
memorial, the government made the pawnshops in monasteries
subject to the *ho-mai* tax.[17]

[14] In the famous story of HUO Hsiao-yü 霍小玉, translated by E. D. EDWARDS,
Chinese Prose Literature of the T'ang Period, London, 1938, 2.136-148 (esp. 143)
and by Chi-chên WANG, *Traditional Chinese Tales*, New York, 1944, pp. 48-59
(esp. p. 54).

In addition to the above names, pawnshops were also known as *ti-tang k'u* 抵當庫
under the Sung (*Miyazaki sensei hōseishi ronshū*, pp. 15, 22) and *tien-k'u* or *chieh-tien
k'u* 解典庫 under the Yüan (*Yüan tien-chang* 元典章 27.8a-b). The term
chieh-tien k'u was so popular that its transliteration is found in the Mongolian texts
of Yüan decrees. Ed. CHAVANNES in *TP* 5 (1904) .357-447 and 9 (1908) .297-428 translates the term by "bibliothèques" with some hesitation. This mistranslation is
followed by Marion LEWICKI in *Collectanea Orientalia* 12 (1937) .21-22. E. HAENISCH,
in his *Steuergerechtsame der chinesischen Klöster unter der Mongolenherrschaft*, 1940,
pp. 58, 63, 69, and N. N. POPPE in his *Kvadratnaya pis'mennost'*, 1941, pp. 118-119,
note 46, however, have rendered the term correctly. For pawnshops in monasteries
under the Yüan, also see P. RATCHNEVSKY, *Un code des Yuan*, 1937, p. 208, note 1.
I am indebted to Professor F. W. CLEAVES for the references in Western languages.

[15] *Ho-mai* means literally "harmonious (i. e. non-compulsory) purchase" of articles,
especially silk, from the people. As an institution, it went through considerable
changes under the Sung dynasty. When it was first introduced, public money was
advanced to the people who were to pay it back in silk; later on the people were
still required to turn in silk, but were not paid for it; finally, under the Southern
Sung, the government asked the people to commute the silk into money and collected
the sum in proportion to the property owned by a given household. See article by
SOGABE Shizuo 曾我部靜雄 in *SR* 23 (1938) .266-294, 535-570.

[16] *Sung hui-yao kao, ts'ê* 163, "Shih-huo" 7.102a-b.

[17] A reason why the government had exempted these pawnshops from the *ho-mai*
tax was that the monasteries claimed to be accumulating funds in order to purchase
monks' certificates (*tu-tieh* 度牒) from the government. According to the *I-chien
chih, chih-kuei* 支癸 8.2b, toward the end of the 12th century such fund-raising

The importance of mutual financing associations in modern China has been noted by Western observers. For example, A. H. Smith in his *Village Life in China* [18] describes " coöperative loan societies " toward the end of the 19th century, which may be considered the principal form of such associations. To use his words:

The simplest of the many plans by which mutual loans are effected, is the contribution of a definite sum by each of the members of the society in rotation to some other one of their number. When all the rest have paid their assessment to the last man on the list, each one will receive back all he put in and no more. The association is called in some places the " Clubs of the Seven Worthies " (*Ch'i hsien hui* [七賢會]). The technical name for any association of the kind in which coöperation is most conspicuous, is *Shê* [社].[19] The man who is in need of money (*Shê-chu* [社主]) invites some of his friends to coöperate with him, and in turn to invite some of their friends to do the same. When the requisite number has been secured, the

pawnshops were very common in Buddhist monasteries in certain districts of modern Kiangsi province. For a thorough study of monks' certificates under the Sung, see Yüan Chên 袁震, 兩宋度牒考 in the *Chung-kuo shê-hui-ching-chi-shih chi-k'an* 中國社會經濟史集刊 7.1 (1944) .42-104; 7.2 (1946) .1-78.

Yang Chao-yü 楊肇遇 in his *Chung-kuo tien-tang yeh* 中國典當業, Shanghai, 1932, p. 1 points out a reference which might be earlier (also mentioned in the *T'ung-su pien* 23.16a). In the biography of Liu Yü 劉虞 (d. 193) in the *Hou-Han shu* 103.3b there is the line 虞所賚賞,典當胡夷 which could be rendered by " What [Liu] Yü bestowed was pawned to barbarians." Although it is known that foreign merchants from the northwest were active in China under the Han dynasty, it is doubtful whether the expression *tien-tang* 典當 here means pawnbroking as in its comparatively modern usage, because the passage certainly refers to gifts made by Liu to barbarians in order to appease them. See *San Kuo chih* 8.5a commentary.

The character *chih* 質 is often found in ancient texts to mean " hostage " but not " pawnbroking." For studies on *chih-jên* 質任, a system of hostages in the third and fourth centuries to guard against revolt, see articles by Ho Tzǔ-ch'üan 何茲全 and Yang Chung-i 楊中一 in *Shih huo* 食貨 1.8 (1935) .25-27, and article by Ho Tzǔ-ch'üan in *Wên-shih tsa-chih* 文史雜誌 1.4 (1941) .39-47. The term *chih-chi* 質劑 in the *Chou-li* 周禮 (*Shih-san-ching chu-su* 十三經注疏 ed.) 15.1a, 16.1a which Biot translates as " les titres ou conventions que gardent les contractants " (*Le Tcheou-li*, Paris, 1851, 1.318) refers to legal documents similar to deeds.

[18] New York, 1899, pp. 152-160.

[19] The history of *shê* goes back to very ancient times as a major institution of worship. To mention a few references: Ed. Chavannes " Le dieu du sol dans la Chine antique " in *Le T'ai Chan*, Paris, 1910, pp. 437-525. Ch'ên Mêng-chia 陳夢家, 高禖郊社祖廟通考 *CHHP* 12.3 (1937) .445-472. Naba Toshisada, article in *SR* 23.2 (1938) .224-233. Lao Kan 勞榦, 漢代社祀的源流 in *CYYY* 11 (1943) .49-60.

members (*Shê-yu* [社友]) assemble and fix the order in which each shall have the use of the common fund. This would probably be decided by lot.[20]

In many such associations, however, the use of the fund involves the payment of interest.

In societies where the rate of interest is fixed, the only thing to be decided by lot, or by throwing dice, will be the order in which the members draw out the common fund. . . . But if, as often happens, the interest is left open to competition, this competition may take place by a kind of auction, each one announcing orally what he is willing to pay for the use of the capital for one term, the highest bidder taking the precedence, but no member ever has a second turn.[21]

This description gives us an idea of the functioning of the coöperative societies, their close relationship to the *shê* (i. e., coöperative associations in general), and their frequent use of lottery and auction. It is evident that these institutions interacted upon one another. The coöperative loan associations, however, are not the only form of mutual financing associations or *ho-hui* 合會. By the latter term, we include at least coöperative societies to provide mutual help for weddings, funerals, and travel.

According to the conjecture of a modern author,[22] *ho-hui* or mutual financing associations may have existed from T'ang times and they may have been introduced from India. Although he offers practically no documentation, the first part of his theory can be substantiated by information from old manuscripts discovered in Tun-huang, especially if we take the term in its broader sense. The Japanese scholar NABA Toshisada, who is a leading authority on such documents, has published several valuable articles on social and economic institutions of the T'ang period. Among these are two articles on the *shê-i* 社邑 or *shê* 社, i. e., "clubs," under the T'ang and Five Dynasties.[23]

Religious clubs known as *i-i* 義邑 or *i-hui* 邑會 existed as early

---

[20] *Village Life in China*, pp. 152-153.

[21] *Ibid.*, p. 154.

[22] WANG Tsung-p'ei 王宗培, *Chung-kuo chih ho-hui* 中國之合會 Shanghai, 1931, pp. 4-6.

[23] 唐代の社邑に就きて in *SR* 23.2, 3, 4 (1938) .223-265, 495-534, 729-793; 佛教信仰に基きて組織せられたる中晚唐五代時の社邑に就きて in *SR* 24.3, 4 (1939) .491-562, 743-784.

as the Northern and Southern dynasties,[24] when lay adherents organized themselves to finance religious activities in Buddhist monasteries, notably for the erection of stone monuments bearing images of Buddhas and Bodhisattvas. Monks and nuns might become officers or members of these religious clubs, or at least they were glad to work through patron groups. Inscriptions [25] on the numerous steles which are preserved indicate how active these religious clubs were from the Northern Wei to the early T'ang.

From the middle of T'ang times, fewer monuments were erected, but this does not mean the religious clubs had ceased to function. According to references derived from late T'ang manuscripts found at Tun-huang, similar clubs known as *shê-i* or *shê* financed activities like vegetable dinner parties given to monks and nuns, recitation and copying of sutras, popular sermons known as *su-chiang* 俗講,[26] and printing of images of Buddhas and Bodhisattvas. NABA estimates that in the ninth and tenth centuries there were usually ten to fifteen such clubs attached to one monastery and the membership of each club numbered about twenty-five to forty people.

Many of these religious clubs performed also social and economic functions. Contributions were made jointly to a fellow member to help him pay for a funeral or for travel. The practice was known as *chui-hsiung chu-chi* 追凶逐吉 " to follow up when there is a happy or unhappy event." In such mutual financing associations, hereditary membership was naturally encouraged. Many circulars from club officers, known as *shê-ssŭ chuan-t'ieh* 社司轉帖,[27] to call meetings or to ask for contributions have been preserved. NABA notices that many of these clubs had no clerical members and were no longer religious in nature. This he inter-

---

[24] For Japanese articles on such early religious clubs, see bibliography in *SR* 23.2 (1938).249-251.

[25] For example, see CHAVANNES, *Six monuments de la sculpture chinoise (Ars Asiatica* II), Paris, 1914.

[26] Held three times a year in the first, fifth, and ninth moons. See HSIANG Ta 向達, 唐代俗講考 in *Wên shih tsa-chih* 3.9, 10 (1944).40-60.

[27] For a discussion of such circulars, see also Lionel GILES, *Six Centuries in Tun-huang*, 1944, pp. 36-38.

prets as a sign of the rise of secular interests in the ninth and tenth centuries. This is certainly significant, but the facts that in some cases monks were also members of these mutual financing associations and that in most cases their meeting places were at monasteries nevertheless indicate a close connection between them. It is probably not far fetched to suggest that these mutual financing associations were offspring of the purely religious clubs.[28]

The disposal of personal belongings of deceased monks naturally provides a problem for monastery organizations. According to Buddhist texts of discipline (*vinaya* or *lü* 律) which were translated in the early fifth century,[29] the clothing and certain belongings of a deceased monk were to be distributed among his fellow monks, given for charity, or sold to pay debts.[30] The principles behind the practice were to intensify the cordial relationship between the dead and the living, and to make the living realize that the same end awaited them so that they might free themselves from mundane desires.

A *vinaya* text translated in the early T'ang period,[31] however, indicates that in India sale by auction was used to dispose of such personal belongings. The practice probably was known to the Chinese even before this text was translated, since it was already followed in Chinese monasteries in the early seventh century. In 626, the monk Tao-hsüan 道宣 (596-667)[32] criticized

---

[28] The *Hsin T'ang shu* 197.16a tells about WEI Chou 韋宙, who was prefect of Yung-chou 永州 (in modern Hunan province) c. 850. The people in the prefecture were poor and in plowing used only man-power. WEI Chou organized them into twenty *shê* or clubs. Each household was to contribute a certain sum per month to its club. He whose lot was drawn could first use the fund to buy a cow. After a long period, there was no shortage of cattle. NABA quotes this story in his article (*SR* 23.4.775) and suggests that this kind of club may have been influenced by those associated with monasteries.

[29] For instances, see the *Wu-fên lü* 五分律 20, trans. in 423-424 (*Tripitaka*, Taishō, vol. 22, No. 1421, 139a); the *Ssŭ-fên lü* 四分律 41, trans. from 408 (Taishō, vol. 22, No. 1428, 859b-c, 862c); and the *Shih-sung lü* 十誦律 28, trans. in early fifth cent. (Taishō, vol. 23, No. 1435, 202b-203a).

[30] Monks and nuns were free to leave wills. For examples in China, see NIIDA Noboru, *op. cit.*, pp. 638-648.

[31] *Kên-pên shuo i-ch'ieh yu-pu mu-tê-chia* 根本說一切有部目得迦 8 trans. by I-ching 義淨 (635-713) (Taishō, vol. 24, No. 1452, 446c).

[32] *Ssŭ-fên lü shan-fan pu-ch'üeh hsing-shih ch'ao* 四分律刪繁補闕行事鈔 3.1 (Taishō, vol. 40, No. 1804, 117a).

auction sale as contrary to the monastic code, especially attacking
the laughter and noise accompanying the auctions in his time as
shameless excitement 今時分賣, 非法非律, 至時喧笑, 一何顏厚. A
similar attack was made in the *Tsêng-hui chi* 增輝記, quoted in
the *Shih-shih yao-lan* 釋氏要覽 of 1019.[33]

These attacks, however, did not check the spread of the practice
in Buddhist monasteries. In the various compilations and editions
of rules and regulations for monasteries in Sung and Yüan times,
we find detailed descriptions of auction sales. For example, in
the *Ch'an-yüan ch'ing-kuei* 禪苑清規 compiled by Tsung-tsê 宗
賾[34] in 1103, there is a lengthy account of *ch'ang-i* 唱衣, lit.
" auction of clothing," which may be summarized as follows:
The auction is to be announced to the community in the monastery by posting a placard. The clothing and other things to be
auctioned are to be displayed in the Hall before auction time.
When the bell rings, the monks will enter the Hall. First, sutras
will be recited for the deceased monk. Then his belongings will be
offered for sale by auction. This is conducted by the *wei-na*
維那 (*karmadāna*) of the monastery. The *wei-na* must know
the normal price of each of the belongings and describe its condition—new, old, or worn out. He has to announce the unit of
cash, by strings of a full hundred or less than a hundred. If the
bidders refuse to raise the price, the article should be sold cheaply.
If they are bidding the price up too high, the *wei-na* will remind
them, saying " Better be thoughtful. You might regret it later."
Unless the monastery treasury has articles to be offered in a
" subordinate auction " 寄唱, no articles from other monks will
be accepted for sale at the same time. The auction will be concluded with another recitation of sutras for the deceased monk.
The net income after deduction of the funeral expenses will be
distributed among the monks who have read sutras for the deceased monk, attended his funeral, or appeared at the auction.

[33] Taishō, vol. 54, No. 2127, 309b-c. I have no information on the *Tsêng-hui chi*
which is quoted several times in the *Shih-shih yao-lan*. A work by the Japanese monk
Sōei 僧濬 (1654-1738) bears the same title *Zō-ki-ki* 增輝記 (not available), but it
is too late to be quoted in 1019.

[34] *Zoku zōkyō* 續藏經 case 16, vol. 5, pp. 457a-b, 468a-b.

If the income is a large amount, a portion (known as ch'ou-fên 抽分) will go to the monastery treasury. The accounts of the auction will be signed by officers of the monastery and posted for the community.

According to the same Ch'an-yüan ch'ing-kuei,[35] if an abbot should retire or have to leave the monastery because of old age, illness, or any other reason, his personal belongings were to be auctioned in a similar manner, because a monk traveling with many possessions would arouse criticism. Another important text is the Pai-chang ch'ing-kuei 百丈清規 [36] re-edited by Tê-hui 德輝 in 1336-1338, but based upon earlier versions of rules and regulations laid down by the Ch'an Master Huai-hai 懷海 (749-814) in the Pai-ching Mountains 百丈山 in modern Kiangsi province. This Yüan work gives more details of ch'ang-i, or auction sales, but labels the institution as ku-fa 古法 or " old method." It says, " In order to reduce the noise and confusion, lottery has been recently introduced in many cases " 近來爲息喧亂，多作鬮拈法 so that the monk whose lot is drawn may have the option of purchasing a certain article. The competitive bidding element is thus taken away, although the sale is still known as ch'ang-i. Any articles not wanted by the monks at the sale will be sold to the secular public. According to an early eighteenth century version of the Pai-chang ch'ing-kuei with commentaries,[37] the articles are simply priced at 70 per cent of current prices and offered for sale to the monks, among whom the itinerant monks (hsing-tan 行單) enjoy an option. The institution is also called ku-ch'ang 估唱.[38] From these references, we may infer that

---

[35] Ibid., p. 459a.

[36] Zoku zōkyō, case 16, vol. 3, pp. 257a-b.

[37] Ibid., case 16, vol. 4, p. 353b.

[38] For additional references, see bibliography at the end of the article on shōe 唱衣 in MOCHIZUKI Shinkō 望月信亨, Bukkyō daijiten 佛敎大辭典 2553b-2554a.

Dealers of secondhand clothing in Chinese markets and fairs often chant the quality and prices of their goods while displaying them in their hands in order to attract attention. This is known as ho ku-i 喝故衣, a term which is also found in the Tung-ching mêng-hua lu 東京夢華錄 (Hsüeh-chin t'ao-yüan 學津討源 ed.) 2.6a by MÊNG Yüan-lao 孟元老 with author's preface in 1148. For references to ho ku-i or ch'ang ku-i 唱估衣 in Peking under the Ch'ing dynasty, see LI Chia-jui 李家瑞 Pei-p'ing fêng-su lei-chêng 北平風俗類徵, Shanghai, 1937, pp. 160-161. It is possible that ho ku-i was influenced by ch'ang-i in Buddhist monasteries.

auction sales in Buddhist monasteries had declined from the end of the Yüan period.

Keeping the institution of *ch'ang-i* or auction sale in mind, we may better understand at least two important documents from Tun-huang, in which the character *ch'ang* 唱 appears several times. Both documents are financial accounts for Buddhist monasteries. So far as I know, no satisfactory interpretation has hitherto been advanced for the character *ch'ang*, which, as now appears probable, is a simple abbreviation of *ch'ang-i* or auction sale.

The first manuscript is on the back of a *Mu-lien pien wên* 目連變文 [39] in the collection of the national Library of Peiping. It was first published in the Bulletin of the Library in 1931 [40] and later utilized by HSIANG Ta in the original version of his " T'ang-tai su-chiang k'ao " in 1934.[41] HSIANG, however, misunderstood the names of articles auctioned by several monks as titles of ballads sung by these monks to lay groups in order to collect donations. No doubt realizing the improbability of his interpretation, he has omitted this reference in a revised version of his work in 1944.

The articles mentioned in the manuscript include *tzŭ-lo hsieh yü* 紫羅鞋雨 (to be read *liang* 兩), i. e., a pair of purple gauze slippers, which was auctioned for 580 *ch'ih* 尺 of cloth; a *fei-mien-ling pei* 緋綿綾被, i. e., a crimson silk quilt filled with floss, auctioned for 1520 *ch'ih*; a *shan* 扇 i. e., a fan, for 55 *ch'ih*; *pai-ling wa* 白綾襪 i. e., a pair of white silk socks, for 170 *ch'ih*; another pair of *pai-ling wa* for 300 *ch'ih*; and a *huang-chin p'o* 黃盡坡 (to be read *huang-hua pei* 畫被) i. e., a painted yellow quilt, for 500 *ch'ih*. These articles probably had been donated to the monastery

[39] *Pien-wên* is a type of literature (usually stories) with illustrations to popularize religious teachings. It flourished in the T'ang period. According to Dr. CHOU Yi-liang 周一良 (in his review of Hsiang Ta's " T'ang Tai su-chiang k'ao " in the *T'u-shu chou-k'an* 圖書周刊 no. 6 of the *Ta-kung pao* 大公報, Tientsin, Feb. 8, 1947) the character *pien* probably came from *pien-hsiang* 變相 " (Buddhist) illustrations."

[40] *Kuo-li Pei-p'ing T'u-shu-kuan kuan-k'an* 國立北平圖書館館刊 5.6 (1931) .79. Another interesting point is that in this manuscript the character *yü* 餘 seems to be used to indicate a " shortage " instead of a " surplus."

[41] *YCHP* 16 (1934) .119-132.

and the proceeds from the auction were to be distributed among the monks, who received 150 *ch'ih* each. The prices of the articles are very high, as one would expect at an auction for benevolent purposes. There is, of course, a general correspondence between the normal value of the objects and the sums listed here, and it is possible that the articles mentioned in this manuscript may have been plural.

The other manuscript is Number 2638 in the collection of the Bibliothèque Nationale. NABA Toshisada has quoted it in part in a supplementary note (pp. 80-81) to his important article on *liang-hu* 梁戶 [42] (i. e., oil-making households attached to monas-

---

[42] *Ryōko kō* 梁戶考 pp. 1-82, reprinted from *Shinabukkyō shigaku* 支那佛教 史學 2.1, 2, 4 (1938).

To this excellent article I wish to add two supplementary notes. First, under the Ch'ing dynasty oil-making households known as *yu-liang hu* 油樑戶 existed in the Ta-t'ung area of northern Shansi. Apparently not belonging to any monastery, they paid regularly to the government taxes, which, together with other taxes, were forwarded to Peking. According to the *Kuang-hsü k'uai-chi piao* 光緒會計表 (1901 ed.) 2.13b by LIU Yüeh-yün 劉嶽雲, the Board of Revenue received from Shansi 2404.20 taels in 1887 and 2195.55 taels in 1888 as *yu-liang ts'ai-kang yen-chien têng-hu k'o* 油樑躧缸鹽碱等戶課, i. e., levies on oil-making, yeast-making, soda-making and other households. These amounts were the regular sums to be collected in a year with an intercalary month and an ordinary year respectively. According to the *Ta-t'ung fu-chih* 大同府志 (1782 ed.) 13.49a-b, such levies in this area can be traced back to about 1751.

Second, the term *po-shih* 博士 meaning something like "master" and referring to craftsmen and the like from T'ang to Ch'ing times is discussed at length on pp. 27-35. In modern Chinese the term has largely been replaced by *pa-shih* 把勢, which is probably its variant form. In Mandarin, we say *ch'ê pa-shih* 車把勢 "a professional cart driver," *hua-êrh pa-shih* 花兒把勢 "a professional gardener," etc. In the Tsinan dialect of Shantung, even prostitutes are called *pa-shih*. This use may have been influenced by the older term, *ch'a po-shih* 茶博士 referring to a waiter or waitress, because a leading prostitute in Tsinan is sometimes playfully called a *ch'a-hu kai-êrh*, 茶壺蓋兒, lit. "top cover of a teapot." For information on the Tsinan dialect I am indebted to Mr. Zunvair YUE 于震寰 of the Chinese-Japanese Library of the Harvard-Yenching Institute.

The *Kuo-yü tz'ŭ-tien* 國語辭典, Shanghai 1943, 1.16 and 1.37 defines *pa-shih* 把式(把勢) as "one who is specialized in a trade" 專精一藝者 and *po-shih* as "a professional title" 職業稱號, but fails to connect the two terms. On *pa-shih* also see Rolf STEIN, *TP* 35 (1939) .97, note 2. Professor F. W. CLEAVES has pointed out the possibility that *pa-shih* may have been a borrowing back from the Turkish *baγši*, Mongolian *baγsi*, or Manchu *bahši*, which was of course borrowed directly or indirectly from the Chinese *po-shih*. Such borrowings back and forth are fairly common. See PELLIOT, *TP* 27 (1930) .14-15, 45-46, note 3.

teries) but offered no interpretation of the character *ch'ang* 唱 in the manuscript. It is a financial report made in 936 by three monks, who were in charge of donations 僿司, on the income and expenses of a number of monasteries in the preceeding three years. Since it bears the red imprints of a seal, *Ho-hsi Tu-sêng-t'ung yin* 河西都僧統印, the report evidently was presented to the Tu-sêng-t'ung or Chief Superintendent of monks in the Sha-chou 沙州 area in modern Kansu province. Under receipts the first entry reads: 已年官施衣物唱得布貳阡參佰貳拾尺, which means, "In the *chi* 已 (read *ssǔ* 巳) year (i. e., 933) clothes and other things donated by the government were auctioned for 2320 *ch'ih* of cloth." Although I do not have access to the original document and NABA does not list the entries immediately following this one, it is more than probable that *ch'ang* here means auction sale. According to this report, each monk or nun received sixty *ch'ih* as a share of the donation, and the young disciples, male and female, each received thirty *ch'ih*, or half that amount.

If my interpretation is correct, these two manuscripts provide us with more information on auction sales. The second manuscript is dated 936; the first one cannot be much later; it may even be earlier. From them we may infer that donated articles were auctioned (probably to the public), that the auction was conducted not by one monk alone, but by several monks, and that the income was distributed among various members of the monastic community on an established scale.

As for lottery tickets, there is an early reference in the collection of Yüan statutes entitled *T'ung-chih t'iao-ko* 通制條格. In the year 1288, it was reported to the central government that in various places south of the Yangtze River, it was the usual practice for disciples who were newly admitted to the monasteries 新附寺院僧徒 to hold public lotteries for profit 拈鬮射利 on the excuse of raising money for more buildings. They provided a few tens of prizes 利物 and made lottery slips of bamboo or wood 籤籌 in thousands or tens of thousands. These lottery slips were then distributed and entrusted to powerful and influential families for sale. On the day designated for drawing the lots, people would assemble like clouds from far and near, not infrequently in thousands. Of course, the monasteries made good profits in running these lotteries. At first only monasteries in or near cities sponsored them; later the example was followed by even more secluded monasteries in quiet mountains and forests. Considering such lotteries to be a form of gambling, the government prohibited them immediately.

After the Yüan, the history of lottery tickets is obscure until the nineteenth century when they were issued in Kwangtung province to gamble on the *wei-hsing* 闈姓, i. e., surnames of successful candidates in the next civil service examination. People who bought tickets could bet on a list of surnames. Those who hit the most surnames of successful candidates won. It became very popular, and those who ran them made a good profit. The *wei-hsing* lottery was prohibited by the government in 1875, but then the gamblers moved to Macao to continue their business under Portuguese protection. In 1885, upon a joint memorial by the Imperial Commissioner P'ÊNG Yü-lin 彭玉麟, Governor CHANG Chih-tung 張之洞, et al., the *wei-hsing* was legalized and made subject to taxes.[44]

Although the *wei-hsing* as basis for lottery may have been a purely native discovery, it is remarkable that foreign lottery tickets were widely circulated in nineteenth century China. From an editorial in an issue of the short-lived *Ching-hua pao* 京話報 in 1901,[45] we read:

---

[43] *T'ung-chih t'iao-ko* 28.7b-8a.

[44] *Kuang-hsü chêng-yao* 光緒政要 compiled by SHÊN T'ung-shêng 沈桐生 (1909 ed.) 11.6a-7a. According to this memorial, *wei-hsing* gamblers were arrested and fined from 1864 to 1871. Also see *Fo-shan Chung-i-hsiang chih* 佛山忠義鄉志, 1923, 11.17a-b.

[45] According to a handwritten note signed by J. S., presumably an original owner of the copies which are now in the Chinese-Japanese Library of the Harvard-Yenching Institute, the *Ching-hua pao* was " a magazine issued at Peking, after the Boxers' trouble. Only six copies [i. e., issues] were brought into circulation, after which the Editor was arrested, press and all records confiscated by order of the Empress Dowager who considered it to be too pro-foreign, and injurious to her government, especially as it was printed in plain and simple language within grasp of the simple folks." The magazine was a semi-monthly. The number quoted here was the fifth issue for the middle of the tenth moon in 1901.

Some days ago, a proposal was made to Prince Ch'ing 慶王 requesting the issue of lottery tickets 請開發財票. At present, this has not been started in Peking, but the Luzon tickets 呂宋票 of the South Seas, the German lottery tickets 德國彩票 of Kiaochow, the *wei-hsing* tickets of Kwangtung, and the relief lottery tickets 賑捐彩票 in the northern and southern provinces, under numerous names, are sold everywhere. Since our government cannot prohibit them, it may be better to issue something like them ourselves so that some of our interests will be saved. Consequently now in Hupei province, people are planning to issue a kind of lottery tickets. They imitate the foreign regulations and call the tickets *fu-ch'ien p'iao* 富籤票.[46]

It is clear that the editor considered lottery tickets a foreign institution.[47]

The use of lottery in general, however, was known to the Chinese for many centuries and was not an importation. The ancient work *Hsün-tzŭ* 荀子[48] says, "Lot-drawing and buckle-throwing are used for the sake of impartiality" 探籌投鈎者，所以爲公也 Another ancient work, the *Shên tzŭ* 愼子,[49] informs us that money or land was divided by buckle-throwing and horses were divided by stick-throwing 投鈎以分財，投策以分馬；分馬之用策，分田之用鈎 in order to prevent complaints. It is reported in the *Hou Han shu* 41.12a-b that in 25 A.D. the peasant revolutionists or bandits known as the Red Eyebrows 赤眉 cast lots to select a nominal leader from among three candidates. From *Hou Han shu* 68.1b we learn that about the same time a commander of government

[46] The term *fu-ch'ien* probably was borrowed from the Japanese *tomikuji* 富籤 "lottery tickets." It is interesting to note that lottery tickets were issued mostly by monasteries in Japan in the middle of the Edo period. See the article on *tomitsuki* 富突 in the *Nihon keizaishi daijiten* 日本經濟史大辭典, 2.1193b-1195a.

[47] The lottery tickets in Hupei mentioned in this magazine were issued when CHANG Chih-tung was the viceroy. CHANG's petition (dated Jan. 11, 1902) for imperial permission mentions several kinds of native and foreign lotteries. CHANG's tickets, named *ch'ien-chüan ts'ai-p'iao* 籤捐彩票 were to be distributed in the prefectures and districts, which for this purpose had been graded into three classes. This semi-voluntary sale did not meet with a good response from the people. On Oct. 25, 1902, the Viceroy had to present another petition to change the lottery to a compulsory *p'ei-k'uan chüan* 賠款捐 or "indemnity contribution (or tax)." See *Chang Wên-hsiang kung ch'üan-chi* 張文襄公全集, Tsou-kao 奏稿 33.16b-17a; 34.1a-2a. Also see Hsü K'o 徐珂, *Ch'ing-pai lei-ch'ao* 清稗類鈔, *ts'ê* 35, *Tu-po lei* 賭博類 pp. 4-5, 22-23.

[48] *Hsün-tzŭ chi-chieh* 荀子集解 (1891 ed.) 8.1b; not translated in H. H. DUBS, *The Works of Hsüntse*, London, 1928.

[49] *Erh-shih-êrh tzŭ ch'üan-shu* 二十二子全書 ed. 1b-2a, 4a.

forces wrote the names of his generals on bamboo slips, which he put in a tube. The general whose name was drawn was to cover the rear while the others were retreating.

Moreover, the history of lottery is hardly separable from that of games and methods of divination.[50] The character *ch'ien* 籤

[50] In this connection I wish to call attention to two terms, *kuan-p'u* 關撲 and *p'u-mai* 撲賣 (not to be confused with *p'u-mai* 撲買 in note 2 above), which appear many times in works describing city life in the two capitals of the Sung dynasty. The two terms are discussed by A. C. MOULE in two notes in his article "Wonder of the Capital" in *The New China Review* 3 (1920) .12-17, 356-367, which is a translation of passages from the *Tu-ch'êng chi-shêng* 都城紀勝 (author's preface dated 1235). In the first note MOULE defines *p'o-mai* (i. e., *p'u-mai*) as "to sell by auction (more commonly 拍賣)" and identifies *kuan-p'o* (i. e., *kuan-p'u*) with *hsiang-p'u* 相撲 "to wrestle" or "box" (p. 16). In the second note, he corrects himself on *kuan-p'u* and concludes "it would seem that . . . *kuan-p'o* had at Hang-chou some connection with *p'o-mai* and described the sale by some kind of auction, or perhaps, lottery of sweets and other delicacies and toys and so forth" (p. 356).

Kuan-p'u definitely referred to gambling by means of games of chance like coin-throwing and lot-drawing for prizes, which from the dealers' point of view meant the sale of goods. It was probably similar to the hoop-, ring-, and dart-throwing games in American fairs and amusement centers. According to the *Tung-ching mêng-hua lu* 7.12b the prizes included not only delicacies and toys, but also curios and other valuables, even chariots, horses, real estate, and sing-song and dancing girls. In some cases one could gamble one *hu* 笏 (a large unit of silver or gold, synonymous with a *ting* 鋌) for thirty *hu* 有以一笏撲三十笏者. Coin-throwing for *kuan-p'u* is reported in the *Kuei-hsin tsa-chih* 癸辛雜識 (*Hsüeh-chin t'ao-yüan* ed.) *Hsü-chi* 續集 A.37a, which says, "One hears that in the reign of Li-tsung 理宗 (1225-1274), in the spring the market game *kuan-p'u* was imitated in the imperial gardens. It was done by small eunuchs among themselves. When it came to [the turn of] the Emperor, they would provide him with coins having tails (or heads?) on both sides 純鏝骰錢 at the second or third throw so as to make fun." Since *kuan-p'u* was in theory prohibited as a form of gambling, the restriction was lifted officially for only a few days (known as *fang kuan-p'u* 放關撲) during festival seasons.

The term *p'u-mai*, meaning "gamble" or "sell," seems to have applied to games of chance played by hawkers and peddlers with their customers, as a sideline to regular sales. Thus it may be considered synonymous with *kuan-p'u*, only on a smaller scale. There is no evidence that *p'u-mai* was sale by auction. The identification of *kuan-p'u* with *hsiang-p'u* "wrestling" is, of course, unjustified. In the terms *kuan-p'u*, *p'u-mai*, and *hsiang-p'u*, as well as in *p'u-mai* "bidding for tax farming," the only element common to the meanings of the character *p'u* is "to hit."

The *p'u* in *p'u-mai*, "to gamble or sell," is also written *po* 博, a character for "gambling" in general. In the Yüan play *Yen Ch'ing po yü* 燕青博魚 (*Yüan ch'ü hsüan* 元曲選, Han-fên-lou ed. *ts'ê* 8, 15a-17a), we learn that fish could be gambled for by throwing six coins and won if five or six of the coins fall alike, described as *wu-ch'un, liu-ch'un* 五純六純, "five-unmixed" or "six-unmixed." The coins to be thrown were called *t'ou-ch'ien* 頭錢 (same as 骰錢 in the *Kuei-hsin*

refers to sticks used for either gambling or divination. The character *ch'ou* 籌 is used for chips, tokens, or sticks representing prizes in various games, in addition to lottery tickets. The character *chiu* 圖 for the lottery itself, according to traditional philologists,[51] is closely related to *kou* 鈎 in *t'ou-kou* 投鈎, " buckle-throwing " mentioned above. But its phonetic *kuei* or rather *ch'iu* 龜 [52] may also indicate a general connection with the tortoise shells used by ancient Chinese for divination.

Since the earliest references to the four money-raising institutions invariably link them to the Buddhist organization, we may tentatively assume their monasterial origin. This however does not mean that each of them was an importation from India. Sale by auction in medieval monasteries is the only case in which the Indian influence is fairly certain. The other three institutions may have been a Chinese innovation, because the general concepts and practices of moneylending, mutual help, and lot-drawing were undoubtedly familiar to the Chinese prior to the introduction of Buddhism. The remarkable point is that Buddhist monasteries and their communal wealth apparently have provided favorable conditions for the growth of financial institutions and thus exerted considerable influence on the social and economic life of the secular world.

tsa-chih quoted above) " coins used as dice." In the famous novel *Shui-hu chuan* 水滸傳 chap. 37, we also find Li K'uei 李逵 gambling with *t'ou-ch'ien*. Cf. Pearl Buck, *All Men Are Brothers*, 1937, p. 657 and J. H. Jackson, *Water Margin* 1937, 2.523. Both translators have rendered *t'ou-ch'ien* incorrectly as " dice."

[51] *Shu-wên chieh-tzŭ ku-lin* 說文解字詁林 pp. 1224-1225.

[52] The ancient name 龜茲 for Kucha is traditionally pronounced 丘慈 *ch'iu-tz'ŭ.* The character *ch'iu* 秋 is sometimes written 禾 plus 龜, with the latter as its phonetic.

[53] The modern term for auction is *p'ai-mai* 拍賣, in which the character *p'ai* 拍 may have been related to *p'u*, " to hit," discussed above. Sale by auction is generally considered to be an imported practice. In guides to cities like Peiping and Shanghai compiled under the Republic, auction stores 拍賣行 are classified in the category of *yang-hang* 洋行 (i. e., " foreign companies "); several of them even have *yang-hang* as part of their titles. Pawnshops periodically invite dealers to inspect unredeemed articles and to make bids for them. Such sales are known as *ta-tang* 打當, meaning something like " to get rid of pawned articles " and the bidding is known as *fêng chia-êrh* 封價兒, literally " to put a price in an envelope." (Cf. *Pei-p'ing fêng-su lei-chêng*, p. 433.) This is believed to be a native practice, but its history is not known. In the *Yüan tien-chang* 27.8a-b the disposal of unredeemed articles is called *hsia-chia* 下架 " to remove from the shelves," but there is no information as to how the articles were sold.

THE FORM OF THE PAPER NOTE *HUI-TZU*
OF THE SOUTHERN SUNG DYNASTY

LIEN-SHENG YANG

HARVARD UNIVERSITY

In my *Money and Credit in China, a Short History* [1] published in 1952, I wrote:

Unlike the *chiao-tzŭ* of Szechwan which bore stamp prints of three colors, *hui-tzŭ* is reported to have been printed from single brass plates in one color. A Japanese work on numismatics of Eastern Asia reproduces the photograph of a note-printing plate, and suggests that it may have come from the Sung dynasty. It is 3 Chinese inches wide and 5.3 inches long. The top quarter of the plate contains a drawing of ten coins. The next quarter bears twenty-nine characters reading, "With the exception of Szechwan, this may be circulated in the various provinces and districts to make public and private payments representing 770 cash per string." The bottom half is a picture of a courtyard of a granary and three persons carrying bags of grain. Three characters at the corner of the picture read, *ch'ien ssŭ ts'ang*, "May there be a thousand of such granaries," which is, of course, an allusion to a line in the *Book of Odes*. According to the Japanese author, the plate may have been used to print *hui-tzŭ*.

The Japanese work referred to is OKUDAIRA Masahiro 奧平昌洪, *Tōa senshi* 東亞錢志 10.92a-93a.

In a letter dated May 15, 1953, Dr. HU Shih called my attention to a series of six memorials in the collected works of CHU Hsi 朱熹,[2] in which CHU impeached T'ANG Chung-yu 唐仲友,[3] prefect

---

[1] For corrections and a reply to criticisms of my book see the " Appendix."

[2] *Hui-an Hsien-sheng Chu Wen-kung wen-chi* 晦庵先生朱文公文集 (*SPTK* ed., referred to hereafter as *Wen-chi*) 18.17a-32a, 19.1a-27a.

[3] In spite of CHU's impeachment, T'ANG is reported in his biographies to be a capable and accomplished scholar. See CH'IEN Shih-sheng 錢士升, *Nan Sung shu* 南宋書 (1797 ed.) 63.3a-b, *Chin-hua fu-chih* 金華府志 (1909 reprint of 1683 ed.) 16.6b-7a, and esp. LU Hsin-yüan 陸心源, *Sung shih i* 宋史翼 (1906 ed.) 13.11a-12b. T'ANG's *Ti-wang ching-shih t'u-p'u* 帝王經世圖譜 in 16 vols. is included in the *Chin-hua ts'ung-shu* 金華叢書 and the *Wu-ying-tien chü-chen-pan ts'ung-shu* 武英殿聚珍版 (Canton ed.). His other writings on government, studies on the Classics, and his literary works (many fragmentary) have been collected under the title *Chin-hua T'ang-shih i-shu* 金華唐氏遺書 in the *Hsü Chin-hua ts'ung-shu*.

216

of Tʻai-chou 台州,[4] for corruption and other offenses. These memorials, dated 1183, contain interesting details about the political, social, and economic life of China in the 12th century. Of special interest is the report in the last three memorials about a case of counterfeiting the paper note *hui-tzu*, from which we can derive considerable information about the form of *hui-tzu*. The counterfeiting case involved TʻANG Chung-yu and a professional wood-block cutter 開字匠,[5] CHIANG Hui 蔣輝, who was also known as CHIANG Nien-chʻi 蔣念七.[6]

Two depositions of CHIANG Hui, quoted in memorials no. 4 and no. 6 may be translated as follows:

(1) In the 4th year of Chʻun-hsi 淳熙 (1177), I, CHIANG Hui, forged 450 *tao* 道 or sheets of *hui-tzu* in Kuang-te-chün 廣德軍.[7] The matter was discovered at Lin-an-fu 臨安府 and I was sentenced to be exiled [as a tatooed soldier] to Tʻai-chou. On the 14th day of the 12th moon of the 7th year of

---

TʻANG's interpretation of the Classics differed considerably from that of CHU Hsi, and TʻANG and CHU are reported to have exchanged slighting remarks concerning the scholarship of each other. Some thirteenth century and later writers, therefore, questioned whether CHU's impeachment of TʻANG was entirely unbiased. See YEH Shao-weng 葉紹翁, *Ssu-chʻao wen-chien lu* 四朝聞見錄 (*Tsʻung-shu chi-chʻeng* 叢書集成 ed.) *I-chi* 乙集, p. 39, CHOU Mi 周密, *Chʻi-tung yeh-yü* 齊東野語 (*Tsʻung-shu chi-chʻeng* ed.) 17.226, 20.264-265, and colophon by CHANG Tso-nan 張作楠 to TʻANG's *Chiu-ching fa-tʻi* 九經發題 in the *Hsü Chin-hua tsʻung-shu*.

According to *Sung shih i* 13.11b, in his impeachment, CHU Hsi was influenced by slanderous information from KAO Wen-hu 高文虎, a subordinate official of TʻANG. KAO's name does appear in *Wen-chi* 18.22b. The details in CHU's memorials of impeachment, however, read very convincingly. On KAO Wen-hu and his scholarly son KAO Ssu-sun 高似孫 see article by Professor William HUNG, 高似孫史畧箋正序之一 in *Shih-hsüeh nien-pao* 史學年報 1.5 (1933) .1-9. On the possibility of CHU's being unconsciously influenced by TʻANG's enemies in general, see CHʻEN Liang 陳亮 *Lung-chʻuan wen-chi* 龍川文集 20.3b-4b and *Wen-chi* 36.19a-b.

[4] Around the modern Lin-hai 臨海 hsien, Chekiang.

[5] The character *kʻai* 開 is used as a verb synonymous to *kʻe* 刻 "to cut, to engrave."

[6] It is an old custom to use a number after a surname to refer to a person by indicating his position of seniority among children of the same generation in his family or clan. See my review of WANG Li's 王力 grammar in *HJAS* 12 (1949) .249. In Sung and Yüan times, however, such numeral indicators were often large numbers, sometimes including the character *pai* 百 or *chʻien* 千 or *wan* 萬, so that it appears doubtful whether they served exactly the same purpose. The CHIANG Nien-chʻi means CHIANG 27. Compare the HUANG 25, FANG 102, and 36 *Hsüan-chiao* below.

[7] The modern Kuang-te-hsien, Anhwei.

Ch'un-hsi (1180, actually early in 1181), I and HUANG Nien-wu 黃念五 cut six counterfeited [government] seals, copied the official signature, and cut pictorial illustrations of human figures and other objects 出相人物 [8] for *hui-tzu* in the house of LOU Ta-lang 樓大郎 in Su-hsi 蘇溪, Wu-chou 婺州.[9] We manufactured 900 sheets of *hui-tzu* in the denomination of one *kuan* or string, which I shared with HUANG Nien-wu and others. Early in the 2nd moon of last year (1182), I returned [to T'ai-chou]. On the 12th day of the 8th moon, *kung-shou* 弓手 (" police archers ") from I-wu-hsien 義烏縣 of Wu-chou came to apprehend me. I evaded and took refuge in the house of the Prefect. The above is truth.[10]

(2) I, CHIANG Hui, was originally a native of Ming-chou 明州.[11] In the 6th moon of the 4th year of Ch'un-hsi, because I forged *hui-tzu* with the already exiled criminal FANG Pai-erh 方百二 and others and because the matter was discovered, the authorities of Lin-an-fu sentenced me to be exiled to the prisoners' quarters 牢城 in T'ai-chou. I was assigned to serve at the *Tu chiu-wu* 都酒務 or General Wine Bureau.[12] To render the service there, I hired a substitute CHOU Li 周立, a native of the prefecture, and paid him with my monthly provisions. I supported myself by cutting wood-blocks for books every day. In the 3rd moon of last year (1182), T'ANG Chung-yu called me in and asked me to cut printing blocks for the works of YANG-tzu (YANG Hsiung 揚雄) and HSÜN-tzu (HSÜN Ch'ing 荀卿) etc.,[13] in the office

---

[8] The term *ch'u-hsiang* 出相 (or 像) appears also in titles of illustrated novels. For examples, see SUN K'ai-ti 孫楷第, *Chung-kuo hsiao-shuo shu-mu* 中國小說書目, Peiping, 1933, p. 44 and p. 84. The terms *ch'üan-hsiang* 全相 (像) and *hsiu-hsiang* 繡像, of course, are more common.

[9] Wu-chou was around the modern Chin-hua, Chekiang. Su-hsi is perhaps a misprint for Lan-hsi 蘭溪.

[10] *Wen-chi* 19.10b-11a.

[11] Around the modern Ningpo. According to *Wen-chi* 19.9b, CHIANG may have come from Wu-chou.

[12] Under the Sung dynasty, for the most part of the country, the government held a monopoly over the manufacture and sale of wine. The offices in charge of the monopoly were called *Chiu-wu* 酒務. The actual charge, however, was often in the hands of annual tax-farmers. The brewing of wine and connected works were done by hired laborers or soldiers (with or without a criminal record). See *Sung hui-yao kao* 宋會要稿, *Shih-huo* 食貨 20 and 21.

[13] These and the works of two other thinkers, WANG T'ung 王通 and HAN Yü 韓愈, were printed together with government funds by T'ANG Chung-yu who used the copies as personal gifts. *Wen-chi* 19.2b-3a, 19.22a-b. CHU Hsi also received a copy of the works of the four philosophers, but estimated its cost and paid for it at the prefectural treasury *Chün-tzu k'u* 軍貲庫. *Wen-chi* 19.1a.

Interestingly enough, a copy of the *Hsün-tzu* of which the blocks were cut by CHIANG Hui, WANG Ting, and others, is still preserved in Japan. Reproductions of the work are in the *Ku-i ts'ung-shu* 古逸叢書 and the *SPTK*. The names of CHIANG Hui and WANG Ting appear on many sheets in the corner where the cutter's

of the *Kung-shih k'u* 公使庫.[14] I, and WANG Ting 王定 and others, altogether 18 people, did the cutting in the office.

On the 13th day of the 8th moon, police archers from I-wu-hsien of Wu-chou suddenly arrived at T'ai-chou and arrested me, stating that they wanted me because I was involved in a case of HUANG Nien-wu and others who counterfeited *hui-tzu*. Under arrest, I was going to follow [the police] to testify in the case. T'ANG Chung-yu, at this time, ordered TUNG Hsien 董顯, an attendant serving the office 承局學院子 [15] of *Kung-shih k'u*, and two others to recapture me. Chung-yu decreed to the police: " You are police archers coming to arrest a soldier under my jurisdiction. [How dare you] arrest him without presenting your credentials! " The archers were sent back under custody. I was taken back to live in the original office.

In the 10th moon documents again came from the *T'i-hsing-ssu* 提刑司 (" Office of the Circuit Judicial Intendant ") [16] to arrest me. Chung-yu sent *San-liu Hsüan-chiao* 三六宣教 [17] (i.e., his brother's son) to order me to gather my tools and move to Chung-yu's house. I reached a back hall called *Ch'ing-shu t'ang* 清屬堂 where I was lodged and boarded. Food was sent in by Grandma CHIN 金婆婆. Three days after, Chung-yu came in and said to me, " I have kept you in safety here. I have some matter to ask you. Will you be willing to consent? " I answered him right away, " I don't know what matter. You'd better tell me." Chung-yu said, " I want to manufacture some *hui-tzu*." I then said, " I am afraid it will be humiliating if we get discovered later and caught." Chung-yu said, " Let me have my way. If you do not obey me, I shall send you to the prison where you may die of imprisonment. Since you are an exiled criminal soldier, there will be no harm." Fearful of his severity, I consented.

The next day, seeing Grandma CHIN sending in my food, I asked her, " How can we get paper? " She said, " Leave it to us. Chung-yu will send my son, CHIN Ta 金大, to the countryside of Wu-chou and have paper made 撩 [18] and sent here in sealed cases 使箬頭封來.[19] The next day, Grandma

---

name is normally found. See colophon dated 1822 by the Japanese scholar KARIYA Mochiyuki 狩谷望之 (Ekisai 掖齋) who owned the copy of the *Hsün-tzu*. I am indebted to Dr. HU Shih for this reference.

[14] Treasury of funds in local governments intended primarily for the entertainment of transient guests. Actually, the funds were often used or abused by local officials to make lavish gifts to each other or to their superior officials. See *Wen-hsien t'ung-k'ao* 文獻通考 (*Shih-t'ung* 十通 ed.) 24.237c-238a, which quotes *Chien-yen i-lai ch'ao-yeh tsa-chi* 建炎以來朝野雜記 (*Ts'ung-shu chi-ch'eng* ed.) *Chia-chi* 甲集 17.255-256. Also see WANG Ming-ch'ing 王明清, *Hui-chu hou-lu* 揮塵後錄 (*Chin-tai pi-shu* 津逮祕書 ed.) 1.11b-12a.

[15] The term *hsüeh-yüan-tzu* 學院子 also appears in *Wen-chi* 19.4b-6b, 11a, 12a, 22b.

[16] *T'i-hsing* was shortened from *T'i-tien hsing-yü* 提點刑獄. See E. A. KRACKE, Jr., *Civil Service in Early Sung China*, Cambridge, Mass., 1953, pp. 50-51.

[17] *Hsüan-chiao lang* 宣教郎 was a prestige title 散官. See *Wen-hsien t'ung-k'ao* 577b, KRACKE, *ibid.*, p. 82.

[18] The word *liao* 撩 (synonymous with *lao* 撈 " to drag for," " to fish up ") refers to

CHIN brought me a traced master-copy of *hui-tzu* of *i-kuan-wen sheng* 一貫先省 (i. e., 770 cash). The figure was that of Chieh-lü Hsien-sheng 接履文生.[20] I asked Grandma CHIN who did it, and she said it was Ho Hsüan 賀選, who lived in Ta-ying-ch'ien 大營前,[21] who traced the copy in [T'ANG Chung-yu's] inner study 裏書院.[22] This Ho Hsüan was good at copying pictures and tracing characters and he was a confidant spy of Chung-yu and [his nephew] the *Hsüan-chiao*. At that time, she gave me a block of pear wood. I finished the cutting in ten days. Grandma CHIN put it in a wicker box[23] made of vine and took it into the house for safekeeping.

Two days later, I saw Grandma CHIN and *San-liu Hsüan-chiao* coming in with ten pear-wood blocks which were smooth on both sides and also 20 pages of a master-copy of the 1st chapter of the *Hou tien-li fu* 後典麗賦 or *Supplement Collection of Dignified and Flowery Rhymed Prose*.[24] The *San-liu*

---

the process of paper-making by dipping the mould-frame into the vat of macerated fibre. The process is better known as *ch'ao-chih* 抄紙. See *Chien-yen i-lai ch'ao-yeh tsa-chi*, *I-chi* 乙集 17.572, *T'ien-kung k'ai-wu* 天工開物 (Japanese reproduction of 1637 ed.) B.71b-72a, and Dard HUNTER, *Paper Making, the History and Technique of an Ancient Craft*, 2nd ed., New York, 1947, pp. 84-94. Also compare the expression *ch'ao-tsao hui-tzu* 抄造會子 in *Wen-hsien t'ung-k'ao* 9.100b.

According to CHOU Mi, *Kuei-hsin tsa-chih* 癸辛雜識 (Chin-tai pi-shu ed.), *Hsü-chi* 續集 B.47b-48a, the process of *liao-chih* 撩紙 can be facilitated by adding juice squeezed from stems and leaves of *huang shu-k'uei* 黃蜀葵, i. e., *Hibiscus mainhot* (or certain other plants) which will prevent the moist paper from being sticky.

[19] I do not know the second character, which probably refers to a bamboo case or a basket with cover. This character also appears in *Lung-ch'uan wen-chi* 20.12a referring to a container of fifty large tangerines.

[20] This perhaps refers to I-yin 伊尹. The *Han-shih wai-chuan* 韓詩外傳 (SPTK ed.) 2.13b says, 伊尹接履而趨、遂適於湯、湯以爲相 Thereupon I-yin made haste without stopping until he came to T'ang, who made him minister. (J. R. HIGHTOWER, *Han shih wai-chuan*, Cambridge, Mass., 1952, p. 61).

Since the reference does not seem to have been popular, Dr. HU Shih has suggested to me that the depiction may have been the famous story of the old man Huang-shih-kung 黃石公 who intentionally dropped his shoe from a bridge to ask CHANG Liang 張良 to pick up and put on for him. (*Shih chi* 55.2a-b).

[21] A place called *Ta-ying-ch'ien* is found on a map showing the district of Ning-hai 寧海 in *T'ai-chou fu-chih* 台州府志 (1722 ed.). It is located to the east of the city walls.

[22] This use of the term *shu-yüan* is also found in *Wen-chi* 19.9b, 11a, 23a-b. Compare the Japanese *shoin* "study."

[23] 乘 stands for 盛.

[24] Information on this title is found in CH'EN Chen-sun 陳振孫, *Chih-chai shu-lu chieh-t'i* 直齋書錄解題 (1883 ed.) 15.19a-b: "*Hou tien-li fu*, in 40 chapters, compiled by T'ANG Chung-yu, [tzu] Yü-cheng 與政, of Chin-hua. Chung-yu was known for his literary works. This compilation includes pieces by famous writers

Hsüan-chiao said, "I am afraid you have nothing to occupy your hands. At present, you may cut blocks for the rhymed prose until the arrival of the manufactured paper." At that time, he also said, "If you are careful in your manufacturing of *hui-tzu* for Chung-yu, when he completes his term of office here, he may take you back to Wu-chou and take care of you. There will be no difficulty."

I cut blocks for the rhymed prose for a month. In the 2nd ten-day period of the 12th moon, Grandma CHIN brought to me, in the wicker box, paper for making 200 sheets of *hui-tzu*, and the block I had cut, together with such articles as native red, indigo blue, and brownish black (pigments or ink). She handed me those things. I printed 200 sheets of *hui-tzu* but did not apply any seals on them. Again the things were put into the case for Grandma CHIN to carry into the house. On the next day, Grandma CHIN took out [master-copies of the words] *i-kuan-wen sheng* in seal characters and three characters for the signature of the official in charge, and, in addition, a blue pattern with the two characters *tzu* 字 and *hao* 號 (i. e., the serial character and number). Only at that time [25] did I begin to apply three red seals to the notes. I asked Grandma CHIN and *San-liu Hsüan-chiao*, "Who made these seal characters *i-kuan-wen* and the official signature?" Grandma CHIN said they were by Ho Hsüan.

In the last ten-day period of the 12th moon, 150 more sheets were printed. From the 1st moon to the end of the 6th moon of this year (1183), 2600-odd sheets were printed at about 20 times. The number printed each time was 100, 150, or 200. No notes were printed in the 7th moon. On the 26th day of the 7th moon, I saw Grandma CHIN rushing to tell me, "Run away quickly! The *T'i-chü* 提舉 [26] has sealed all the treasuries. I am afraid they may find you by searching." In a hurry, I climbed over the back wall by putting up a ladder, and ran to a pavilion behind the house, but I was caught by soldiers of CHAO *Chien-ya* 趙監押 [27] and delivered to Shao-hsing-fu 紹興府 for imprisonment and investigation.[28]

---

from the end of the T'ang to the glorious period of our dynasty. It stops with the Shao-hsing era. There was formerly a *Tien-li fu* in 93 chapters collected by WANG Wu 王戊; therefore, this work has the title *Hou tien-li fu*. I have not seen WANG's compilation."

According to *Wen-chi* 18.27a, T'ANG Chung-yu used government funds to print collections of rhymed prose in small characters 小字賦集. The books were sent to a bookstore owned by him for sale. According to *Wen-chi* 18.24b-25a, 27a-b, T'ANG also owned a dyed silk shop 綵帛鋪 and a fish shop 魚鮺鋪.

[25] 是實 probably should read 是時.

[26] CHU Hsi's title was *T'i-chü Liang-che tung-lu ch'ang-p'ing ch'a-yen kung-shih* 提舉兩浙東路常平茶塩公事.

[27] *Chien-ya* was a local police officer.

[28] *Wen-chi* 19.24a-26a. Strangely enough, notwithstanding his depositions, CHIANG Hui was finally released. T'ANG Chung-yu merely lost his new job as *Chiang-nan hsi-lu t'i-tien hsing-yü* 江南西路. CHU Hsi, disappointed by the result of his impeachment and further embarrassed by his appointment to take T'ANG's position

From the above depositions, we learn that in order to manufacture *hui-tzu* of the denomination of one string, the counterfeiter CHIANG Hui cut on a block of pear wood, perhaps among other patterns, the picture of Chieh-lü Hsien-sheng. The work was undoubtedly elaborate, because it took a professional wood-block cutter and professional counterfeiter ten days to accomplish it. He also cut wooden stamps for the words *i-kuan-wen sheng* in seal characters, the official signature, and a blue pattern with serial character and number. He must have also cut government seals or perhaps he used the ones he forged earlier in other places. At least three colors were used for the printing, namely, red, blue, and black. Apparently, red was for the seals, blue for the serial character and number, and black (and, perhaps, other colors) for the rest of the note. A special kind of paper was manufactured for the note.[29]

The colorful appearance of *hui-tzu* thus resembled that of its predecessor and contemporary note *chiao-tzu* as described by Ts'AO Hsüeh-ch'üan 曹學佺, *Shu-chung kuang-chi* 蜀中廣記,[30] who quotes FEI Chu 費著 of the Yüan dynasty. The description has been summarized in my *Money and Credit in China, a Short History*, p. 54. The fact that the counterfeiter used pear wood, however, does not mean the government made its plates with the same material. Actually, the expression *t'ung-pan* 銅板 " brass

in Chiang-nan hsi-lu, turned in his resignation. Minister WANG Hui 王淮 was a relative of T'ANG and probably helped T'ANG's case with other friends of T'ANG. *Wen-chi* 19.16a-b, 18a; 22.22a-23b, 25b.

[29] The Sung government manufactured its *hui-tzu* paper in Hui-chou 徽州, later in Ch'eng-tu, and from 1168 in Lin-an-fu. In the middle of the 13th century, there were 1200 government workers to make *hui-tzu* paper and 204 printers to turn out the note. *Hsien-ch'un Lin-an chih* 咸淳臨安志 (1830 reprint) 9.7b-8a; WU Tzu-mu 吳自牧, *Meng-liang lu* 夢粱錄 (*Ts'ung-shu chi-ch'eng* ed.) 9.77.

According to observations made by contemporaries, the fact that the Sung government resorted to the use of local paper inferior to Szechwan paper, together with the fact that regulations against counterfeiting of paper currency were not enforced, accounted for the prevalence of counterfeiting. Cf. SOGABE Shizuo 曾我部靜雄, *Shihei hattatsu shi* 紙幣發達史, Tōkyō, 1951, pp. 72-76. An earlier article by SOGABE on the counterfeiting of paper money in the Southern Sung period in *Bunka* 文化 7.2 (1940) is unfortunately not available.

[30] *Ssu-k'u ch'üan-shu chen-pen, ch'u-chi* 四庫全書珍本初集 ed., 67.13a-23b.

plate " appeared in documents of the Southern Sung period concerning government printing of *hui-tzu*.[31] Therefore, my first
sentence in the paragraph quoted at the beginning of this article
is not completely wrong, although it should be revised in the light
of the additional information. It is still possible for the brass
plate reported in OKUDAIRA's book to have been used to print
hui-tzu, but it is almost certain that such a plate would not suffice.
The note required the official signature, government seals, and at
least another stamp for the serial character and number.

APPENDIX

I should like to take this opportunity to make a few corrections and to reply
to a few criticisms of my book. The corrections are as follows:

Page 24, line 26: *For* the official reading *read* the popular reading.

Page 24, line 28: *For* the popular reading *read* the other reading. For these
two corrections on the *K'ai-t'ung yüan-pao* or *K'ai-yüan t'ung-pao* I am
indebted to Professor Chi-chen WANG of Columbia University.

Page 26, line 27: *For* 1898 *read* 1889. For this correction on *t'ung-yüan*
and for the correction on page 89 on the establishment of the Russo-Chinese
Bank, I am indebted to Mr. E. KANN, author of *The Currencies of China*,
Shanghai, 1926 and 1927.

Page 27, line 20: *For* bearing a square hole *read* bearing an intended square
hole. For this correction on the *pao-tsang* 寶藏 coin, I am indebted to
Mr. H. F. BOWKER, compiler of *A Numismatic Bibliography of the Far East*,
New York, 1943.

Page 48, lines 33-34: *For* the British Hongkong dollar (issued 1866-1868)
read the British (Hongkong) dollar (minted 1866-1868 in Hongkong, and from
1895 in India).

Page 49, line 1: *For* the British Hongkong dollars *read* the British dollars.
For the corrections on the British dollar I am indebted to Mr. Dickson H.
LEAVENS, author of *Silver Money*, Bloomington, 1939.

Page 89, line 41: *For* 1911 *read* 1896.

Page 107, line 20: (and several other places in the book) *For* Okutaira *read*
Okudaira.

Page 108, line 29: *For* Okutaira Mashahiro *read* Okudaira Masahiro.

Page 109, line 33: *For* 3.24 *read* 3.23.

Page 133, line 31: *For* Okutaira Masaniro 1.14n *read* Okudaira Masahiro
1.12n.

In a letter dated April 2, 1953, in which Mr. BOWKER made the correction
" bearing an intended square hole," he raised the following criticism:

" In par. 6.12 you state that no Sung notes have survived. If you will

---

[31] *Wen-hsien t'ung-k'ao* 9.98c-99a.

go to the Boston Museum of Art you will find in their collection two Sung notes, as well as notes of the T'ang, Western Liao, Ming, and Ch'ing eras. These are fully described and pictured, some being in colors, in item 180 of my Bibliography. The colored plates, however, are not to be found in the original article, but only in the reprint.

"I have noted that CARTER has raised doubts of the authenticity of the notes found in *Ch'üan Pu T'ung Chih*, on the authority of Professor PELLIOT. I have noted that the Western Liao note pictured by DAVIS opposite page 270 of the above-mentioned work is practically identical with the one figured in *CPTC*, which leads me to believe that PELLIOT did not know what he was talking about."

To this criticism, I have replied in a letter dated April 8, 1953:

"On the matter of early paper money, I am afraid I cannot share your uncritical opinion concerning the *Ch'üan pu t'ung-chih* 泉布統志 and A. M. DAVIS, *Certain Old Chinese Notes*. The T'ang and Sung notes in these books are not reliable. To mention a few obvious objections, the use of the term *pao-ch'ao* 寶鈔 for notes, the use of the terms *Nei-ko* 內閣 and *Ko-pu* 閣部 for the Cabinet or Government authorities, and the important position assigned to silver are all anachronistic."

The *Pacific Historical Review* 22.2 (1953) .201 contains a review of my book by Professor W. EBERHARD. I am grateful for his comment that " The book can, therefore, be regarded as a compact, critical, and reliable account of money and credit in China as far as is known today." However, his statement " the question of round coins between the first and the seventh centuries A. D. is covered by one sentence only (p. 24) " is incorrect. Information on this subject can be found also in paragraphs 3.13 (p. 23), 4.2, 4.3, 4.4 (pp. 30-31) and 4.20, 4.21, 4.22 (p. 36). His criticism of the lack of a bibliography is dubious. It is obviously impractical for a small book to list all the available materials. Moreover, nearly all the important references can be located either directly or indirectly in my notes.

ADDITIONS AND CORRECTIONS

In the following notes, the numbers in parentheses indicate the volume and page of the *Harvard Journal of Asiatic Studies* where the article was published. These are followed by the page number in the present volume and in many cases by a further number indicating the line or the footnote. Thus (17.339)11.14 means *HJAS*, volume 17, page 339, new page 11, line 14.

(17.331).3 — On the meaning of the year-title T'ung-chih, cf. Mary C. WRIGHT, "What's in a Reign Name: The Uses of History and Philology," *JAS* 18.1(1958).103–106. According to a reply by Wen-hsiang to an inquiry from Thomas WADE, the name T'ung-chih expresses the desire *t'ung-kuei yü chih* "to return to (or, see restored) together a state of order." Dr. WRIGHT's assertion that "Private papers, including the diary of the well-informed and gossipy LI Tz'u-ming, yielded nothing" (p. 104), however, is incorrect. See Note 5. In Harry HUSSEY, *Venerable Ancestor, the Life and Time of Tz'u Hsi, 1835–1908, Empress of China*, 1949, T'ung-chih is translated "Universal Tranquillity" (p. 117).

(17.335)7.12 — *For* Arthur *read* Alfred.

(17.339)11.14 — *For* 1125 *read* 1225.

(17.341)13.Note 25 — On the "natural life" of a dynasty, it is interesting to note that a tradition gives the name *yun-wei* 閏位, "intercalary position" (first used in *Han shu* 99C.30a to refer to the Hsin Dynasty of WANG Mang), to those dynasties (Ch'in, Sui, Yuan) which ruled over the whole of China but lasted less than a century. Cf. Ho Tung-ju 何棟如, *Huang tsu ssu ta-fa* 皇祖四大法, 6.17a.

(18.302)19 — According to *Li-hsüeh chih-nan* 吏學指南, a handbook for government clerks included in the encyclopedia *Chü-chia pi-yung shih-lei ch'üan-chi* 居家必用事類全集 *hsin-chi* 辛集 15.11b, in Yüan times a distinction was made between *chia* 假 "leave (borrowed time)" and *chia* 暇 "holiday (leisure time)." This distinction seems rather arbitrary and probably was not strictly observed. The two characters, of course, were used interchangeably for "leave" and "holiday" in ancient texts, and between the two characters, the latter is considered the original for such meaning.

(18.318)35.35 — *For* slipers *read* slippers.

(15.513)49.Note 20 — On hostages known as *Ki-in* 其人 in Korean history, cf. article by Lee Kwang Rin 李光麟 in *Hak Lim* 學林 3(1954) 1–25.

(15.516)52.Note 29 — On hostages in Wei and Chin times, cf. article by Sakuma Kichiya 佐久間吉也 in *Fukujima Daigaku Gakugei Gakubu ronshū* 福島大學學藝學部論集 8.1(1957)1–16.

(15.518)54.Note 37 — According to Lɪ Wei-chung 李惟中, *Hsing ch'ü t'u-shuo* 涇渠圖說 (preface 1342, included in *Ch'ang-an t'u-chih* 長安圖志, 1784 ed.) *hsia* 18b, in military agricultural colonies under the Yüan dynasty, two oxen constituted a *chü* 具. The translation on this page probably should be corrected accordingly.

(15.520)56.Note 46 — A translation of Hsɪ Ch'ao's essay, "Feng fa yao," can be found in E. Zürcher, *The Buddhist Conquest of China*, 1959, pp. 164–176.

(20.50)72 — The article by Mɪʏᴀᴢᴀᴋɪ on *hsien pu-tsu* 羨不足 has been included in his *Ajiashi kenkyū* アジア史研究, 1957, pp. 1–26.

(12.218)77.Note 10 — Cf. Cʜᴏᴜ Fa-kao 周法高, "Ku-tai ti ch'eng-shu" 古代的稱數 in *Chung-yang yen-chiu-yüan yüan-k'an* 1(1954)129–212.

(12.219)79.Note 11 — Cf. article by Nᴏɴᴜᴍᴇ Chōfū 布目潮渢 in *Ritsumeikan bungaku* 立命館文學 148(1957) 633–543.

(12.217)76.24 — *For* 13,000,000 *read* 4,000,000.

(12.222)81.Note 22 — Arthur Wᴀʟᴇʏ (*The Real Tripitaka*, 1952, p. 278) understands differently this passage including the terms *erh-fen-pan* and *ta-erh-fen-pan*. E. O. Reischauer, (*Ennin's Diary*, 1955, pp. 34, 44) follows the interpretation given in this article.

(13.581)92.Note 17 — This economic history of ancient China by Li Chien-nung has appeared under the title *Hsien-Ch'in Liang Han ching-chi shih kao* 先秦兩漢經濟史稿, 1957. Cf. esp. pp. 127–140.

(13.540)101.Note 35 — On the meaning of *k'ai ch'ien-mai* 開阡陌, cf. article by Mᴏʀɪʏᴀ Mitsuo 守屋美都雄 in *Chūgoku kodai no shakai to bunka* 中國古代の社會と文化, 1957, pp. 211–238.

(13.541)101.Note 37 — It has been suggested that, instead of *lu-fu* or "radishes," *lu* may have referred to *hu-lu* 瓠盧 or "gourd."

(13.547)108 — On the problem of military and labor services under the Han dynasty, cf. article by Nɪsʜɪᴅᴀ Taichirō 西田太一郎 in *Tōhōgaku* 東方學 10(1955) 37–47 and article by Yᴏɴᴇᴅᴀ Kenjirō 米田賢次郎 in *Tōhō gakuhō*, Kyoto, 27(1957) 189–212.

(9.109)121.4 — *For* two *read* three.

(9.115)127, Note 44 — *For* T'ang *read* T'an.

(9.118)130.18 — *For* millenia *read* millennia.

(9.123)135 — On the problem of the land system and tax system of Wei and Chin, cf. articles in *Chung-kuo li-tai tʻu-ti chih-tu wen-tʻi tʻao-lun chi* 中國歷代土地制度問題討論集, 1957. On the interpretation of the terms *chan-tʻien* 占田 and *kʻo-tʻien* 課田, cf. article by AMANO Motonosuke 天野元之助 in *Jimbun kenkyū* 人文研究 8.9 (1957).963–980.

(9.126)138.28 — *For* perfect *read* prefect.

(9.130)142.Note 114 — *For* chih *read* chin.

(9.130)142.Note 115 — Cf. Étienne BALAZS, "Le traité économique du 'Souei-chou,' " *TP* 42 (1953).

(9.133)145.10 — It has been suggested that instead of "the old [established] levies of 3 *pʻi* of silk and 3 *chin* of floss," the text may have read "the old [established] levies of 2 *pʻi* of silk and 2 (or 3) *chin* of floss." However, I hesitate to make this emendation.

(9.143)155.Note 48 — *For* SBAW *read* SPAW.

(9.151)163 — On military agricultural colonies under the Wei and Chin dynasties, cf. article by Nishijima Sadao 西島定生 in *Tōyō bunka kenkyūjo kiyō* 東洋文化研究所紀要 10(1956).1–84.

(9.153)165.Note 19 — *For* damned *read* dammed.

(9.159)171.13 — *For* Emperformed *read* Emperor performed.

(9.161)173.1 — *For* Yu-yei *read* Yu-pei.

(9.166)128.15 — *For* and *read* yet.

(9.169)181.4 — The original Chinese text for "fifty" perhaps should read "fifteen."

(13.174)198.Note 1 — Cf. Jacques GERNET, *Les aspects économiques de Bouddhisme dans la société chinoise du Ve au Xe siècle,* 1956.

(9.180)192.Notes 34 and 35 — *For* OKUHIRA *read* OKUDAIRA.

(13.184)208.13 — *For* Pai-ching *read* Pai-chang.

(13.186)210.Note 42 — In 1952 I consulted the manuscript "Pelliot chinois 2638" in the Bibliothèque Nationale and verified the usage of *chʻang* 唱 as auction sales.

(13.190)214.Note 50 — On *pʻu-mai* 撲買, cf. A. C. MOULE, *Quinsai, with Other Notes on Marco Polo,* 1957, p. 39, and article by IRIYA Yoshitaka 入矢義高 in *Tōyōshi kenkyū* 東洋史研究 11.4 (1951) 54–76. The article is very scholarly, but IRIYA's understanding of a difficult passage describing *pʻu-mai* from the *Hsi-hu lao-jen fan-sheng lu* 西湖老人繁勝錄 (*Han-fen-lou pi-chi* 涵芬樓祕笈 ed.) 19a is inadequate and his punctuation of the text contains errors.　Tentatively, I would translate this passage as follows: "When the Winter Solstice draws near, it is customary in the Capital [for peddlers] to carry prizes for people to gamble for by tossing coins.　[The prizes include] jumbo shrimps, chestnuts, the Young Lord's dried salt fish, etc. (for *fen* 糞 read *hsiang* 鯗).　In most cases, people gamble for "ten-unmixed" (i.e., ten coins falling alike, ten heads or ten tails). [One pays] three coins for one throw, to gamble for one fighting cock plus an additional prize of 2,000 coins in the paper money *hui-tzu* or 1,500 coins in cash counted in full string.　If all coins but one fall alike, one is permitted to make three free throws. This kind of gambling is done everywhere in the streets."

(16.365)216 — P'ENG Hsin-wei, *Chung-kuo huo-pi shih*, 1954, vol. 2, plate 43, illustrates a bronze plate which may have been used for printing *hui-tzu* in Hangchow under the Southern Sung. Cf. also his discussion on pp. 266–269.

(16.365)216.13 — It is interesting to add that Ch'ien-ssu Ts'ang 千斯倉 and Wan-ssu Ts'ang 萬斯倉 were names of government granaries under the Yüan dynasty.　Cf. *Yüan shih* 85.14a.

ABBREVIATIONS

BEFEO	*Bulletin de l'École française d'Extrême-Orient*
BMFEA	*Bulletin of the Museum of Far Eastern Antiquities*
CHHP	*Ch'ing-hua hsüeh-pao (Tsing Hua Journal)*
CS	*Chin shu*
CSCC	*Chin shu chiao-chu*
CYYY	*Chung-yang Yen-chiu-yüan Li-shih Yü-yen Yen-chiu-so chi-k'an (Bulletin of the Institute of History and Philology, Academia Sinica)*
FEQ	*Far Eastern Quarterly*
HHS	*Hou Han shu*
JAOS	*Journal of the American Oriental Society*
JAS	*Journal of Asian Studies*
JNChRAS	*Journal of the North China Branch of the Royal Asiatic Society*
MSOS	*Mitteilungen des Seminars für orientalische Sprachen*
SBE	*Sacred Books of the East series*
SG	*Shinagaku*
SKC	*San Kuo chih*
SPAW	*Sitzungsberichte d. preussischen Akademie d. Wissenschaften*
SPPY	*Ssu-pu pei-yao*
SPTK	*Ssu-pu ts'ung-k'an*
SR	*Shirin*
SZ	*Shigakuzasshi*
TG	*Tōyō gakuhō*
TP	*T'oung pao*
TSCC	*Ts'ung-shu chi-ch'eng*
TSFYCY	*Tu-shih fang-yü chi-yao*
YCHP	*Yen-ching hsüeh-pao (Yenching Journal of Chinese Studies)*